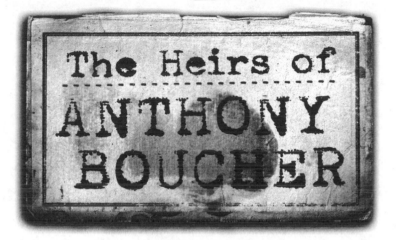

The Heirs of ANTHONY BOUCHER

A History of MYSTERY FANDOM

REVISED & UPDATED

MARVIN LACHMAN

Poisoned Pen
PRESS

The Heirs of Anthony Boucher

Also by Marvin Lachman

Encyclopedia of Mystery and Detection
(with co-authors Chris Steinbrunner, Otto Penzler,
and Charles Shibuk)

A Reader's Guide to the American Novel of Detection

The American Regional Mystery

Detectionary (with co-authors Chris Steinbrunner,
Ottor Penzler, Charles Shibuk, and Francis M. Nevins)

The Villainous Stage

Cover design by The Book Designers
Cover images © lekseykolotvin/Shutterstock, andreiuc88/Shutterstock, Arcady/Shutterstock, AWP76/Shutterstock, Dark Moon Pictures/Shutterstock, Gavran333/Shutterstock, Hitdelight/Shutterstock, Irina Kozorog/Shutterstock, LiliGraphie/Shutterstock, Liu zishan/Shutterstock, Maria Isaeva/Shutterstock, Nejron Photo/Shutterstock, Stephen Coburn/Shutterstock, Stocksnapper/Shutterstock, Taigi/Shutterstock, zef art/Shutterstock
All internal photographs © Art Scott, unless otherwise noted

Published by Poisoned Pen Press, an imprint of Sourcebooks
P.O. Box 4410, Naperville, Illinois 60567-4410
(630) 961-3900
sourcebooks.com

Library of Congress Cataloging-in-Publication data is on file with the publisher.

Printed and bound in the United States of America.
SB 10 9 8 7 6 5 4 3 2 1

CONTENTS

DEDICATION

This book is dedicated to Allen J. Hubin. He was the first great heir of Anthony Boucher. When he founded *The Armchair Detective* (*TAD*) in 1967, it gave the fans of crime fiction a publication for which to write and eventually a reason to meet. For more than ten years he published and edited *The Armchair Detective,* which set a standard of excellence by which later fan journals would be judged. It published articles, check lists, reviews, and letters that often sparked controversy and provided humor.

For three years Hubin replaced Boucher as mystery reviewer for the *New York Times Book Review*. He also replaced Boucher as the editor of the annual volume *Best Detective Stories of the Year* from 1970 through 1975. Meanwhile, Hubin had a full-time job as a research chemist, a family (wife and five children), and the magazine to edit and publish. Even after he was no longer publishing *The Armchair Detective,* Hubin continued as an unpaid reviewer for it, and *The Mystery FANcier, The Mystery*File,* and *Deadly Pleasures.*

It was while publishing *TAD* that Hubin began the project that may well place him above all other fans: *The Bibliography of Crime Fiction, 1749–1975.* This listing of virtually every book published in our field is arguably the most indispensable reference work ever in crime fiction. Hubin updated it through 2000 via the internet and CD-ROMs. To this very day, he continues to add new titles, and dates of birth and death of mystery writers as they are discovered. Hubin expanded his bibliography to include thousands of films based on crime fiction as well as the titles of short stories in collections.

The Armchair Detective gave fans a place to "meet" in writing. Soon, there were small, intimate parties (in apartments such as mine). Eventually, there was Bouchercon, the World Mystery Convention, with up to 2,000 fans attending, and other conventions.

Mystery fandom as we know it today would eventually have come about without Al Hubin, but it would have been later, less scholarly, and not as much fun.

Photo by Jennifer Hubin

Allen J. Hubin

All knowledge is contained in fandom.
—Anthony Boucher

PREFACE

This history of mystery fandom is called *The Heirs of Anthony Boucher* because it was to Boucher that fans turned before "The Fan Revolution" was launched in 1967. There were fans before 1967, and I shall discuss them. However, it was in 1967 that the mystery developed a fandom that was not limited to specific authors or characters such as Sherlock Holmes.

Boucher was an excellent mystery writer, but he gave up writing novels—though he continued to write the occasional short story—to review mysteries for the *San Francisco Chronicle* in 1942. In 1951 he became the mystery critic for the *New York Times Book Review.* In addition, he reviewed for *Ellery Queen's Mystery Magazine.* He was considered the outstanding reviewer of crime fiction in America and on three occasions received Edgars from Mystery Writers of America for his writing.

Boucher mentioned fan activities in his column, but there were few except for those involving Sherlock Holmes. Boucher reviewed what was perhaps the earliest general fan scholarship, *A Preliminary Check List of the Detective Novel and Its Variants* (1966), an annotated list of recommendations by Charles Shibuk. In 1966 Boucher also wrote of a bibliography of the works of John Dickson Carr, compiled by Rick Sneary of California.

I had been reading mysteries for almost twenty-five years before I had the opportunity to write or speak to another fan. In 1967 I was only one of millions of mystery readers, but I also considered myself a fan. I kept notes on the books I read, prepared checklists of favorite authors, and compiled brief biographies of them and their series detectives. They were only for my own use then.

My isolation was ended in 1967 when Allen J. Hubin surveyed the people who had requested Sneary's work, asking if they were interested in a journal *about* mystery fiction. The answers he received were positive. I was one of those replying enthusiastically. Those interested subscribed and provided enough articles and reviews to fill the first issue. *The Armchair Detective* and the "Fan Revolution" were born. In a delightful coincidence, at about the same time, Lianne Carlin founded her fan magazine, *The Mystery Lover's Newsletter.*

Hubin wrote to me about a mystery fan, Charles Shibuk, living, as I did then, in the Bronx, and I telephoned him. We spoke of mysteries for an hour, my first conversation with another fan, and it was the start of a long friendship.

Since I was there at the beginning and have continued to be active in fandom to the present, it would be false modesty not to mention myself in this history. I have tried to be objective, but because I care about the mystery, its past, present, and future, I do not avoid expressing opinions on possibly controversial subjects.

In 1967 Boucher's advice and strong encouragement were major factors in Hubin's going ahead with *The Armchair Detective.* Boucher enthusiastically reviewed the first issue on December 3, 1967. He spoke for mystery fans when he described it as the kind of journal for which he had been looking for many years. He wrote letters that were published in the second and third issues of *The Armchair Detective.*

We expected Boucher would play a major role in the newly born fandom, but that was not to be. I can still recall the shock of reading Boucher's obituary in the newspaper on May 1, 1968. It was as if a friend had died. I had read his column on Sundays for almost twenty years. Everything that has been done in mystery fandom since he died is part of Anthony Boucher's legacy.

Life (and death) being what they are, many fans who were my friends have died since 2005. Many of them are listed in my Acknowledgments page.

I set out to write a history of mystery fandom because none had been written before. Mystery fandom has had a profound effect on many lives: the fans (and often their families), writers, and people in the publishing industry.

The first edition of this book was published in 2005. Much has happened to fandom since I completed my research and writing for it in 2004. The major United States mystery conventions that were held in 2005 are still active and have thrived. However, since then Great Britain has come into its own as a place for new conventions and fandom. All the major American and British fan journals that I wrote about in 2005 continue to be published, as you shall read later in this book. The internet has permitted far greater communication among fans due to the huge growth in the number and variety of blogs. Websites provide research data, once only available in reference books, within seconds. All that happened in the last fourteen years convinced me that it was time for this revised, updated edition.

Millions of people read mysteries, but there will never be more than a relatively small number, perhaps several thousand, who enjoy reading, writing, and talking *about* mysteries and attending conventions. If you're reading this book, you're probably one of them.

—Marvin Lachman, 2019
Santa Fe, New Mexico

INTRODUCTION: THE MAKING OF A MYSTERY FAN

by Edward D. Hoch
Past President of Mystery Writers of America and Recipient of Its Grand Master Award

When Marv Lachman first told me of his plans for this book and asked me to write an introduction for it, I was pleased to be part of the project. I've known Marv for some thirty-five years, and can think of no one better equipped to tell the story of mystery fandom. And the more I thought about it the more I realized that I too have always been a mystery fan.

I've written elsewhere that the first adult novel I ever read was the Pocket Books edition of Ellery Queen's *The Chinese Orange Mystery,* purchased at the corner drugstore for twenty-five cents. The year was 1939. I was nine years old and a faithful listener to the weekly Ellery Queen radio show since it had become a Sunday night fixture a few months earlier. About a year later, when I was bedded down with chicken pox, my grandfather brought me the complete Sherlock Holmes, another radio favorite. I read both books eagerly, and a whole new world opened to me.

Some time after that I discovered Green Dragon books, a series of monthly digest-size paperbacks that I read and collected for almost three years. When they were joined by a companion series, Black Knight books, I read those too. The authors were unknown to me, and years later I discovered that many of the titles were reprinted from Phoenix Press and Mystery House hardcovers, not exactly the cream of the mystery crop.

It wasn't until 1945, when I answered an ad and joined the new Unicorn Mystery Book Club, that I started discovering writers I liked almost as much as Queen and Doyle. The first four-in-one Unicorn volume introduced me to Margaret Millar and Thomas B. Dewey, and many others followed. By this time I was beginning to realize that I loved a mystery, to paraphrase another favorite radio title. I subscribed to *Ellery Queen's Mystery Magazine* and started searching used bookstores for the issues I'd missed. I went on to discover Carr, Christie, Chesterton, Chandler, Cain, and Charteris, and the "C" section in my bookcase began to sag.

In 1949 Clayton Rawson invited Unicorn subscribers to join Mystery Writers of America as affiliate members, an offer I readily accepted. I'd started writing short stories while still in high school, and though I didn't become a published author until 1955, I found myself attending MWA meetings in New York, when my army service took me there during the Korean War. After my discharge I worked a year for Pocket Books in New York, continuing my close ties to MWA.

I'd never attended an Edgar Awards dinner until I won the Edgar myself in 1968. This intensified my relationship with both writers and fans. Already a regular contributor to *EQMM* and other mystery magazines, I sold my first novel and quit my advertising job in Rochester to write full time. I believe it was in 1971 that my wife Patricia and I were invited to a party of mystery fans at the Bronx apartment of Carol and Marv Lachman. It was attended by Al Hubin, Otto Penzler, Chris Steinbrunner, Charles Shibuk and others who were to become important cornerstones of mystery fandom. These parties, held after the Edgar dinners in late April, were an event that I still remember fondly.

When the first Bouchercon was announced for Santa Monica, California, in 1970 we skipped it only because it was held in May, shortly after the Edgar Awards dinner. Patricia and I were at the second one in Los Angeles, and we have now attended twenty-six of those thirty-five annual events. In many ways Bouchercon has become the perfect mystery convention, a seamless blending of writers and fans that not only helps publicize the mystery and encourage new writers but also provides a lively meeting place for practitioners of a sometimes lonely profession.

I think there are times when many writers wonder if there's really anyone out there reading their words, caring about the characters and plots they shape from their imagination. At Bouchercon and other fan events I'm always pleased when someone tells me they've enjoyed a recent story. I often seek out authors myself, to express my pleasure at their latest book. Though I've been a published writer for fifty years now, I'm still a fan.

The history of mystery fandom is a story that needed to be told. Many readers, and even some writers, are unaware of what has gone before. They know little or nothing of the fans from the past, and what they contributed to the genre. It is, after all, mystery fandom that keeps alive all those great names from yesterday while discovering the new classic writers of our own day. With this book Marv Lachman has done an amazing job of chronicling it all, from the earliest Sherlockians through the popular fanzines and mystery conventions to the latest internet websites.

Read it and rejoice!

Chapter One

FANDOM BEFORE THE "REVOLUTION"

Mystery fandom followed many of the paths trod by science fiction fans, but it was over thirty years behind. In 1930, inspired by Hugo Gernsback's *Amazing Stories,* fans began forming organizations, beginning with the Science Correspondence Club, and publishing "fanzines," their term for fan magazines. In 1939 they held the first World Science Fiction Convention (Worldcon) in New York City, where a world's fair emphasizing the future was being held. Worldcons have been held annually since 1946, and beginning in 1953 Hugo Awards (named after Gernsback) have been presented by fans.

There has been speculation as to the reasons for the relatively slow start by mystery fandom. It is possibly because science fiction fans are younger, have fewer responsibilities, have more energy for fandom, and are less inhibited. Wearing costumes is important at science fiction gatherings. A few mystery conventions have attempted costume events, with indifferent results. The fedora and trench coat do not permit much imagination, whereas *Star*

Wars and *Star Trek* costumes appeal to the young. There have been significant increases in the size of Bouchercon, the World Mystery Convention, but it still lags far behind its science fiction cousin. In 2016 when it was held in New Orleans, a popular tourist city, Bouchercon drew about two thousand people. That year, Worldcon was held in Kansas City and over four thousand attended. About 1,500 attended Bouchercon in 2017 in Toronto, while Worldcon in Helsinki drew over 7,000.

The first history of science fiction fandom published in book form was *The Immortal Storm* (1954) by Sam Moskowitz, chairman of the first Worldcon. As far as I can determine, the book you are reading is the first history of mystery fandom.

The Edgar Allan Poe Society of Baltimore (1923–)

There was fandom before Sherlockians organized. Honoring the man usually credited with writing the first detective story, the Edgar Allan Poe Society of Baltimore started in 1923 and remains active. Its object: "promoting the understanding of Poe's life and writings, and his association with Baltimore." Since 1997 the primary means of providing information about Poe has been a website which as of 2015 contained six thousand individual pages, called by the society "the most extensive collection of Poe-related material available in any single resource."

***Happy Hours Magazine* (1925–1936) and *Dime Novel Round-Up* (1931–)**

The term "dime novel" refers to paper-covered books, usually priced at a dime, that were popular in the United States, mainly from 1860 through 1915, when they were largely replaced by pulp magazines. Thousands of dime novels were published, with detective stories especially popular. After they were no longer published and were becoming increasingly scarce, their fans began to organize. Ralph F. Cummings founded the Happy Hours Brotherhood, a group of dime novel readers and collectors in 1924. In 1925 he began a bimonthly, *Happy Hours Magazine.* In January 1931 that magazine was succeeded by *Dime Novel Round-Up,* with Cummings as editor-publisher. However, *Happy Hours Magazine* was revived by Ralph P. Smith and published until June 1936. Cummings published *Dime Novel Round-Up* until July 1952 when Edward T. LeBlanc of Fall River, Massachusetts, took over. LeBlanc presided for an incredible forty-two years and 390 issues, until J. Randolph Cox of Dundas, Minnesota, replaced him after the June 1994 issue. Cox, also a scholar of the mystery, continued as editor-publisher until December 2012 when he retired. He was replaced by Marlena Bremseth of Virginia. Among mystery-related articles to appear over the years have been those about early series detectives "Old Sleuth" and King Brady, and Cox's monumental bibliography of the most famous dime novel detective, Nick Carter.

Sherlockian Fandom (1934–)

The "revolution" to which I have referred was in 1967, and this book is primarily about fandom since then. However, no history of fandom is complete without mentioning fans of Sherlock Holmes. Their history has been published; one volume of Jon L. Lellenberg's multi-volume history of Sherlockians devotes 508 pages to the years 1947–1950 alone.

In 1934, author Christopher Morley founded the Baker Street Irregulars (BSI). Its name is that of the London street urchins who help Holmes in his cases. In June 1934 BSI's first meeting was held in New York City, followed in December by the first BSI dinner. Now, to celebrate Holmes's "birthday," as suggested in Arthur Conan Doyle's writings, the BSI dines on the Friday closest to that date, January 6. At first, the banquets were for males only, with the exception of a token female who represented "The Woman," as Holmes called Irene Adler. Many women now attend the dinners.

The Irregulars write of and debate various aspects of the Holmes canon. As Vincent Starrett wrote, "A very considerable literature has accumulated—for the most part essays in fantastic scholarship—solemn tongue-in-cheek fooling in the fields of textual criticism and imaginary biography." Typical was Rex Stout's "Watson Was a Woman," in which he purported to show that a female shared the rooms at 221B Baker Street and John D. Clark's theory, also advanced by William S. Baring-Gould, that Nero Wolfe was the illegitimate offspring of Holmes and Adler.

In 1944, Edgar W. Smith, a leading Irregular (in his business life he was a vice-president at General Motors), edited a collection of essays, *Profile by Gaslight: An Irregular Reader About the Private Life of Sherlock Holmes,* that Simon & Schuster published. Smith had enough material left over to edit a second collection, *A Baker Street Four-Wheeler,* published by his own private press, Pamphlet House. The favorable reaction to these books led Smith to edit a magazine, *The Baker Street Journal,* which first appeared in January 1946 and whose purpose was to continue this speculation and scholarship. The publisher was Ben Abramson, owner of Manhattan's Argus Book Shop. Circulation never went beyond two thousand. As Morley said, "Never has so much been written by so many for so few."

The list of BSI members included "ordinary" fans, but also noted mystery authors Vincent Starrett, August Derleth, Frederic Dannay, and John Dickson Carr. Anthony Boucher was leader of The Scowrers, the BSI group in the San Francisco Bay area, one of many "scions" (local Chapters) that had sprung up.

Franklin D. Roosevelt was made an honorary member of the BSI in 1942, and in a letter (later published in *The Baker Street Journal*) he proved himself adept at mock scholarship, postulating that Holmes was born in America to a criminal father but chose to go to England to fight crime. Roosevelt dubbed a portion of "Shangri-La," the Presidential retreat, "Baker Street." His successor, Harry S Truman, was made an honorary member, and he, too, was a knowledgeable Sherlockian fan.

Abramson's financial resources proved inadequate for what

had become a 132-page, typeset, quarterly journal, and he suspended publication after the January 1949 issue. Smith began publishing it himself in January 1951 as a more modest forty-page, mimeographed magazine. Dr. Julian Woolf became editor in 1960. In 1975 Fordham University began publishing it, returning it to its status as a typeset, illustrated journal. It is now published and edited by Steven Rothman of Philadelphia. The *Journal* is also on the internet, and a searchable set of CD-ROMs reproduces its first fifty years.

At about the time Holmes's American fans organized in 1934, his British counterparts formed the Sherlock Holmes Society. It was a casualty of World War II, but in 1951, inspired by the popular Sherlock Holmes Exhibition at the Marylebone Public Library during the Festival of Britain, it was resurrected, thanks to Anthony Howlett, a young barrister. Howlett spent considerable time helping the exhibition, though he admitted also being attracted by Freda Pearce, the assistant librarian and his future wife. He was joined by some of the original British Sherlockians. Renamed the Sherlock Holmes Society of London, it held its first meeting at the Victoria and Albert Museum on July 17, 1951. In May 1952 it started publishing *The Sherlock Holmes Journal* and over a half-century later, despite many changes of editors, it is still published semiannually.

The Sherlock Holmes Journal started as a mimeographed magazine, but as membership increased, the society was able to publish it on slick paper, using, appropriately, the Baskerville typeface, and including illustrations. There have been news, reviews, poetry, articles, and much material on Doyle, including a 1959 issue honoring the centennial of his birth.

Howlett continued his work on the magazine until his death in 2003. He was instrumental in a statue of Holmes being placed near the Baker Street Underground station, and he was a major force in the society's 1968 pilgrimage to Switzerland that included a recreation, in Victorian costumes, of the battle between Holmes and Professor Moriarty at the Reichenbach Falls. At the end of the battle two clothed dummies were thrown off the cliff into the Falls.

The 2003 obituary for Anthony Howlett gave a positive view of Sherlockian fandom in England, as, at first, did the death notices in 2004 for Richard Lancelyn Green, former chairman of the Sherlock Holmes Society of London. Green had joined the society at age twelve in 1965, after reading his first Holmes story. He was an obsessive collector of material relating to Doyle and Holmes, owning one of the few surviving copies of *Beeton's Christmas Annual* for 1887, the first printing of *A Study in Scarlet.* Green was also a scholar, earning a Special Edgar for his bibliography of Doyle. Ten days after Green's obituary was published, a Reuters dispatch reported there were mysterious circumstances concerning Green's death, saying he had been garroted with a shoelace. There was an inquest, and the coroner proclaimed an open verdict saying there was insufficient evidence to rule whether Green's death was murder, suicide, or a mistake. Green had mentioned a mysterious American who had damaged his relationship with Dame Jeanne Doyle, the last of Sir Arthur's children.

The popularity of Sherlock Holmes continues, and it is an international phenomenon. Peter Blau, who maintains a list of Sherlockian societies, reports, according to the website *Sherlockian.net,* that there have been over 900 at one time or another, with 417 active as of July 2017. Twenty-six nations have Sherlockian groups, including fifteen in Japan alone. There is even one in Kyrgyzstan! Forty-two of the states in the United States have such groups, with California and Illinois each having more than twenty. (New York State has eighteen.) They invariably have names derived from the Holmes tales, for example, Mrs. Hudson's Cliff Dwellers in New Jersey and the Sons of the Copper Beeches in Philadelphia.

The Saint Club (1936–)

The first non-Sherlockian group devoted to one character was The

Saint Club, founded in 1936 for those interested in Leslie Charteris and his creation, Simon Templar ("The Saint"). Charteris was active in its founding and in addition to providing publicity for him, it has always had a charity component, using its membership fees and selling Saint-related merchandise. That allowed the club, still active, to contribute to hospitals in its early days and now to facilities for youth at risk. The club published a newsletter, edited by Ian Dickerson, on an irregular basis. It was first called *The Saint Club* and then *The Saint*. In about 1992 it became *The Epistle*, but there is no record of an issue since Summer 1994.

The Saint Club has always been irreverent and the back of its membership card says:

"The bearer of this card is probably a person of hideous antecedents and low moral character, and upon apprehension for any cause should be immediately released in order to save other persons from contamination."

The Pulp Era (1950–1971, 1993)

Fans of dime novels are often fans of the "pulps." (Pulps were fiction magazines printed on untrimmed pulpwood paper that were popular from 1915 through the early 1950s.) Lynn Hickman began publishing magazines for pulp fans in 1950 while a few pulps were still published. He produced fifty-nine issues, under several titles, of a magazine once jokingly titled *JD-Argassy* (*The Pulp Era*). It began as a fanzine for fans of *Argosy*, the most varied of pulps, which though known for adventure fiction, usually had a mystery story in each issue. In the winter of 1963 Hickman changed the title to simply *The Pulp Era* and continued that fan magazine until spring 1971. It was revived briefly in 1993, but then Hickman died.

Patricia Wentworth Fan Club (1961)

Fans of Patricia Wentworth, the British writer who created that most extraordinary private detective, Maude Silver, an elderly, white-haired lady who knitted booties while interviewing her clients, formed a fan club in 1961. According to Boucher, they published a newsletter in Newport, Rhode Island. However, no other information is available regarding this club, which is no longer active.

JDM Bibliophile (1965–2004)

A more hard-boiled writer than Patricia Wentworth became the subject of a fan magazine in March 1965 when Len and June Moffatt of Downey, California, first published the *JDM Bibliophile* (*JDMB*), devoted to the work of John D. MacDonald. MacDonald starting writing for pulp magazines in 1946 during their waning days. He then switched to paperback originals, mostly for the Fawcett's Gold Medal line. In 1964 Gold Medal launched the series that made MacDonald famous when they published four novels about Florida adventurer-detective Travis McGee.

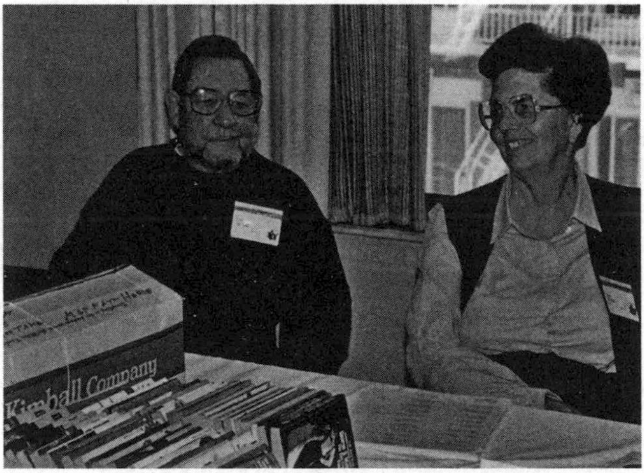

Len and June Moffatt, creators of *JDM Bibliophile*

JDMB, a mimeographed magazine at the time, was described in its initial issue as a "non-profit amateur journal devoted to the readers of John D. MacDonald and related matters." A goal was to obtain complete bibliographic information on all of MacDonald's writings, and this was partly achieved with *The JDM Master Checklist,* published in 1969 by the Moffatts. They had help from many people, including MacDonald himself. Though he kept good records, he, like most authors, didn't have complete publishing data on his own work. Especially helpful to the Moffatts were William J. Clark and another couple, Walter and Jean Shine of Florida. The Shines published an updated version of the *Checklist* in 1980, adding illustrations, a biographical sketch, and a listing of articles and reviews of MacDonald.

JDMB offered news and reviews of MacDonald's writings and their adaptation to various media. There were also contributions from MacDonald, including reminiscences and commentary. The Moffatts contributed a column ("& Everything"), as did the Shines ("The Shine Section"). Other *JDM* fans sent articles, letters, and parodies. One issue, #25 in 1979, included the Shines' "Confidential Report, a Private Investigators' File on Travis McGee," describing information gleaned from the McGee canon about his past, interests, cases, and associates. MacDonald once said of Walter Shine, "He knows more about Travis than I do."

After the Moffatts had published twenty-two issues of *JDMB,* it was transferred in 1979 to the University of South Florida in Tampa, with Professor Edgar Hirshberg as editor. It continued until 1999. One final issue, #65, was published as a memorial to Hirshberg who had died in June 2002. It was edited by Valerie Lawson.

On February 21, 1987, about a hundred McGee fans gathered at his "address," Slip F-18 at the Bahia Mar Marina in Fort Lauderdale, Florida, where McGee kept his houseboat *The Busted Flush*. The mayor of Fort Lauderdale unveiled a plaque honoring McGee.

Doc Savage Fandom (1965–)

In 1964, Bantam began reprinting the Doc Savage pulp stories as paperbacks. Lester Dent had written most of these under the pseudonym "Kenneth Robeson." *Bronze Shadows,* a fan magazine edited and published by Fred Cook and devoted to the crime-fighting hero, often referred to as "The Man of Bronze," appeared in October 1965. It lasted fifteen issues, until November 1968. It was followed by Lynn Meyers, Jr.'s *Doc Savage Journal* (1969), but that only had one issue.

The success of Bantam's Doc Savage reprints, continuing into the 1970s, eventually led to publication of at least ten more fan magazines about Savage. *The Doc Savage Reader,* a mimeographed magazine, whose first issue was January 1973, was published by John Cosgriff of Illinois and Mark J. Golden of Virginia. Other commitments forced this magazine to be discontinued after October 1973. *The Doc Savage Reader* was notable for the earliest fan writing of Will Murray, considered the most knowledgeable person about Doc Savage; he later wrote new novels about Savage. All issues of *The Doc Savage Reader* contained Dave McDonnell's satire "Doc Garbage." Another parody, in 1979, showing that fandom need not be serious, was George Chastain's "Dog Sausage," with the hero depicted as a pig.

Murray was also a contributor to the similarly titled *The Doc Savage Club Reader,* begun in 1977 by Frank Lewandowski of Berwyn, Illinois, as an outgrowth of the Doc Savage Fan Club, started by paperback cover artist Jim Steranko. Like Sherlockians, Doc Savage fans formed local chapters. Lewandowski formed two in the Chicago area. When Bantam suspended reprints of the Doc Savage series, Lewandowski led a letter campaign that resulted in their resumption. Because of non-Savage material he was also receiving, Lewandowski changed the magazine's name to *Nemesis, Inc.* It continued until 1991.

The *Doc Savage Fan Magazine,* founded in 1974, had five issues. *The Man of Bronze* (1975), *Doc Savage and Associates* (1976), and the *Doc Savage Forum* (1979) lasted only one issue each.

The *Doc Savage Quarterly* was started in January 1980 by Bill Laidlaw of San Luis Obispo, California. Despite its title, it also offered articles and reviews on non-Savage subjects, for example Richard Benson, the pulp hero known as "The Avenger." Most of the Benson stories, like those about Doc Savage, were published under the pseudonym "Kenneth Robeson," the name Lester Dent also used for writing *Doc Savage*. The *Doc Savage Quarterly* lasted for fourteen issues.

The *Quarterly* was followed by still more Doc Savage fan magazines. *The Savage Society of Bronze* (1982–1985) and *Zine of Bronze* (2007–2012) lasted seven issues each. There is only one Savage fan journal that is not defunct. *The Bronze Gazette* (formerly *The Doc Savage Gazette*) was published from 1990 to 2015 (75 issues) by Howard Wright's Green Eagle Publications of Modesto, California. Since 2015 it has been published by Terry Allen's Fantom Press in a colorful format as the "Unofficial Magazine for the Fan of Bronze." Continuing "gimmicks" of past pop culture, it offers a "decoder bookmark" to subscribers; it is published three times yearly.

Edgar Wallace Organizations (1965–2011)

The Edgar Wallace Club was organized by Penelope Wallace, daughter of the popular and prolific English author. (About 1930 it was estimated that one of every four books published in England was by Wallace.) The purpose was "to bring together all who have an interest in her father's life and work; to keep his name alive in the memories of older readers; to introduce new generations to his stories." The club first met in December 1965. A souvenir program from that meeting became part of first issue of *The Edgar Wallace Club Newsletter*, a quarterly publication, when it was published in January 1969. One feature of the newsletter was a listing of Wallace in print, and in 1969, 37 years after Wallace died, fifty-three of his books were still in print, mainly in England, but also in Germany, where he was very popular. The newsletter facilitated exchanges of Wallace books and also published lost Wallace material, including poems, short stories, and even his lyrics to a song.

In January 1971 the name was changed to The Edgar Wallace Society. By 1972 there were 120 members, many of whom were Americans, including Lianne Carlin and Allen J. Hubin. Penelope Wallace, though listed as "Organizer," no longer produced the newsletter. However she remained President of the Edgar Wallace Society until her death in January 1997.

In February 1986 the newsletter became *The Crimson Circle,* the title of a popular Wallace novel. There were periods of inactivity, but in August 2000 *The Crimson Circle* resumed, with Penelope Wyrd, Wallace's granddaughter, now "Organizer/Administrator" and Pim Koldewijn of the Netherlands as editor. Issues were brief and sporadic, compared to the earlier days of the club. The last, No.120, appeared in Summer 2004.

During a hiatus of the Edgar Wallace Society, Alan Carter set up the Edgar Wallace Appreciation Society, publishing six issues of its newsletter, *The Edgar Wallace Journal,* in 1999–2000; it resumed in December 2003, usually in the form of a single folded sheet. The last issue appears to have been No. 31 in December 2011.

The Praed Street Irregulars and *The Pontine Dossier* (1966–1977)

Long before the Sherlockian popularity of the 1970s, sparked by Nicholas Meyer's bestseller *The Seven-Per-Cent Solution* (1974), August Derleth began a series of pastiches about a Holmes-like detective, Solar Pons, and his friend and chronicler, Dr. Lyndon Parker. Pons was created in 1928 after Derleth confirmed, through correspondence with Arthur Conan Doyle, that there would be no more Sherlock Holmes adventures. Upon the death of Derleth in 1971, the series was continued by Basil Copper. Eventually, there were almost one hundred novels and short stories about Pons, more than about Holmes.

Luther Norris of California founded a society in 1966 devoted to this pastiche character, using the name Praed Street Irregulars (PSI) after the street on which Pons "lived." In February 1967 Norris founded a journal for the society, *The Pontine Dossier,* which he published until his death in January 1978. The PSI had annual dinners in the Los Angeles area, beginning in April 1967.

The John Dickson Carr Bibliophile **(1966)**

There was only one issue of *The John Dickson Carr Bibliophile,* published by Rick Sneary for the August 1966 mailing of FAPA (the Fantasy Amateur Press Association). Members of FAPA were often fans of the mystery too, and early issues of the *JDMB* were part of FAPA mailings. Because Anthony Boucher mentioned the Carr bibliophile in his column, this four-page document played a vital role in mystery fandom. When Allen J. Hubin contemplated publishing *The Armchair Detective,* he asked the people who had ordered Sneary's list to determine if there was sufficient fan interest for such a journal. (Anthony Boucher gave him their names.) Only when most of those who responded to Hubin said they were interested did Hubin go ahead with the magazine.

Chapter Two

THE ARMCHAIR DETECTIVE (1967–1997)

The Armchair Detective (TAD) was a *catalyst* for the fan revolution, perhaps an appropriate term considering that its founder, Allen J. Hubin, was a research chemist. It gave fans an outlet for their enthusiasm about mystery fiction and led to other fan publications. *TAD* encouraged fans to write scholarly works about the mystery, many of which won MWA Edgar Awards. It brought the mystery a degree of academic respectability reflected in Ph.D. dissertations and courses taught at the university level. It brought fans together, first in informal gatherings, then in increasingly large meetings such as the World Mystery Convention, Bouchercon.

Photo by Marilyn Hubin

Al Hubin and Mike Nevins collating copies of *TAD* in 1969

If Al Hubin had trepidations about starting the magazine, his experience after Boucher's rave review of the first issue (October 1967) only increased them. He expected some responses a few days after the Sunday on which Boucher's review was published, but come Wednesday his mailbox was empty. Some detective work on his part led him to a nearby playground where he found that neighborhood children had—for the first and only time—plundered his mailbox and scattered his mail there. Hubin was able to retrieve all forty new subscriptions. More came, and soon all two hundred copies he had printed were gone, necessitating a second printing.

The early issues of *TAD* show what fans wanted to read—and what they were willing to write. Because most books *about* the mystery were out of print and because bibliographic material was in short supply, fans wanted to read about favorite authors, and they wanted checklists that would allow them to complete their collections of these authors and their series detectives. Furthermore, though the "Golden Age" of detective fiction (usually dated from 1920 through 1939) was far in the past, *TAD*'s early readers seemed primarily interested in it, especially in writers who had flourished then, such as Agatha Christie, R. Austin Freeman, Henry Wade, and Freeman Wills Crofts. Though major writers were eventually covered in *TAD* articles and checklists, one of the joys of early *TAD* was the number of obscure—though worthwhile—writers to whom space was given. Such non-household names as Rodrigues Ottolengui, C.E. Vulliamy, Seeley Regester, and L.T. Meade come to mind.

TAD readers wanted to communicate with other fans, and the letters section quickly became a popular feature. Correspondents corrected and added to what had been written, asked questions, and received answers. Some requested assistance, as did William F. Nolan when he did not receive cooperation from Dashiell Hammett's lover, Lillian Hellman, on the biography of Hammett Nolan was writing.

TAD's first issue contained thirty pages. (The cost of a year's subscription then was two dollars for four issues.) The lead article was by Sherlockian scholar William S. Baring-Gould, to whom the issue was dedicated because he died three weeks after submitting it. His article was not about Holmes; it was about Fu Manchu. Considering the popularity of the Holmes canon, *TAD* contained comparatively little Sherlockian material, undoubtedly because *The Baker Street Journal* was available. However, the second issue had a history of Sherlockian fandom by John Bennett Shaw, perhaps America's leading scholar of the canon.

Another Sherlockian, James Keddie, Jr., contributed "Rambling Thoughts on a Tec Collection," an article about his thirty years of reading and collecting mysteries. Especially valuable was Keddie's suggested reading list of twenty-one books *about* mystery fiction and collecting, including one that had been recently published about Agatha Christie by Gordon C. Ramsey. The first issue of *TAD* included "A Teacher Meets Agatha Christie," an article by Ramsey about his interview with Christie and his nervousness at the prospect of meeting the great lady.

I had promised, in responding to Hubin's original survey, to write for *TAD*. I was now faced with having to write something to keep my promise. I contributed "Religion and Detection: Sunday the Rabbi Met Father Brown," combining a brief survey of authors and detectives who were members of the clergy, along with a pastiche in which the detectives created by Harry Kemelman and G.K. Chesterton meet.

The first issue was noteworthy for "The Paperback Revolution," the first of one hundred consecutive columns by Charles Shibuk reviewing paperback mysteries. There were also film notes by William K. Everson, perhaps the leading expert on detective films. *TAD* was also a source of mystery news that included lists of books recently published.

Hubin found that a fellow Minnesotan, Ordean Hagen, was compiling the first bibliography of crime fiction, and in *TAD*'s second issue Hagen wrote about his project. His book was published in 1969 as *Who Done It?* but, sadly, Hagen died before it came out. In the pages of *TAD,* then in a book that has been updated five times and become a CD-ROM, Hubin corrected Hagen's work, added thousands of titles, and published his massive *Crime Fiction IV A Comprehensive Bibliography 1749–2000.*

Though Edgar Wallace had been dead for thirty-five years, crime writer Nigel Morland was still alive and able to reminisce about "The Edgar Wallace I Knew" in *TAD*'s third issue. Frank Gruber and Steve Fisher wrote of their early days as pulp writers, with Fisher recalling the reclusive Cornell Woolrich, about whom there was much interest. Meanwhile, Francis M. Nevins began his writing about Woolrich that eventually led to his Edgar-winning biography. With the help of Bill Thailing and Hal Knott, he published a Woolrich bibliography. Thailing, the ultimate Woolrich fan, wrote that he first read Woolrich on a troopship going to the South Pacific in World War II, but he let his enthusiasm carry him away when he described Woolrich as "the greatest writer the world has ever known."

Enthusiasm was also apparent in other early work published in *TAD.* Nolan provided the first complete checklist of Hammett's Continental Op stories. Keddie wrote about crime plays, and Frank P. Donovan authored a four-part series on railroad mysteries.

Before *TAD* was born, Robert E. Briney and William J. Clark started a checklist of the works of John Creasey. With Creasey's help, Briney completed the bibliography (521 novels) of the man then considered mystery's most prolific writer. Hubin later discovered and interviewed for *TAD* Lauran Bosworth Paine, who wrote over 600 books.

Another Minnesotan, J. Randolph Cox, wrote about a course on the mystery, possibly the first for college credit, he taught at St. Olaf's College in January 1971. (Cox also wrote for *TAD* on Nick Carter, A. A. Milne, and George Harmon Coxe.) That the mystery had begun to achieve academic status was reflected in *TAD,* beginning with Joan M. Mooney's Ph.D. dissertation, "Best

Selling American Detective Fiction," published in five issues beginning in 1970. Another doctoral dissertation, "The Problem of Moral Vision in Dashiell Hammett's Detective Novels," by George J. Thompson, appeared in seven parts, starting in 1973. These articles met with the approval of some *TAD* readers, but others complained that they were dry and lacked the enthusiasm of the fans who had been writing for *TAD* without the prospect of academic advancement.

A problem raised early in *TAD*'s history (and still discussed today) is whether it is possible to write intelligent criticism of a mystery without disclosing vital plot elements and/or the ending. Frank McSherry complained that Donald Yates had given away too many solutions and surprises in his 1970 piece on locked rooms. Hubin devised a compromise: warning in advances if articles contained plot spoilers.

Because *TAD*'s readers felt strongly about their favorite escape reading, they sometimes disagreed with each other and had wildly divergent opinions about the same book. Shibuk thought Barzun and Taylor's *A Catalogue of Crime* (1971) was "the greatest contribution to the genre in the last thirty years." However, George Wuyek thought Barzun and Taylor "highly biased and selective." Bill Pronzini, also a fan and supporter of *TAD*, criticized Barzun and Taylor for emphasizing classic detective puzzles, calling their book the "most exasperating, depressing, and irritating book I've ever come across."

In 1971 Bruce Monblatt attacked *TAD* for "the shenanigans of the Baker Street Irregulars" and "frivolous attempts to talk of eccentric author Harry Stephen Keeler." He praised efforts to make the mystery "academically respectable and relevant." He thought detective novels were now "preempting the mainstream novel as the mirror of modern society" and told of how moved he was by scenes of violence in the novels of Ed McBain. Nevins replied that there was a surprising amount of social relevance in Keeler.

Like Sherlockians, I used mock scholarship in my 1971 *TAD*

article "The Secret Life of Perry Mason." I "proved" that Lieutenant Tragg was really Mason's brother and that Mason and Della Street had a love affair. R. Gordon Kelly wrote to punch holes in my theories, missing the point of my perhaps feeble attempt at humor.

Fred Dueren wanted more about Golden Age authors, while Frank Eck and Jon Jackson thought there was too much on early writers. In 1974, Regina Cohen felt Mickey Spillane had been underrated, while James Sandoe, a leading expert on hardboiled writers, responded by welcoming a debate on Spillane, whom he called a "dreadful fellow," and said about the Mike Hammer novels, "I don't have stomach enough to reread them to speak for the prosecution."

The Daughter of Time by Josephine Tey is often considered one of the ten greatest detective novels, so it was with surprise that *TAD* readers read in 1977 an attack on that book by Guy M. Townsend, a historian who said, "Tey makes a mockery of scholarly research by ignoring and distorting evidence." Many wrote objecting to Townsend's thesis, pointing out he was not distinguishing between historical writing and fiction, and that Tey was writing for mystery readers, not scholars. Strongest in criticizing Townsend was Myrna J. Smith, whom he then implied was a hysterical female, leading her to reply that he was "snobbish and arrogant." She might have called him sexist too.

Despite its considerable scholarship and disagreements, *TAD* was not all seriousness. Jon L. Breen, Veronica Kennedy, Robert Aucott, and R.W. Hays provided quizzes. There were poems by Ola Strøm. Ed Lauterbach told Sherlockian jokes. Other articles of mock scholarship, in addition to mine, included Thomas D. Waugh's "The Missing Years of Nero Wolfe" and Eileen Snyder's "Was Watson Jack the Ripper?" Beginning with Vol. 18 No. 1, (Winter 1985), Louis Phillips began a humor column "Dial N for Nonsense."

Though Francis M. Nevins was serious in writing about Harry Stephen Keeler, the wackiness and length of Keeler's plots (some Keeler novels were seven hundred pages long) lent themselves to readers' chuckling at such Nevins articles as "The Worst Legal Mystery in the World," "The Wild and Wooly World of Harry Stephen Keeler," and "Hick Dick from the Sticks: Harry Stephen Keeler's Quiribus Brown." Nevins, calling himself "Hellgate Newlander," a deliberate variation on Newgate Callendar, the pseudonym of the *New York Times Book Review* mystery reviewer in the 1970s and 1980s, wrote humorous reviews, especially of the books of Michael Avallone.

Bill Pronzini contributed funny articles on Phoenix Books, a publisher known for its poor mysteries, and on his choice as "the *worst* mystery novel of all time," *Decoy,* by the pseudonymous "Michael Morgan." William F. Deeck wrote of James Corbett, another unconsciously funny mystery writer who somehow published over forty books despite prose that included lines such as "Nothing could have surprised the astonishment on his countenance."

For almost ten years Al Hubin produced *The Armchair Detective* single-handedly, with only help from his five children or an occasional visitor in collating *TAD* for mailing. In addition to his large family, he had a responsible full-time job and from 1968 through 1971 was mystery critic for the *New York Times Book Review.*

In 1976 Hubin accepted an offer from Publisher's Inc. of Del Mar, California, an adjunct of the University of California at San Diego (UCSD), to publish *TAD,* thus relieving him of the chores of typing copy, addressing, stuffing and mailing over a thousand envelopes, managing subscriptions, and finding sources of revenue through advertising and new subscribers.

Publisher's Inc.'s proprietorship of *TAD,* began with Vol. 9, No. 3 (June 1976), and the immediate reaction was favorable, especially because their professional printing permitted double columns that were easier to read than the long horizontal lines that Hubin used. Saddle stitching was another improvement over the stapled *TAD,* from which the last pages sometimes came loose. Answering Jim Goodrich, who worried that he was losing control of *TAD,* Hubin admitted that work on his bibliography prevented his commenting on most letters but that he still had editorial control, though "the selection of the final contents, and their arrangements in the issue, is largely outside my activity." Hubin also said that *TAD* was receiving fewer letters and articles. Perhaps that was because other magazines started in the 1970s had the more personal, fan focus of early *TAD.*

The stewardship of *TAD* by Publisher's Inc. lasted only two years. Their ambitions exceeded their resources. As late as their final issue (July 1978), C. David Hellyer, managing editor, was promising to make available nationally, through UCSD, a college-level course on the mystery, mystery lecture tours, seminars, and a volume of the best of *TAD.* Promises were not kept; they were having severe financial problems, which also led to the demise of their Mystery Library. They used a mailing service that proved inefficient for subscriptions, and they did not answer letters from subscribers who did not receive their issues.

Otto Penzler, the fan who became a one-man industry

By the summer of 1978, *The Armchair Detective* was on the brink of death in California when in New York a rescuer appeared: Otto Penzler, long-time (though he was only thirty-five) fan and writer. Penzler had collaborated on *Detectionary* (1971) and *Encyclopedia of Mystery and Detection* (1976) and had founded a publishing company, Mysterious Press. He took over *TAD* effective with the October 1978 issue, and though he initially had difficulty getting the material for that issue from Publishers, Inc., to whom it had been submitted, Penzler produced the issue.

Despite further problems in receiving subscription information from California, Penzler worked to restore *TAD*'s good reputation. By Summer 1979, *TAD* had an outstanding issue devoted to Ellery Queen on the fiftieth anniversary of *The Roman Hat Mystery.* The covers of *TAD* were improved, thanks to artwork by Carolyn Hartman (then Mrs. Penzler). However, there were still delays in mailing, and as Penzler said in the Spring 1980 issue, almost 10 percent of copies mailed were never received, the fault, he implied, of the Postal Service. With great personal effort, he eventually kept his promise that "we'll do the best we can to make the magazine appear regularly and that everyone gets all the issues due them."

With the end of Volume 13 in 1980, Hubin relinquished the editorship of *TAD,* though he continued as consultant and book reviewer. Hubin had edited fifty-two issues (4,062 pages), without any remuneration, but he thanked those who had contributed to *TAD.*

Hubin was replaced by Michael Seidman, an editor with Charter Books. Seidman, writing in *TAD* and elsewhere, displayed a writer/editor viewpoint regarding fandom, believing that fans should support writers by buying books. Of course, he was writing before the genre achieved greater success in the late 1980s. In Vol. 14, No.3 (Summer 1981), his editorial expressed the opinion that fans were not supporting writers sufficiently, finishing with the admonition "READ AN AMERICAN MYSTERY" (Seidman's emphasis).

Seidman called Bouchercon "a celebration of the writer," ignoring that it had been started by fans. When bookstores reported rising sales of mysteries in 1983, he told *TAD*'s readers, "Obviously, it will now be up to us to make certain we support the bookstores and publishers." On the subject of awards, he closed his editorial in Vol. 17, No. 3 (Summer 1984) by saying, "It is our support for the writers—through book purchases and fan mail—that is the most meaningful recognition."

By the autumn of 1985, Seidman said that the request *TAD*

most often received was for more reviews. He offered to send review copies to fans who promised to review them. By the following spring, seventeen of *TAD*'s 110 pages were reviews. Opening the floodgates to reviewers led to some negative reviews. These probably troubled publishers, who were increasingly advertising in *TAD*, more than they bothered fans. Seidman then said that he would like to avoid negative reviews in the future "unless there is some depth to the review and some point is made." By Volume 29, about 25 percent of the magazine consisted of reviews of new books. *TAD* also tried to be friendly to booksellers and publishers. It ran a fifteen-page list of American mystery booksellers in 1992 and the Independent Mystery Booksellers Association's best-seller lists, starting in 1993.

Readers bemoaned the paltry number of letters compared to *TAD*'s early days. Vol. 17, Nos. 3 and 4, had only two letters each. Assuming all letters received were published (a generous assumption since several letters I sent never appeared), *TAD*'s readers seemed less interested in writing. Jon L. Breen in Vol. 18, No. 3 (Summer 1985), perceptively questioned whether the shortage of letters wasn't at least partly caused by the time lag between an issue and the publication of letters responding to material in it. For example, the two letters in Vol. 17, No. 4, referred to Vol. 17, No. 1.

TAD began publishing original short stories in 1990, justifying this as providing another market for writers. This proved unpopular with many *TAD* readers who expressed opinions; they felt the magazine should stick to writing *about* the mystery.

In William L. DeAndrea *TAD* acquired its most controversial contributor, an Edgar-winning novelist whose column "J'Accuse" was either loved or hated by fans, but seldom ignored. His opinions on mysteries as well as the Gulf War and political correctness seldom failed to draw either praise or ire. He was at his angriest reacting to a lengthy *TAD* article in the Summer 1986 issue by Bill Delaney, titled "Ross Macdonald's Literary Offenses." DeAndrea called this article that was critical of Macdonald "dreck" and "an attack of alphabetical dysentery." Several letters also criticized Delaney, and one reader canceled his *TAD* subscription because of him.

Volume 20, No. 4 (Fall 1987), included comments on possible discrimination against women. *TAD* was reflecting not only American society but also MWA, where there were complaints by Phyllis Whitney and others that women writers had not won a fair share of the Edgars. Member of the 1987 Edgar committees were told to be "gender conscious." In his column, DeAndrea frowned upon another Whitney suggestion, one never adopted by MWA, that there be a separate Edgar for romantic suspense, presumably because women often wrote in that subgenre. However, since 2001 MWA has given the Mary Higgins Clark Award for the best book that met guidelines set forth by Clark. These guidelines discourage the use of unnecessary violence, explicit sex, and four-letter words.

Not willing to depend only on articles submitted, *TAD* assembled, in addition to DeAndrea, an impressive stable of columnists. Shibuk continued until he had completed twenty-five years. Jacques Barzun and Wendell Hertig Taylor updated their 1971 book. John L. Breen's columns, "What About Murder?" and "Novel Verdicts," continued his two Edgar-winning books. The prolific Edward D. Hoch found time to write a short story column, "Minor Offenses." Richard Meyers reviewed television mysteries; Thomas Godfrey reviewed crime films; Chris Steinbrunner reviewed old-time radio mysteries; and Dick Lochte and Tom Nolan reviewed audio mysteries. I reviewed first mysteries in a column I called "Original Sins." Janet A. Rudolph, founder of Mystery Readers International, wrote "Murderous Affairs," which told of mystery conventions, fan magazines, awards, and other activities. There was a Baker Street column by Scott and Sherry Bond and two columns in the form of ongoing newsletters about Rex Stout and Dorothy L. Sayers.

Seidman said he was growing stale as editor of *TAD* and relinquished that job to Kathy Daniel effective Vol. 22, No. 1 (Winter 1989). Daniel reached the point, beginning in 1989, where *TAD* was able to pay, albeit modestly, contributors for articles and columns. She instituted the practice of guest editorials, though she invariably used professional writers or editors rather than the fans who had supported *TAD*.

With Vol. 25, No. 3 (Summer 1992), Kate Stine replaced Daniel, maintaining *TAD*'s standard of quality. In 1995 Judi Vause became managing editor and advertising manager and then bought the magazine from Penzler. *TAD* seemed as strong as ever when in 1996 at Bouchercon it won an Anthony as Best Magazine, while *The Armchair Detective Book of Lists*, edited by Stine, won as Best Critical Work. If *TAD* was in financial trouble, its readers were not aware of it. At the beginning of Vol. 30, almost 15 percent of the magazine's space consisted of ads. *TAD* had over six thousand readers who bought it either by mail or from dealers. That was far more than any other fan magazine.

TAD's luck ran out. DeAndrea died in October 1996, only forty-four years old, of liver cancer. Elizabeth Foxwell replaced Stine as editor in 1997 for Vol. 30, No. 3, only to find she was boarding a sinking ship. The magazine was suspended after that issue. Foxwell wrote in *Mystery & Detection Monthly* that Judi Vause was having "physical and financial problems." Vause never answered mail, nor did she pay contributors or reimburse subscribers for issues they never received. One can understand how illness or financial problems can befall a publisher. However, it was inexcusable for someone not to tell her subscribers there are difficulties, and that she will try to reimburse them when she can. Rumors circulated that someone else would buy *TAD*, but that never happened, and the magazine that meant the most to mystery fandom died.

TAD's importance to fandom cannot be overstated. It encouraged fans to share their knowledge and enthusiasm with others and helped to create an international fan base, with subscribers from Australia, Belgium, Denmark, Great Britain, Germany, Israel, Italy, Japan, The Netherlands, Norway, Portugal, and Sweden. The articles and scholarship that first saw the light in its pages led to a significant increase in the number of books *about* the mystery. *TAD*'s longevity and professionalism set a standard by which all other fan journals are judged.

Chapter Three

THE MYSTERY LOVER'S/READER'S NEWSLETTER (1967–1973)

Coincidentally, a second general-interest fan magazine appeared in the same month as *The Armchair Detective:* October 1967. It actually appeared before *TAD* because a prospectus issue was sent in August to potential subscribers who answered a notice in *The Baker Street Journal. The Mystery Lover's Newsletter* (*TMLN*) was the creation of Lianne Carlin of Revere, Massachusetts, then a stay-at-home mother of a two-year-old, who was anxious to use her journalism training. A mystery reader, she wondered why there was no journal for mystery fans.

TMLN's first issue had twelve pages. Two articles were reprints: a brief biography of Alfred Hitchcock and the remainder of W.B. Stevenson's chapbook, *Detective Fiction,* the first part of which formed half of the prospectus. Mrs. Carlin's husband, Stanley, using the pseudonym "S. Carl Linn," wrote an article "Detective Fiction and Hemingway," revealing Hemingway as a fan of Raymond Chandler and Georges Simenon. There was also publishing news, queries from readers, and a "Book Mart" page for subscribers to list book wants and books they had for sale.

Gradually, *TMLN* published more original material and attracted most of the same cadre of fan-scholars as *TAD.* Robert Washer, Luther Norris, Robert Sampson, John McAleer, and Bill Crider appeared first in *TMLN.* They wrote articles and checklists about writers, including Ellery Queen, Ernest Bramah, Nick Carter, Anthony Gilbert, Clayton Rawson, and Josephine Tey. Because some checklists contained errors or were incomplete, *TMLN*'s readers used their considerable knowledge for corrections. Charles Shibuk, a movie fan, adapted the annotated checklist, a common practice in film scholarship, to the mystery with his list of Chandler on screen.

TMLN may have been strong on scholarship, but it wasn't solemn. Nevins published his earliest writing about Harry Stephen Keeler, whom he called "the sublime nutty genius of the crime genre," as well as "Department of Unrelated Miscellanea," a running series about lighter aspects of the mystery. I wrote a parody-pastiche in which Della Street, Nikki Porter, and other secretaries to famous detectives form a union and go out on strike. It ended with Perry Mason forced to answer his own phone.

Not having as large a list of subscribers, nor the benefits of a Boucher review, as did *TAD, TMLN* began more modestly. It grew larger but only reached twenty-two pages at the end of its second year and never went beyond fifty-one pages. Carlin changed its name to *The Mystery Reader's Newsletter (TMRN)* in 1969 because she found that a "smoother, more professional" title. Helped in part by a notice in Hubin's column in the *New York Times Book Review* and an ad in *Ellery Queen's Mystery Magazine, TMRN* eventually had about five hundred subscribers.

TMRN was strong on interviews, with Mary Stewart, Nicholas Blake, Ira Levin, Joyce Porter, Howard Haycraft, John Ball, and Elizabeth Linington among the subjects. The Linington interview by Ann Waldron drew a heated response from Linington in the next issue because she thought that Waldron overemphasized her

Photo by Carol Lachman

(left to right) Charles Shibuk, Lianne Carlin, and Marv Lachman at the first Mystery Readers' Party in 1969

involvement in the John Birch Society, a right-wing organization, making her seem "a very foolish and fanatical person."

It wasn't only about politics that readers of *TMRN* felt strongly. Shibuk and Nevins, who later became good friends after they met in person, came to verbal blows as a result of Shibuk's letter in Vol. 2 No.1: he disagreed with Nevins, who called Hammett's *Red Harvest* "subtle." Nevins defended his point and then, in turn, criticized Shibuk's opinions denigrating Hitchcock's later films, remarking that he couldn't expect to "see eye-to-eye" with someone holding those views.

James Mark Purcell's "All Good Mysteries Are Short Stories" was a self-styled "polemic" which began, "I'd like to start an argument. I think the novel is the wrong length for the straight detective story." He drew an unfortunate analogy to racism to describe what he perceived as prejudice against the short story. He was criticized in the following issue by Bill Crider and Randy Cox. Even I, arguably the biggest fan of short stories, thought he overlooked much, including that novel length allows deeper characterization and more complex plotting.

However, I welcomed his infusion of controversy into the pages of *TMRN*.

TMRN published a column by Rona Randall on the mystery scene in the United Kingdom. In 1972 Randall wrote about the birth and growth of England's Crime Writers Association. Pat Erhardt wrote a report on the first Bouchercon. Professional writers, including Howard Haycraft, Phyllis Whitney, Helen McCloy, and John Creasey, sent letters to *TMRN*. In 1970, acting on a suggestion from Lianne Carlin, I started a series, "The American Regional Mystery," in which I described how mysteries captured the distinctive geography, customs, and speech of each U.S. region. I eventually turned it into a book of the same name, published in 2000.

Having fallen behind in *TMRN*'s schedule, Carlin wrote in Vol. 5 No. 6 of her problems as she juggled publishing with raising two small children and holding down a part-time job. Originally bimonthly, *TMRN* became quarterly. A prescient letter writer, William Ruble, wrote in Vol. 6 No. 1, "I hope this is not the first step toward ceasing publication altogether." After the following issue (Autumn 1973), personal problems forced Carlin to terminate publication. When, thirty years later, I interviewed her for this book, she remembered fondly "the newsletter's talented and loyal contributors and readers. They were the true essence of the publication. The newsletter turned out to be an eye-opening enterprise (so much knowledge out there!) as well as fun!"

Chapter Four

MYSTERY READERS' PARTIES (1969–1976)

Mystery fans began to communicate, but in the days before email it was via letters or phone calls. I learned in April 1969 that Al Hubin, Lianne Carlin, and Bob Washer were attending the MWA Edgar Awards banquet in New York City, along with their spouses. Also present would be out-of-town fans Bob Briney, Francis "Mike" Nevins, Patricia Erhardt, and Hal Knott. I lived in New York then and looked forward to meeting people I had only known through the written word. With the enthusiastic agreement of my wife, Carol, I sent invitations for Saturday night to what I called "The First Mystery Readers of America Party." That organization didn't exist; I made it up as a reason to have a party for mystery fans. Because most of the people were staying in Manhattan, I included subway directions to the northern reaches of the Bronx where we resided. Also invited was Charlie Shibuk, a fellow Bronxite.

We lived on the nineteenth floor of a large apartment building, and, for the first time since we moved there, all the elevators went out of commission on the evening of the party. Early arrivals Erhardt and Knott decided to walk up the stairs, an easy job for Hal, a mountain climber. Pat, on the other hand, was a sedentary person and a heavy smoker. She arrived out of breath.

Fortunately, the elevators were quickly repaired because Al and Marilyn Hubin came with a frail, seventyish Canadian mystery fan, Estelle Fox, in tow. She was one of many uninvited people who came as word spread that mystery fans and writers were welcome at the Lachmans. Estelle was proud of her collection of twenty-four scrapbooks containing reviews, articles, correspondence, and autographs of mystery writers. In her will, she left those to the Toronto Reference Library. She also had a collection of the first mysteries of over a thousand authors.

The conversations, unfortunately never recorded, were memorable. In a *TAD* editorial, Hubin commented, "What a pleasure to sit among knowledgeable people and talk of things mysterious on into the night!" Lianne Carlin called the party "the mystery buff's answer to LSD: habit-forming, heady, but harmless." A highlight of the evening was Nevins describing the wacky plots of Harry Stephen Keeler. Tales of what Nevins called Keeler's "Screwball Circus" had everyone laughing. The conversations weren't only about mystery; some spouses weren't even mystery fans. We learned a great deal about each other's personal lives.

Two regulars at our parties, beginning in 1971, were Otto Penzler and Chris Steinbrunner, with whom Shibuk and I collaborated on two books about the mystery. One year when Chris had a good bit of alcohol to drink, he was feeling warm and decided to get some fresh air. Not seeing the screen door, he accidentally pushed it aside, emerging on to our terrace where only the railing prevented his falling nineteen floors.

Other occasional attendees included Bob Aucott, a Philadelphian who was a poet, Sherlockian, and expert on baseball; Randy Cox, the world's leading expert on Nick Carter; Amnon Kabatchnik, theatre director and leading expert on crime plays;

Jon L. Breen, reviewer and master of the art of pastiches and parodies; mystery film expert Norman Nolan; and Richmond Pugh, a friendly Manhattanite who smoked cigars. Many attendees smoked, but, though this was after the Surgeon General's 1964 report, we weren't as health-conscious then and I didn't think of asking our guests not to.

Mystery writers attended because they were fans as well as writers. One early guest was Edward D. Hoch, *the* legendary short story writer. Ed brought another writer, Dan J. Marlowe, who gave up a business career to become a writer and became successful in his new field after publishing the novel *The Name of the Game is Death* (1962), about which Dan told a fascinating story. His book turned fugitive bank robber Al Nussbaum into a fan of Marlowe's work. After Nussbaum's arrest, an admiring phone call Nussbaum had previously placed to Marlowe, was traced by the FBI, who interrogated Marlowe, hoping to get information about Nussbaum's confederate, who was still at large and wanted for murder. Marlowe took an interest in Nussbaum, encouraged him to write while he was in prison, where he became a model prisoner. Marlowe was also instrumental in Nussbaum receiving parole. Later, Nussbaum became a published writer, and in the 1980s, when Marlowe suffered a disabling stroke, Nussbaum became his guardian.

The 1969 party was a huge success and our parties became an annual event through 1976. The Bronx seemed to be the gathering place for mystery fans, which was probably appropriate since Edgar Allan Poe had lived about a mile from where I did.

In 1977, Carol and I did not have time to prepare for our usual Saturday party. Friday, we were attending the MWA banquet because Penzler, Shibuk, Steinbrunner, and Lachman were nominated for an Edgar for *Encyclopedia of Mystery and Detection.* Anyway, Bouchercon was becoming *the* place for fans to meet, and the Mystery Readers' Parties became a pleasant memory.

Chapter Five

OTHER FAN MAGAZINES AND ORGANIZATIONS: 1960S

With two general-interest fan magazines established in the United States in 1967, another began in Sweden, and other fans started magazines devoted to favorite authors. It was early days in a publishing revolution that would eventually see dozens of fan magazines. Most did not last; the time, effort, and money involved usually defeated even the most enthusiastic fans.

The Rohmer Review (1968–1981)

An early journal devoted to a specific author was *The Rohmer Review,* edited and published for the Sax Rohmer Society by Dr. Douglas A. Rossman, zoology professor at Louisiana State University. It first came out in July 1968. Robert E. Briney, later chairman of the computer sciences department at Salem State University in Massachusetts, was Associate Editor, and a highlight of the first issue was his article "An Informal Survey of the Works of Sax Rohmer."

Rossman and Briney were among those who believed the creator of Dr. Fu Manchu deserved greater fame. Fu Manchu was once one of the most famous characters in crime fiction, and the description of him as "the yellow peril incarnate in one man" is famous, though relatively little was known about Rohmer by most fans. By its second issue, *The Rohmer Review* had 134 subscribers. Briney, who started his own Rohmer collection because he couldn't find books by him in public libraries, became editor/publisher with the fifth issue, August 1970. *Rohmer Review* was published semi-annually until 1974, and then other pressing matters forced Briney into "irregular" publication. Sometimes a year would go by between issues, and then two would be published within a month. Four years elapsed between #17 and the last issue, #18, dated Spring/Summer 1981. At its peak, about three hundred copies of *The Rohmer Review* were distributed, though Briney lost money on it.

Among the material appearing in *The Rohmer Review* were reprints of articles and fiction by Rohmer; bibliographies (generally by Briney); an illustrated article about a forgotten Rohmer play, *The Eye of Siva* (1923); reviews of a 1972 Rohmer biography; John Ball's childhood reminiscences, "My Hero—Fu Manchu"; Ray Stanich's article on Fu Manchu on radio; and a reprint of a Ron Goulart parody, "The Hand of Dr. Insidious." There was even "The Polyglot Mr. Rohmer," the reprint of a lecture by Pulitzer Prize-winning author Jean Stafford.

On several occasions, members of the Rohmer Society met informally in New York City when Chris Steinbrunner showed Fu Manchu films as part of his Armchair Detective Cinema. (That film group was founded by Steinbrunner shortly after *TAD* began.) It operated in a machine shop near Times Square called "Joe's Place," whose owner was film fan Joe Judice.

The contents of all issues of *The Rohmer Review* are available on a website, *The Page of Fu Manchu,* edited by Dr. Lawrence J. Knapp.

DAST-Magazine (1968–); *Jury* (1972–2008)

Iwan Hedman-Morelius was the Swedish Al Hubin: a mystery

scholar and collector who founded a Swedish-language fan journal, *DAST-Magazine* (its name is short for Detectives–Agents–Science Fiction–Thrillers) in September 1968, when he was still unaware of Hubin and *The Armchair Detective*. His collection, about 20,000 books, was almost as large as Hubin's.

Hedman was a professional soldier in the Swedish Army, retiring as a captain at age fifty in 1982. He started *DAST* as a mimeographed publication he sent free to thirty-four friends. After one year he had one hundred subscribers, and eventually he had a circulation of over fifteen hundred and could print it in offset thanks to the Swedish government, which partly subsidized it as a "cultural magazine." He had readers in the United States, Japan and Australia, in addition to those in European countries. Like Hubin, he had the help of his family in assembling his magazine for mailing.

Hedman—he adopted the last name of Morelius, his grandfather's original name—gave up publishing *DAST* in 1995 after 143 issues. He had moved to Spain for his health in 1986, and, though costs were less, it became increasingly difficult to publish a Swedish magazine from there. His friend Kjell E. Genberg took it over. *DAST* ceased being a print magazine in 2007, becoming a web magazine. Genberg is editor of reviews, and Leif-Rune Strandell is chief editor and publisher. *DAST* remains the longest active general-interest mystery fan magazine. However, Morelius was not satisfied with being "idle," so in 1997 he started a Swedish language newsletter, *Läst & Hört I Hangmattan* (Read & Listened to in the Swingbed... or Hammock in English usage) to recommend mysteries.

Hedman-Morelius's ability to read and write English as a second language made him a prolific contributor to American fan magazines. In 1974, he published the equivalent of Hubin's bibliography, a listing of the crime fiction published in Sweden between 1864 and 1973, which he later updated. He also published books and articles about thriller writers, including Leslie Charteris, Dennis Wheatley, Desmond Bagley, and Alistair MacLean.

Morelius hosted writers and fans when they visited Sweden. In 1981, when the Crime Writers International Congress was held in Stockholm, seventy miles from his home in Strängnäs, he invited delegates to a party, hiring buses to bring 150 people there. Morelius died in 2012.

In 1972 Bertil Widerberg started *Jury,* a quarterly journal that, though in Swedish, attempted to be international in scope. It included articles, interviews, reviews, and occasionally short stories. It ended in 2008.

The Queen's Canon Bibliophile, The Ellery Queen Review (1968–1971)

Though many current readers have never read an Ellery Queen mystery, Anthony Boucher said in 1961, "Ellery Queen *is* the American detective story," recognizing Queen's preeminent roles as detective, author, and editor. In October 1968, the Reverend Robert E. Washer, a Baptist minister from Oneida Castle, New York, published the first issue of a fan journal, *The Queen's Canon Bibliophile (TQCB),* devoted to all aspects of the work of Frederic Dannay and Manfred B. Lee, who wrote as Queen. Washer even named his son "Frederic" after Dannay.

So popular was Queen then that soon leading fan-scholars were submitting articles, checklists, and letters. Francis M. Nevins began *Royal Bloodline,* his Edgar-winning book about Queen, in the pages of Washer's magazine. Joe R. Christopher interrupted his doctoral dissertation to write an article, "The Retirement of Richard Queen," about Ellery's father.

My first regional writing was an article about Ellery's New York City, and then I wrote a history of *Ellery Queen's Mystery Magazine.* In November 1968 Washer and his wife came to the New York area to visit Dannay and Lee, stopping first in the Bronx to visit the Lachmans. It gave me the idea for the first "Mystery Readers of America" party the following spring.

TQCB acquired a new—and better—title. *The Ellery Queen*

Review, in October 1971, but unfortunately that issue was the last because illness and family matters caused Washer to suspend publication and become much less active in mystery fandom. He died in 2017.

Chapter Six

THE FIRST BOUCHERCON: 1970

Bouchercon began in a bar. Writing about its origins in the 1991 Bouchercon program, Len and June Moffatt recalled that in a bar, at the close of a July 1969 science fiction convention they were reminiscing with Bruce Pelz about Anthony Boucher and his enthusiasm for both science fiction and mysteries. Pelz said, "I wonder if it is time to put on a mystery convention." There had never been one.

Pelz asked Phyllis White, Boucher's widow, for permission to use his name. She readily agreed, writing, "The only misgiving I have is that calling a convention a memorial—to anyone—sounds rather anti-festive. Tony would never want to turn up as a wet blanket at a convention. If the committee thinks that there is no danger of anyone being downhearted, I am very much in favor of the idea." Phyllis White was given membership number 000, an honor continued until it was retired after her death.

Pelz and Chuck Crayne were Co-Chairmen, but in the first Anthony Boucher Memorial Mystery Convention program Pelz said that the Moffatts, who originally agreed to be liaison with MWA, were far more active and that there might never have been what has become known as Bouchercon without them. He referred to the convention as "this experiment, which could not guarantee any particular results."

During Memorial Day weekend 1970, eighty-two fans gathered at the Royal Inn in Santa Monica. Most were from California, but some from far afield, including Pat Erhardt and her father from Utica, New York, and editor Donald A. Wollheim from New York City.

Bouchercon began May 29 with a Friday evening opening reception. This became a tradition, though future receptions became elaborate, with food served and awards presented. The reception was followed by several room parties, which, because of the relatively small attendance, almost everyone attended.

Photo by June Moffat

Robert Bloch, author of *Psycho*, Guest of Honor at the first Bouchercon in 1970

The official opening was at 1:00 p.m. on Saturday, and Poul and Karen Anderson, writers who had known Boucher, spoke about his work and varied interests. (This was a time of single-track programming, so attendees did not have to choose which panel to attend.) They were followed by a panel called "Mysteries in the Old Pulps," moderated by Len Moffatt, that included writers and editors Howard Browne, William P. McGivern, Larry Shaw, and Robert Turner, as well as bibliographer Bill Clark. It was so successful, with so much audience participation, that Moffatt finally had to stop it so the rest of the day's program could continue. Enthusiasm was so great that fans were asking, "Why haven't we done this before?"

Next came an auction to raise money to help pay the costs of the convention; advance registration was only four dollars for the weekend. Auctions later became a regular Bouchercon event, but they would raise funds for charities, often those promoting literacy.

The next panel, called "The State of the Art," moderated by Pelz, included three people primarily known for their science fiction writing and/or editing: Larry Niven, Jerry Pournelle, and Wollheim. There were also mystery writers Bill S. Ballinger and Clayton Matthews. A question by Pournelle to the audience, asking what readers want in the way of crime fiction, led to the creation of an unscheduled panel to be held that evening to discuss that topic.

Because this convention had its roots in science fiction, there was a masquerade, a frequent event at science fiction meetings. One teenager came as a vampire, but other costumes were mystery-related. Pelz was Dr. Gideon Fell and challenged people to spot the deliberate mistakes in his costume. Niven was "Flavius Maximus," Roman private eye investigating the murder of Julius Caesar.

An unfortunate tradition was started at Sunday's banquet-luncheon with food that was generally described as "mediocre," a word applied to most Bouchercon meals thereafter. Guest of Honor Robert Bloch spoke, talking of Boucher and how they met at a science fiction convention. Bloch joked, "We met, we fell in love, got married and lived happily ever after." He also spoke of the mystery in general and said that literary critics did not take it seriously enough. He predicted that in 1990 historians would read John D. MacDonald to find out what life in the U.S. was like, rather than the works of mainstream writers.

The convention closed with a business meeting to discuss the future of Bouchercon. There was agreement that it would become an annual event, although it should be held in October to avoid conflicts with MWA's spring banquet and summertime science fiction conventions. However, one person said she thought Bouchercon was a meeting for writers and would-be writers and that fans should not be included. There was a roar of disapproval, and Clayton Matthews said that it was beneficial for writers to meet readers in relaxed settings so they could find out what they were doing right—or wrong.

Another unpopular suggestion, rejected by the organizers, was that the name of the convention be changed each year to honor others in the mystery. It was decided that the convention would continue to honor Boucher. Because Boucher was known to love both fans and writers, a sentence heard often during the weekend was "It's too bad Tony couldn't be here to enjoy this."

Chapter Seven

OTHER BOUCHERCONS: 1970S

1971: Los Angeles

Bouchercon moved to Columbus Day weekend (October 8–11) at the International Hotel in Los Angeles. Bruce Pelz was chairman, and he was aided by the Moffatts, Gail Knuth, and Drew Sanders. Official attendance was only seventy-six, down from the prior year, apparently due to insufficient advance publicity. It was not the cost; registration was still only four dollars, and a single room at the hotel was fourteen dollars per night. Because of the low attendance, it was decided to end the convention on Sunday, rather than Monday, as scheduled.

Phyllis White was there, along with Boucher's sons, James and Larry White, and their wives. Bill S. Ballinger was the Guest of Honor, but he had to leave the opening reception to finish a teleplay he was writing for the *Cannon* series. This was only one of several problems. The opening session was delayed because one speaker, Joe Gores, was late, his plane from San Francisco delayed by fog. Pelz had to leave to pick up another speaker, Howard Browne. William P. McGivern was unable to appear because he had the flu.

Edward D. Hoch of Rochester, New York, attended and appeared on a panel devoted to "The State of the Art, 1971." The popular 1970 pulp panel was repeated, with Richard Deming and Robert Bloch added. According to Leo Rand's Bouchercon report in *JDMB,* beer was served to the panelists. Bloch spoke from the podium rather than his seat, joking that since he had been the only one not to imbibe, he was the only panelist capable of standing.

Crime movies, an important part of early Bouchercons, were shown on Saturday and Sunday nights. There was also a poker game, a tradition that has lasted into the twenty-first century.

Photo by June Moffatt

Bruce Pelz (right), who first had the idea for Bouchercon, with Bill S. Ballinger, 1971 Guest of Honor

Pelz and the Moffats had suggested in flyers that awards, using Boucher's pseudonym, "H. H. Holmes," be awarded, but there was little positive response, so it was not until 1986 that the first award honoring Boucher, the Anthony, was given.

Assessing the convention, Rand called it a success. He also blamed low attendance on fans and writers not being "used to the idea of an annual convention. They may see a notice about it but still not really know what it is all about." Then, trying to explain the pleasures of such a convention to those who had never attended one, he used words many were to use in the future: "You had to be there to truly appreciate it."

1972: Los Angeles

Bouchercon returned to L.A.'s International Hotel for the weekend of October 20–22, and attendance was larger, though only ninety-three. Rand reported that some attendees remarked that smaller conventions were more fun! The Moffats co-chaired Bouchercon III with Pelz as treasurer.

Frederic Dannay, the surviving half of the Ellery Queen team, was scheduled to be Guest of Honor but was unable to attend due to illness. Robert Washer spoke in his place at Sunday's luncheon, citing the importance of Boucher and Queen in his own life. Before his talk, a tape of Boucher giving one of his mystery reviews on radio was played.

There were more panels than before, and more varied speakers. Rand said, "Programs ran overtime both days, as the question-and-answer sessions with the audience were longer than anticipated and quite lively." Present was John Nieminski of Illinois, who attended every subsequent Bouchercon until his death in 1986. It was obvious that Bouchercon, despite its California roots, was becoming national. Emphasizing this was the announcement that the fourth Bouchercon would take place in Boston.

1973: Boston

The idea of an East Coast Bouchercon came from Stewart Brownstein, another person experienced at putting on science fiction conventions, but also a mystery fan. Robert Briney and Brownstein were Co-Chairmen, with Washer and Lianne Carlin completing the committee.

Bouchercon IV was held Columbus Day weekend (October 5–7) at the Sheraton-Boston Hotel. Illness and accidents continued to plague Bouchercon, as Washer, who spoke for Dannay in 1972, was unable to attend because of illness, while car trouble forced Carlin to miss much of the event. There was no Guest of Honor, but the leading American expert on detective stories in Spanish, Professor Donald A. Yates, was featured speaker, delivering an outstanding talk on Jorge Luis Borges and Anthony Boucher. A Boucher translation in *EQMM* was the first appearance of Borges in English.

Briney had a moment of panic Friday night when he learned that the printer had closed early and he was not able to pick up the programs. Fortunately, the shop opened early Saturday. 105 people registered. Columbus Day weekend coincided with Yom Kippur that year, reducing attendance. Still, many Easterners got to attend their first Bouchercon, including *EQMM* editor Eleanor Sullivan, Ron Goulart, and Charles Shibuk. Friday night's only activity was a get-acquainted party where the conversation was so enjoyable it lasted four hours.

For the first time a book was published in conjunction with Bouchercon: *Multiplying Villainies: Selected Mystery Criticism 1942–1968 by Anthony Boucher*. It was edited by Briney and Nevins and contained a foreword, "Tony Boucher As I Knew Him," by Helen McCloy. Published in a limited edition of 500 copies, it took three years to sell out, but is now highly collectible.

The formal program included Nevins talking about Cleve F. Adams and Randy Cox talking of Nick Carter. Charlotte MacLeod spoke on "The Occult in Mystery Fiction." There was an especially good "Science Fiction and Mystery Fiction" panel with Edward D. Hoch, Goulart, and Briney. A last-minute panel on Cornell Woolrich, with Nevins, Yates, and Hal Knott went as smoothly as if it had been planned months before.

This was my first Bouchercon, and I was drafted for another impromptu panel, "Mystery in Films," though I wasn't sure why since film experts Shibuk and Chris Steinbrunner were panelists. For the first of many Bouchercons, Steinbrunner was responsible for the film program, and it was varied, including *The Laurel and Hardy Murder Case, And Then There Were None,* and the first chapter of the *Drums of Fu Manchu* serial.

This Bouchercon received media attention. An interviewer and camera crew from Boston's WBZ-TV, at the Sheraton to interview Liza Minnelli, filmed part of Bouchercon and an interview with Yates, both of which were aired. There was also coverage by *Boston Globe* columnist Bill Fripp, who called it MWA's fourth annual convention, though the local chapter of MWA had not been helpful. It would not be the last time that credit for Bouchercon would mistakenly go to professional writers instead of the fans who put it on. Later, the editor of a book using Boucher's Sherlock Holmes radio scripts said, inaccurately, "After his death, the Mystery Writers of America named their annual convention after him."

1974: Oakland

Bouchercon returned to California October 4–6 at the Royal Oak Inn at Oakland's Airport, with science fiction writer/editor Adrienne Martine-Barnes as Chairwoman. Because of lack of publicity, attendance dipped to about fifty, and almost all who came were from Northern California. However, John Nieminski and I traveled there, from Chicago and New York respectively, with our wives, and the Moffatts came up from Southern California.

The convention began Friday night with the now traditional reception, this time a wine-and-cheese affair held in the bridal suite, of all places. The formal program on Saturday and Sunday often mentioned Boucher, but that was appropriate since he had lived in nearby Berkeley. Phyllis White gave personal reminiscences, as did colleagues Karen and Poul Anderson, Shirley Dickensheet, and Leonore Glen Offord. Guest of Honor Reginald Bretnor spoke about his friendship with Boucher, describing the latter's many talents, from gourmet cooking to poker playing.

Among other panelists were Joe Gores, Bill Pronzini, and Frank McAuliffe. On Sunday morning, I spoke about "The American Regional Mystery." It was early, and barely a half-dozen people were there at the start, but others drifted in. Oakland was an enjoyable Bouchercon, albeit the smallest, and one forgotten because so few "regulars" attended.

Nieminski asked Len Moffatt how one went about bidding for Bouchercon. Moffat recalled, "I told him he had just won the bid (knowing of no others), and so the sixth Bouchercon went to Chicago."

1975: Chicago

Bouchercon not only moved to Chicago, but it moved to summer (July 18–20) to avoid a conflict with the first International Crime Writers Congress scheduled for October. Nieminski and Robert Hahn were chairmen, and the site was the Midland Hotel, near Chicago's Loop. On arriving, I spotted a sign on the hotel marquee announcing "Boucheron." It was the first, but not the last, time for that misspelling. (Boucheron is the name of a French perfume and also a French winery.) The Midwest location allowed people from the area, including Max Allan Collins, Allen J. Hubin, and Dan J. Marlowe, to attend their first Bouchercons. Attendance was one hundred ten, the highest yet at Bouchercon.

Programming was still single-track, with a total of eight panels. Don Yates chaired a panel on reviewing, which included Hubin and Alice Cromie of the *Chicago Tribune*. With Nicholas Meyer's *The Seven-Per-Cent Solution* on the bestseller list, a Sherlockian panel was logical, and one on Saturday drew four experts: Otto Penzler, Jon Lellenberg, Robert L. Fish, and Nieminski. Another Saturday panel asked "Who is the Big Mac?" in considering John D. MacDonald, Ross Macdonald, and Philip MacDonald. Saturday night's banquet had a witty speech by Fish, the Guest of Honor.

On Sunday, along with Hal Knott, Hubin, and Woolrich expert William Thailing, I was on a "collecting mysteries" panel. I recall Otto Penzler being miffed that he hadn't been selected since he had an outstanding collection of first editions, while my accumulation, consisted mainly of old paperbacks and a complete run of *EQMM*. The last panel had lawyer Mike Nevins on the subject of Perry Mason. No one is more knowledgeable on that subject.

1976: Culver City, California

A projected geographical rotation system (East Coast, Midwest, and Pacific Coast) did not materialize as Bouchercon returned to California and the Pacifica Hotel in Culver City, October 1–3. The

Moffatts chaired their second Bouchercon; John Ball was Guest of Honor. This Bouchercon broke all attendance records with 157 people registered in advance, and a few showing up as daily registrants. The registration fee was only six dollars, with another six-fifty to attend the Sunday Luncheon, which 114 people did.

Ball, an author of police procedurals, was a logical choice to moderate a panel that included three investigators from the Los Angeles Police Department. They commented on the accuracy of police work shown in novels and television. One panelist called *The Rookies* the worst of the current "cop" shows on TV. To the panelist's embarrassment, the creator of that series was in the audience. She defended herself, blaming its producer for changing her scripts. This Bouchercon had more law enforcement procedural panels—five—than previous Bouchercons. One was a talk on "Nitrobenzene and Other Horrors" by James White, Boucher's criminalist son.

Fiction-related panels included "Clergymen-Detectives" and one on the late Fredric Brown, who always complained when his name was misspelled "Frederic," as it was in the convention program.

The most enjoyable event was a talk by British mystery writer Christianna Brand. As Bob Briney wrote in his report for *TAD*, "Miss Brand is a warm, funny, and utterly delightful woman, and she captivated the audience instantly and completely with her anecdotes about herself, the Detection Club, and the behavior of Dorothy L. Sayers, John Dickson Carr, and others."

Bouchercon had its first book dealers, Ruth and Al Winfeldt of the Scene of the Crime bookstore in Sherman Oaks. They sold books at the back of the room in which panels were held. The noise of book selling sometimes interfered with panels.

The program ran long on Sunday so the business meeting, at which the site of the next Bouchercon was to be announced, was canceled. However, the "Dead Dog Party," a science fiction convention custom, was on its way to becoming a Bouchercon tradition too: Those who did not have to leave early gathered for more good talk, including discussion of 1977's location: New York City.

1977: New York City

Bouchercon came to its most prestigious locale thus far, the Empire Room of New York's Waldorf-Astoria Hotel, during Columbus Day weekend, October 7–9. Otto Penzler and Chris Steinbrunner were Co-Chairmen, and they selected Stanley Ellin as Guest of Honor. Past complaints of lack of publicity for Bouchercons did not apply here. There was even a humorous article by Eric Pace in the *New York Times* commenting, "Admission to all these events is a steal at $20." Of the 351 people registered, 331 showed up. Over one-third (119) attended the banquet for another twenty dollars.

In a separate room, Carol Brener, of Murder Ink, sold new and used books. There were also autographing sessions for attending authors and the Bouchercon Mystery Art Exhibit, with works by William Teason and Frank McSherry among others.

On Friday evening Phyllis White spoke of Boucher's personal life and his many interests outside of the mystery and science fiction.

The well-organized convention included imaginative panels and talks. There was one in which John M. Linsenmeyer, editor of *The Baker Street Journal*, portrayed Sherlock Holmes and was questioned by a panel of Sherlockians. Other speakers included Al Nussbaum, the bank-robber-turned-crime writer, who talked about his first "career"; Walter Gibson, who spoke about The Shadow and did

Phyllis White, Anthony Boucher's widow, at one of the many panels she attended for thirty years

magic tricks for an encore; and Brian Garfield, author of *Death Wish*. He expressed his unhappiness with the Charles Bronson film version because it appeared to advocate vigilantism. There were also talks by Phyllis Whitney on romantic suspense, Himan Brown on old-time radio mysteries, and Robert L. Fish, who appeared with a U.S. Coast Guard lieutenant and discussed smuggling.

On Saturday night, there was the American premier of Sax Rohmer's 1923 play, *The Eye of Siva*, in a condensed version by Bob Briney. Christianna Brand was in America again and, with anecdotes, delightfully introduced the film version of her *Green for Danger.*

At Sunday's luncheon, Stanley Ellin was "roasted" by fellow writers, editors, and even his wife. Garfield said that when Ellin, author of the famous story "The Specialty of the House," was asked by the steward on a Cunard ship if he would like to see the menu, Ellin replied, "No, bring me the passenger list." During the speeches, Isaac Asimov, busy perfecting his image as a dirty old man, "goosed" Eleanor Sullivan, much to her embarrassment, as he passed behind her. When Ellin got his chance to talk, he thanked Frederic Dannay, in attendance, for accepting his story when he was an unpublished author, but then he took his revenge on his roasters, turning their words against them.

1978: Chicago

I missed my first Bouchercon in five years because I was in a neck brace due to a herniated cervical disk. Bouchercon IX was October 6–8, at the Bismarck Hotel in Chicago's Loop. Robert Hahn and John Nieminski, who co-chaired in 1975, were joined by Professor Ely Liebow in putting on a successful meeting with about 150 people attending. All Sherlockians, they proved that not only science fiction fans could put on a mystery convention. In writing about it for *The Mystery FANcier*, Don Yates lauded the intimacy of the gathering and made an observation that seemed reasonable at the time. "Indeed, there may not be more than two hundred hard-core mystery fans to be convened anywhere at any one time—outside New York City—and, in any case, ever larger numbers are clearly not necessary to assure success."

Walter Gibson was, at eighty-one, the oldest Bouchercon Guest of Honor, and in addition to speaking wittily at the banquet, he again performed magic tricks. There was a panel on Chicago writers, and Mike Nevins spoke on Harry Stephen Keeler, painting so intriguing a picture of that eccentric writer that all Keeler books in the book room were quickly sold. Another panel discussed "new" writers such as Ruth Rendell and P.D. James, who obviously had not then achieved their later reputations.

Bob Briney spoke about Anthony Boucher; Yates spoke of Agatha Christie; and John McAleer spoke of Rex Stout, subject of his Edgar-winning biography. The Chicago Sherlockian scion, Hugo's Companions, held one of their monthly meetings at the banquet, in the words of Sherlockian Yates, "to perpetrate their arcane rites and ceremonies" while initiating two new members. When a Sunday morning panel was about to be canceled due to the non-appearance of a speaker, a lively impromptu panel of editors of fan journals was substituted.

A notable part of the 1978 Bouchercon was the gatherings of fans that, after the formal sessions, went on into the early hours of each morning. Most party-friendly were the *DAPA-EM*ers, a group to be discussed later in this book. Hal Rice joined the *DAPA-EM* crowd by accident when in a darkened film room Nieminski mistook him for Bob Briney, another big, bearded gent, and invited him to a room party.

1979: Universal City, California

The tenth Bouchercon at the Sheraton-Universal in Universal City, California, October 5–7, was especially sweet to me, having missed the previous year and arriving after a week of family illness. It provided a lift almost from the beginning: a dinner at which fans kicked around such arcane topics as the music mentioned in Cornell Woolrich mysteries. Later that Friday evening was the first of many parties held over the years in Hal Rice's suite at Bouchercons.

Noreen Shaw was listed on the program as "chairman" of this Bouchercon; Larry, her husband, edited the program. Attendance was again about 150. Saturday started for me with a private discussion about opera with Phyllis White, as knowledgeable on that subject as was her husband. There was a good panel on old-time radio and in the afternoon a funny, angry talk by Harlan Ellison, the science fiction writer who has written enough mysteries to have earned two Edgars. His targets: television executives and publishers.

The feature at Saturday night's banquet was the speech generally conceded to be the funniest ever presented at Bouchercon. Guest of Honor Tony Hillerman spoke about the inept bank robbers of Taos, New Mexico. There were gales of laughter, and Ellison laughed so hard he literally fell off his chair.

On Sunday, reformed bank robber Al Nussbaum discussed his fourteen years in prison. I moderated a panel on reviewing at which it was agreed that it is easier to pan a book than to praise it. Jon L. Breen spoke about the sports mysteries of Cortland Fitzsimmons, once popular but now forgotten. They are still fun to hear about (and read), partly for their corniness. Sunday also had a great "Dead Dog" party, at which I finally agreed to join *DAPA-EM*, members Nieminski and Ellen Nehr having made it sound too appealing to miss.

Chapter Eight

DAPA-EM (1973–2011)

"What is a *DAPA-EM?*" is a question its members were often asked. *DAPA-EM* is short for *Elementary, My Dear APA* and was the only APA (Amateur Press Association) devoted to the mystery. *DAPA-EM* was once the core group of mystery fandom. Its members chaired eighteen Bouchercons and have been active in many more, as well as in regional conventions. In addition to producing their APA magazines, they write widely in the field, producing books, articles, and reviews usually for little or no remuneration. Because of their activities, nineteen of those honored as Fan Guests of Honor at Bouchercons have been *DAPA-EM*ers. Many have been similarly honored at regional conventions.

Photo courtesy of Art Scott

Art Scott, "The Emperor," official editor of *DAPA-EM* for over thirty years

DAPA-EM was founded in 1973, as a quarterly fan journal, by Donna Balopole of Floral Park, New York. There were six members then, one of whom, Jeff Smith, continued until its last issue in 2011. APAs are limited-membership groups whose members produce copies of their magazines, which they send to an Official Editor. He or she collates and mails them to members, as well as keeping track of finances, a waitlist, and whether members meet the requirements of minimum activity ("minac"). Balopole, editor for the first twelve mailings, was replaced by Art Scott of California, a research chemist, in mailing number thirteen. He had campaigned on a platform that included a switch to bimonthly status and stronger recruitment efforts. He remained Official Editor until it ended in January 2011. By 1980, the membership reached its limit of thirty-five, and the total pages of each mailing often exceeded three hundred; the first mailing had only twenty-seven pages.

To satisfy "minac," each member had to submit at least four pages, three of which were original material, every four months. The other requirements mainly involved paying dues to cover mailing costs. The magazines produced were as diverse as the individuals. The titles were also varied and often humorous. Among them were Bill Crider's *Macavity,* named after T.S. Eliot's mystery cat, and Bob Briney's *Contact Is Not a Verb*, using a rule of grammar on which Nero Wolfe insisted.

Most members considered their mailing comments to other members the most important part of their magazines. In addition, members wrote about their personal lives, including family, travels, and attendance at mystery conventions. Since many were collectors, they wrote of their "booking" experiences. For example, Crider told of finding $270 inside a used book he bought. Scott, a collector of old paperbacks, was ejected from a bookstore in Buffalo, where he was booking with George Kelley, by a less-than-rational owner. Graeme Flanagan of Australia went booking in the only secondhand bookstore in Port Moresby, Papua New Guinea.

Members put considerable effort into their magazines. Some wrote book reviews and articles. Scott (and others) included photographs taken at Bouchercons. Former member Dave Lewis did considerable research in writing about Frederick

Nebel. Members were generally from the United States, though several lived in Canada, one in Australia, and two in England. Every region of the United States was represented at one time or another. Backgrounds varied, with librarians, teachers and government workers predominating. There were also lawyers, policemen, a fireman, and a pharmacist. With 126 people having been members at one time, space does not permit me to describe each, but some stand out and define *DAPA-EM*.

When Ellen Nehr died in 1995, she was called the "heart and soul of *DAPA-EM*." One year she came to Bouchercon wearing a T-shirt proclaiming her "*DAPA-EM* Den Mother." She enjoyed Bouchercons and *DAPA-EM* room parties so much that she complained loudly if World Series games were played on television, calling them distractions from the yearly conventions she so anticipated.

Ellen had been an officer in the U.S. Air Force, and few were surprised to learn that, considering her strong opinions and personality. For dinner during the 1980 Bouchercon, thirty-one people, members of *DAPA-EM*, their spouses and friends, went to a restaurant where Nehr announced to the waiters, after everyone had been seated, "Separate checks." Yet, despite her hard-boiled exterior (which masked a soul of great generosity), she insisted on calling herself "a typical American housewife," and her reading tastes ran to the coziest of mysteries.

Ellen felt strongly about the authors she disliked, especially Robert B. Parker, creator of Spenser. She read one of his books only because she lost a bet. When I started my book on regional mysteries, she wrote me, "If you promise to leave Parker out of your New England listing, I promise to answer both letters of complaint you get when the book is published." I decided Parker's Boston mysteries were too important to take advantage of her offer.

While Nehr disliked hardboiled crime fiction, she felt equally strongly about other types, opining, "You will never convince me

George Kelley, center, proves to Frank Denton, left, and Jeff Meyerson, right, that he's attending a Bouchercon

that Sherlock Holmes is either readable or viewable." She recommended that people not read an Edgar-winning biography of S.S. Van Dine because he was "a nasty man." Yet, she loved scholarship and discovered a previously unknown pseudonym for Phoebe Atwood Taylor. Her *Doubleday Crime Club Compendium* 1928–1991 won an Anthony in 1993. Her *DAPA-EM* magazine, *The Apron String Affair,* was replete with typos and spelling errors, about which fellow members kidded her. She responded by asking for a moratorium on commenting on these, typically making a mistake when she wrote, "Typo's can happen to anyone."

At the 1980 Bouchercon, when Jon Lellenberg chided John Nieminski for not wearing his convention badge, Nieminski immediately echoed the bandit chief in *The Treasure of the Sierra Madre,* saying, "Bahdgis? We doan need no steenking bahdgis." Behind Nieminski's scholarly exterior was a sense of humor that delighted his friends and those who read his magazine, *Somewhere a Roscoe,* whose title came from S.J. Perelman's parody of private eyes. Though he was not a professional writer, Nieminski's writing was often compared to Perelman's. He was also a serious bibliographer. Without a computer database system, Nieminski lovingly, using thousands of 3x5 cards, prepared indexes to *Ellery Queen's Mystery Magazine* and *Saint Mystery Magazine*.

George Kelley's "non-appearance" at Bouchercons became legendary. He had canceled several times, but though he often attended and was seen by most of the membership, the joke continued to circulate that he had disappeared again. Kelley, a professor at the State University of New York at Buffalo, had one of the largest collections of paperback books in the world and donated 25,000 to his school's library. Andy Jaysnovitch's compulsive collecting of books, magazines, videotapes, and almost everything else also became well known.

Bill Crider wrote that he liked books about alligators in the sewers, and he even wrote an article about them. This became another in-joke in *DAPA-EM,* and at one Bouchercon, Crider was presented with a hand puppet in the form of an alligator, which was promptly named "Bill Jr." Formerly chairman of the English Department at Alvin State College in Texas, Crider was also a prolific and successful writer of crime fiction.

Another Texan, Barry Gardner, joined *DAPA-EM* in 1992 after thirty-one years in the Dallas Fire Department, having risen to second in command. Jeff and Ann Smith expressed the feeling of most members when they said he "fit in so smoothly it was like he'd been there all along." Unfortunately, he wasn't there for long because he died suddenly of a heart attack in July 1996.

Steve Stilwell was the leading exponent of what editor Scott called "The Ferris Wheel theory of APA-ship," dropping off the roster and rejoining more times than anyone wanted to count. When Stilwell was on the roster and wrote, he was invariably worth reading. At Bouchercons, without obviously taking notes, he captured the best lines at parties. He represented *DAPA-EM* at the funerals of Gardner and Hal Rice. Though long married, with two grown daughters, Stillwell promoted the idea of himself as a ladies' man. Able to joke about his reputation, he once reported asking attractive mystery writer

Deborah Crombie for a date. She agreed if she could bring her husband along.

More untoward things happen to Richard Moore and his acquaintances than to any other member. He has had multiple bouts of surgery, once for a broken shoulder when he tripped on his dogs' leashes. His former boss was killed by a letter bomb from the Unabomber, and a friend was murdered in Washington, DC. Richard was *DAPA-EM*'s prime raconteur, captivating audiences at parties with tales of his Uncle Buren in Georgia and also the strange, uninsured motorist, known only as "Mr. Darko," who crashed into Moore's car. During a 2003 hurricane, a tree fell on Richard's car. Richard was another of *DAPA-EM*'s published mystery writers, with three novels and several short stories.

Richard Moore in his role of *DAPA-EM* raconteur

Len and June Moffatt are considered the founding parents of Bouchercon. Their *DAPA-EM* magazine was called *A Flash of Blue,* a tribute to John D. MacDonald, who used a color in each Travis McGee title. They had long been active in science-fiction fandom too, and in 1951 Len was "Tuckerized" by Wilson Tucker, whose name is now used for the practice of including real people as fictional characters in books.

Though usually only seeing each other once a year, *DAPA-EMers* considered themselves part of a family. Typically, two-thirds of the membership attended a Bouchercon, and for many of them *DAPA-EM* room parties were convention highlights. For many years, Hal and Sonya Rice would take a suite and generously host

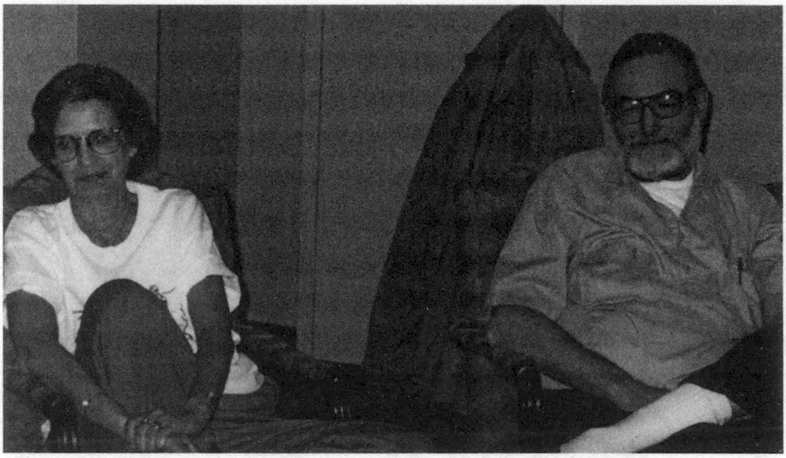

Sonya and Hal Rice, hosts to many *DAPA-EM* parties at Bouchercon

these parties. A smoker himself, Hal would leave his own room to have a cigarette rather than subject people to second-hand smoke. Though little alcohol was consumed, these parties were scenes of considerable mirth, especially when Richard Moore had the floor.

*DAPA-EM*ers cared for fellow members. When newcomer Sandra Scoppettone was nervous about attending her first Bouchercon, Ellen Nehr took her under her wing and introduced Sandra around. When Ellen moved, fellow Ohio member Jo Ann Vicarel helped her. Leslie Slaasted was bothered by a stalker at one Malice Domestic conference until Richard Moore confronted him.

Members have felt they could share the good and bad in life with each other, telling of marriage problems and illnesses, and deaths in the family. Earthquakes, fires, and riots in California led to phone calls to members there, inquiring about their safety. Learning that Bob Briney was hospitalized, members of *DAPA-EM* telephoned him from the Omaha convention in 1990 to wish him well. When members Larry French, Jud Sapp, Trevor Cotton, John Nieminski, Ellen Nehr, Barry Gardner, Don Sandstrom, Hal Rice, and David Rose died, one could sense genuine sadness in the tributes paid them. During Sandstrom's terminal illness, members came from

California, New Mexico, New York, and Wisconsin to visit him in Indianapolis. Two months after Hal Rice's death, Sonya and Hal Jr., their son, came to the Austin Bouchercon Hal had been planning to attend. They said they felt they were with friends. Cotton was the first English member; his magazine was called *My Body Lies Over the Ocean*. When he learned that Jeff Meyerson and his wife, whom he had never met, would be in England at the time of his daughter's wedding, he invited them. In 1986, the Meyersons threw one of their parties in Brooklyn to celebrate a Special Edgar won by Walter Albert.

When the mystery writer Michael Dibdin labeled mystery fans "nerds," *DAPA-EM*ers were quick to respond, pointing out how little he knew of fandom. Another writer, Robert J. Randisi, took what could be considered a "cheap shot" at *DAPA-EM* in the Spring 1983 issue of *The Armchair Detective* when he complained about that magazine's Rex Stout and Dorothy L. Sayers newsletters, claiming *TAD* was turning into "another *DAPA-EM*."

If *DAPA-EM* was a family, it occasionally was a dysfunctional one. Guy Townsend, whose writing in *TAD* and editorship of *The Mystery FANcier* was controversial, proved especially so during his *DAPA-EM* stay. He complained he was dropped because he had been two pages short of "minac." He felt his past contributions warranted an exception. However, Scott, better known as "the Emperor," said that with people on the waitlist, and without a substantive reason, it was not fair to make an exception. Scott was always willing to excuse members when they had reasons such as illness, death in the family, or relocating.

Townsend accepted "demotion" to the waitlist and continued to contribute, eventually coming back to the roster. During this period he engaged in feuds and accused members of conformity and lack of courage, dubbing the membership "old maids" and "a knitting circle." He proposed that annually the membership cast ballots for the five least productive members, who would then be dropped to the waitlist. While some thought there was merit in encouraging some members to submit more substantive magazines, the majority was against Townsend's proposal. Frank Denton said he would not remain a member if this went into effect, and David Doerrer asked, "Do we really want performance evaluations as part of *DAPA-EM* membership?" Townsend's plan was voted down, and Guy sarcastically apologized for "overestimating" the membership and soon resigned.

Walter and Jean Shine were members for only a few years. After quitting, they sent a missive, only signed "Erstwhile Member," that a current member allowed to be included with his magazine. In their letter the Shines complained about those who regard their daily activities, however pedestrian, as worthy of "perpetuity" in the mailings. They singled out people who wrote about their pets. Members pointed out that no one had forced the Shines to read anyone's magazine in its entirety, and it was personal touches that made *DAPA-EM* unique.

When David George joined he, as did most new additions, included a brief biography. He said he had gone from the United States to live in Canada because he did not believe in the Vietnam War. Bob Napier, who had served in Vietnam, expressed his displeasure with this viewpoint because it meant that someone else had to be drafted while service was avoided.

There were other disagreements in *DAPA-EM*. When two members clashed, one asked Scott to make his opponent apologize. Later, he asked Scott, "Will you please, as Official Editor, request that he cease and desist from mentioning the matter any further." The Emperor blew his editorial top and told him, "NO, I will not tell him—or anybody else—what he may or may not discuss in his zines...I am not a Censor, I am not an Ayatollah, I am not your Mommy. Fight your own goddamn battles." As an aside, Scott said, "Revealing the ending to a murder mystery without a warning is 'conduct unbecoming a member of *DAPA-EM*,' and that's about the only action that qualifies."

It soon became quite common to have fewer than thirty-five

people on the roster, with no one on the waitlist. Those remaining seemed as enthusiastic as ever; half had produced at least one hundred issues of their magazines. They generally responded to others via mailing comments, even if family and writing commitments reduced the size and amount of original material in their magazines. An exception was newcomer Steve Steinbock, whose magazines were well-illustrated and imaginative. One issue was devoted entirely to mysteries having their roots in Lewis Carroll's work.

The biggest long-range problem for *DAPA-EM* was that it had an aging roster; the average age was at least fifty-five, and few members were even as young as forty. Younger fans, with whom *DAPA-EM*ers talked at mystery conventions, did not seem interested in the amount of work and commitment needed to produce even a small bimonthly magazine, especially in a world in which one can communicate with other fans immediately in cyberspace.

After several years notice, Scott "retired" in 2011 as Official Editor. There were only twenty-seven people on the roster, and no one volunteered to take his place, thus ending *DAPA-EM*.

Chapter Nine

THE MYSTERY FANCIER (1976–1992)

Because of its editor, Guy M. Townsend, *The Mystery FANcier* was not only one of the earliest but one of the best-remembered fan journals. It started with a preview issue in November 1976, in which Townsend set forth his reason for launching this bimonthly magazine: his belief that there was room for another general fan magazine. What he wanted in *TMF* was "a balance of articles, reviews, and letters," but the third category gave *TMF* its special flavor. Townsend noted a lack of disputation in the letters to *The Armchair Detective.* He hoped to see in *TMF* "a lively letter column with, perhaps, a healthy mixture of back-patting and back-stabbing...The letter column will be open to all opinions, provided they are literately expressed and not libelous." He planned to give contributors of "articles, reviews, or substantial letters of comment" credit against the subscription price, one issue for each submission.

Townsend achieved his aim of producing a frequently impassioned magazine because of his own persona and strong opinions.

In March 1978 Jo Ann Vicarel contrasted it with *TAD*, which she said now had "too many Ph.D.s, too many scholarly works, too much name dropping." She gave praise to *TMF* that was unique in mystery fandom. "When I went to the hospital to give birth to my daughter at the end of September, my husband noted that I was clutching the latest issue of *TMF* to read between contractions and Lamaze breathing." Another reader, Sandy Sandulo, sent a picture of herself reading *TMF* while she donated blood. Nurse Linda Toole wrote of discovering a stack of unread *TMFs* at 1:00 a.m. "I succumbed, and the next thing I knew the birds were singing, the sun was rising, and it was 5:00 a.m.! A bit tough when you have to go to work that day. It was, however, time well spent."

Bibliographer John Nieminski and Guy Townsend, controversial editor-publisher of *The Mystery FANcier*

By the second volume Townsend was engaging in some of the feuds that kept *TMF* interesting. While printing reviews by Martin Morse Wooster, he questioned Wooster's opinions and expressed his anger at having to correct his copy, which used British spelling. Townsend regarded this as an affectation because Wooster is American.

A feature of *TMF* was Townsend's explanations of why issues were late. Most often the post office or his printer was at fault, though he was also willing to blame himself and his hectic life. In 1978, when he announced a price increase from seven-fifty for six issues to nine dollars, Townsend took an approach that was direct, but not likely to win popularity contests, when he said, "Frankly, I don't care to hear any negative comments about the increase. If any of *TMF*'s current subscribers feel that the increase is unjustified, kindly send me an SASE and I will send you explicit instructions as to what you can do with your cheapskate opinions."

The contents of *TMF* were not terribly different from early *TAD*. They included checklists of collectible paperbacks, Bouchercon reports, Chapters from Michael Avallone's biography-in-progress, *Death of a .300 Hitter*, and a book-by-book analysis of the Nero Wolfe saga by Townsend. Robert Sampson wrote about detectives in pulp magazines, and Jeff Banks became *TMF*'s resident expert on nostalgia, with articles about old radio, movie serials, "B" films, and comic books.

There was room for humor. William F. Deeck's "Further Gems from the Literature" was a running compendium of inadvertently funny lines from mysteries. Using the mock scholarship beloved of Sherlockians, I provided a chronology of the life of John Dickson Carr's Gideon Fell, one that suggested he had murdered his wife.

Larry French, a leading expert on the works of John Dickson Carr, had already written a serious article on Carr for *TMF* and was kind to my effort. Then the cover of Vol. 3 (1979), No. 1, carried an obituary for French, who was killed in an auto accident on an icy road.

In July 1978 I began "It's About Crime," the column I would write for *TMF's* remaining fourteen years. It included various features, besides reviews, that I still write for other fan magazines: "Death of a Mystery Writer" (obituaries), "Doom with a View" (reviews of mystery movies and television), and "The Short Stop" (reviews of short stories). Al Hubin, Sue Feder, and Deeck were among *TMF*'s other reviewers.

TMF drew arguments as a flame draws moths. Bill Loeser boasted of "my new campaign to have my say, speak my mind, and thereby make myself obnoxious to everyone else." He was so critical of a Jane Bakerman article that Townsend joked that Loeser "was wise to use a post office box number instead of a street address." Loeser called himself "The Curmudgeon in the

Corner" and claimed that real criticism of mystery fiction was not possible without giving away the solution or important plot elements of books. He proceeded to do this with Christie's *The Murder of Roger Ackroyd* and Carr's *Death Turns the Tables*. In the next issue, I disputed him and wondered if Loeser (or Townsend) had considered giving readers advance warning there would be plot disclosures. Eventually, Loeser claimed he was retiring from writing to *TMF* and its "fannish bleat" and had given up reading mysteries. In the same issue, Carl Larsen praised *TMF*'s letters column, "The Documents in the Case," as "a form of New England town meeting with everyone demonstrating his belief in equality through open discussion."

In his Vol. 4 No. 5 (Sept.–Oct. 1980) editorial, Townsend wrote of the time and labor *TMF* entailed, which he wouldn't mind if he wasn't also losing money. He gave readers a choice as he contemplated raising the subscription price of Vol. 5 to $12 for six issues, asking them to commit to that price. "If I get at least 100 commitments, *TMF* will continue; if I get 99 or fewer, volume 4, number 6, will be the last issue of *TMF* ever printed." More than one hundred agreed. John Nieminski was glad, though he said he would have taken over *TMF* if Townsend ceased publication.

The early 1980s was a period of relative growth for *TMF*, with its paid circulation more than doubling from 214 in September 1981 to 445 in November 1982, as a result of an advertising "blitz" that included giving out a thousand free issues to prospective subscribers. Townsend was embarked on what he termed a "publishing empire" known as Brownstone Books, its name taken from the West Thirty-Fifth Street brownstone in which his favorite detective, Nero Wolfe, resided. Townsend had moved to his wife's hometown, Madison, Indiana, ending his travels temporarily. Brownstone achieved notable success, if not a great deal of money. It began with a facsimile edition of the first volume of *TAD*. It also published Walter Albert's Edgar-winning bibliography of secondary sources, and about a dozen chapbooks.

Strong opinions were frequent in *TMF*. In Melinda Reynolds's "Women Mystery Writers: Thanks, But No Thanks," she said she was unable to enjoy (or in some cases even finish) such highly regarded authors as Dorothy L. Sayers, Ngaio Marsh, P.D. James, Margery Allingham, and Josephine Tey. Teri White, a hard-boiled novelist, agreed with Reynolds, though recommending the work of new female authors such as Marcia Muller. Linda Toole also agreed with Reynolds, though she did recommend Lucille Kallen.

Whatever stability Townsend achieved was vanishing in 1983. Half of his new subscribers failed to renew, so he was left with a circulation of about three hundred. He made the decision, announced in the Nov.–Dec. 1983 issue, to go to law school, while keeping a full-time job. Furthermore, he would be commuting from Madison, Indiana, to law school in northern Kentucky, a round-trip of 150 miles. Because of other commitments, Nieminski couldn't take over the magazine, but Steve Stilwell of Minneapolis agree to assume all editorial duties while Townsend was in law school, with the latter handling publishing, mailing, and subscriptions. In announcing the transition, Townsend said, "Some of you may be leery about continuing your subscriptions, or submitting contributions, under an as yet unknown editorship—although, God knows, if you've put up with my editorial capriciousness over the past seven years the unknown should hold no terrors for you." He then listed Stilwell's credentials, concluding "He is brash, opinionated, obstinate, ornery, and obnoxious—in other words, you probably won't notice any difference when I'm gone."

After the March/April 1984 issue, it became apparent that Stilwell's understanding of the arrangement by which he had become interim editor differed substantially from Townsend's. Matters came to a head when Stilwell cut part of a Townsend letter regarding Jon L. Breen's novel, *The Gathering Place*. The deleted portion, not a large one, concerned a character in the book who had a typing of speed of two-hundred-words-per-minute (a speed I, too, had questioned in my review of that book). When

Townsend protested, Stilwell replied that his cutting of the material was within his purview as editor. He then told Townsend to fire him if he was dissatisfied with the job he was doing. Townsend did so and suspended the magazine, bringing it back in July/August 1986, after finishing law school.

Townsend resumed *TMF* with wrangling, of course. Not having much material for his return issue, due to the hiatus, he allowed himself eight pages for his editorial. After recounting some of his law school experiences, he devoted his attention to *Mystery & Detection Monthly* and Bob Napier's ban on mention of L.A. Morse. (See the Chapter on *MDM*.) Townsend accused Napier of being a censor rather than an editor by not publishing letters about Morse that he disagreed with. Some letter writers agreed with Townsend, while others felt Napier, as editor, had the right to decide what went into his magazine. In Vol. 8 No. 6 (Nov.–Dec. 1986) Townsend used his editorial to summarize his disagreement with Napier. Otto Penzler, referring to what he called Townsend's "one-dimensional political harangues," said "Stuff it. If you want to publish a politically oriented fanzine, go ahead. But don't call it a mystery fiction fanzine."

The argument with Napier was largely over by Vol. 9. Townsend was assessing his problems of time and finances and said he would have to publish quarterly instead of bimonthly. Also, he would increase the price from fifteen to twenty-five dollars. Furthermore, that rate was predicated on his having at least two hundred subscribers. In another ultimatum, he said he would have to cease publication at the end of Volume 9 if he didn't.

In Vol. 9, No. 4 (July–Aug.1987) Townsend announced that *TMF* would continue because 114 of 130 readers who responded were willing to pay the higher rate and, furthermore, he had received a check for a thousand dollars from an anonymous benefactor to help keep the magazine alive. My own attempts at detecting the identity of this patron were unsuccessful. I suspected Bill Deeck because at about this time he was especially active in *TMF*, contributing many articles and reviews and volunteering to type several long articles by others. Townsend rightly called him "a prince among princes." However, when I asked Deeck, near the end of his life, he denied being the donor, so I must leave that generous person nameless, though rumors persist that it was Jane Bakerman.

Most of Vol. 9, No. 6 (Nov.–Dec. 1987) was devoted to Mike Nevins's article covering the last years of Cornell Woolrich. Townsend had ended his brief experiment in paying his contributors and then announced he would only accept contributions from subscribers so, in essence, one had to pay to have one's writing published in *TMF*. In that issue, Townsend explained his reasons. He said his goal was not to increase subscribers, and, in fact, he might have lost some by this policy. However, he wanted *TMF* to be a forum for mystery fans and thought that people who wrote for it should be willing to pay for and read it regularly. "There's something vaguely dishonest about expressing an opinion to an audience and then refusing to listen to the audience's response."

The quarterly *TMF* in Vol. 10 (1988) had a slightly changed, more attractive format, and each issue was larger at 104 pages. It also had *TMF*'s first Associate Editor, Bill Deeck, beginning with No. 2. Besides spending many hours putting *TMF*'s contents on disk, Deeck was preparing an index for *TMF* and wrote a column, "The Backward Reviewer," in which he reviewed old mysteries.

Unable (or unwilling) to avoid provocation, Townsend, in Vol. 10, No. 3 (Summer 1988), went back to bashing Tey's *The Daughter of Time*, accusing her of intellectual dishonesty and saying she had maligned the profession of historian. In Vol. 8, No. 5 (Sept.–Oct. 1986), Townsend had used his editorial column to take umbrage at *The Drood Review*'s criticism of his own novel, *To Prove a Villain* (1985), in which he supported the belief that Richard III was guilty of the murders of "The Princes in the Tower." As a historian, Townsend objected to the *Drood* reviewer questioning his accuracy.

Vol. 10, No. 4 (Fall 1988) saw a new review column, one that would stay with *TMF* until its demise. "The Armchair Reviewer" was Allen J. Hubin, the man with the best claim to using that title. Townsend had complained in the previous issue that he needed more material. Of the 104 pages in this issue, 45 consisted of Deeck's Index to Vols. 6 and 7, and another 40 to William A.S. Sarjeant's article on Sara Woods.

The unknown sponsor donated five hundred dollars to help *TMF* into its eleventh volume (1989). Vol. 11, No. 2 (Spring 1989) was mailed *before* Vol. 11, No. 1 (Winter 1989), with Townsend blaming the delay on his printer. Naturally, there were no letters in No. 2 because readers had not received the prior issue. However, Vol. 11, No. 3 (Summer 1989) had twenty pages of letters.

The anonymous *TMF* backer struck again with five hundred to begin Vol. 12 (1990). Townsend announced that he was running for District Attorney of Jefferson County, Indiana. (He was elected and served in that job until 1994.) Sarjeant began an interesting new column in that issue, "Crime Novelists as Writers of Children's Fiction," with a piece on Manning Coles. Townsend's eccentric mailing continued, and that issue was mailed only a week before No. 2.

The 13th volume of *TMF* began with the announcement of receipt of another five hundred from its unnamed friend. In Vol. 13, No. 2 (Spring 1991), Townsend announced that *TMF* would cease publication after the final issue of that volume. He was down to about a hundred subscribers, and the magazine took a great deal of his time, though Deeck was doing much of the work.

Townsend graciously said goodbye in Vol. 13, No. 4 (Fall 1992), noting how much richer *TMF* had made him, not financially, but in terms of contacts with other mystery fans. "So to all of you who have subscribed to *TMF* over the years, I thank you for giving me the privilege of doing this. To all of you who have written articles and letters and reviews, I thank you for giving me, free, things of such great value."

Townsend did not leave crime and the mystery entirely. He continued to publish fiction. With Joe L. Hensley he published a crime novel, *Loose Coins*. As District Attorney of Jefferson County, he received national coverage when he prosecuted the perpetrators of a crime in which four teen-age girls killed a twelve-year-old schoolmate. In a 1995 interview in the *Indianapolis Star*, Townsend said, "The entire case was gruesome and depressing and I needed something to take my mind off the case once in a while." He turned to an old hobby as an amateur magician and eventually opened a magic store in Jeffersonville, Indiana. He became a prosecuting attorney in Ripley County, Indiana.

Chapter Ten

OTHER FAN MAGAZINES, ORGANIZATIONS, AND CONVENTIONS: 1970S

Pulp **(1970–1981)**

Interest in pulp magazines continued in the 1970s, partly due to a new generation of fans, too young to have read them when they were originally published. *The Pulps* (1970), a book edited by Tony Goodstone, was a survey of pulp magazines. It included fifty stories and one hundred full-color cover illustrations, recapturing the essence of the pulps. That same year the first issue of *Pulp*, a fan magazine edited by Robert Weinberg, was published. The emphasis from the start was on heroes, especially those whose adventures were crime-related. There were interviews with Walter Gibson, creator of *The Shadow*, and Frederick C. Davis, a prolific writer of pulp stories and crime novels. Files from Popular Publications provided bibliographic material, allowing fans to identify some of those who wrote pulp stories under "house names." *Pulp*'s publication schedule was erratic; it seldom published more than one issue a year before ceasing in 1981.

The Mystery Trader **(1971–1980)**
Long active in science fiction fandom, Ethel Lindsay, a retired Scottish hospital head nurse, started *The Mystery Trader* in June 1971. (The first two issues were titled *The Lindsay Trader* and only contained catalogues of books for sale.) By the third issue in 1972, it became a general fan magazine, with a subscription base extending beyond Great Britain. Bob Adey wrote articles about impossible crimes. John A. Hogan wrote about Edgar Wallace. Francis M. Nevins, Mary Groff, and Derek J. Adley were other contributors. There were also reviews, news, and letters. After twenty-one issues, the last in July 1980, Lindsay retired from publishing though she continued writing for CADS and other fan magazines.

Pulp, Paperback, and Other Media Conventions (1972)
Pulpcon, a conference for fans of pulp magazines, was started by three St. Louis fans in 1972, and about one hundred attended it in Clayton, Missouri. It was successful, largely through the efforts of longtime science fiction fan James "Rusty" Hevelin. Mystery pulps were important in panel discussions as well as among the magazines for sale. Though generally held in Ohio, Pulpcon has also been in New Jersey, Arizona, Missouri, North Carolina, and California. Mystery writers Hugh Cave, Michael Avallone, and Francis M. Nevins, among others, have been Guests of Honor.

Pulpcon regulars Walter Albert, Randy Cox, and Bob Briney

Due to diminishing attendance, the last Pulpcon was held in 2008 in Dayton, Ohio. However, members of the Pulpcon organizing committee were loath to abandon annual meetings of fans, and they started PulpFest in 2009. They sought to widen the focus of that convention by showing the effect of pulp magazines on American popular culture in its movies, radio, television, comics, paperbacks, and video games. PulpFest continues to be held. Conventions were held in Columbus 2016 and Pittsburgh in 2017 and 2018.

Following the successful paperback reprints of Mickey Spillane's Mike Hammer books in the 1940s and 1950s, paperback originals became very popular, eventually dealing a death blow to pulp magazines, already in financial distress. These books, especially those in Fawcett's Gold Medal line, are collectible by those who are also mystery fans. Writers such as John D. MacDonald had their first successes in paperback originals. The cover art, often of attractive women in various stages of undress, has been the subject of slide shows at Bouchercons, and some fans are frank enough to say they collect mysteries as much for the covers as for any reason, using "GGA" (Good Girl Art) as their politically incorrect abbreviation. Equally collectible are some paperback reprints, especially those originally published between 1939 and 1959.

The late Lance Casebeer, called "the Godfather of paperback collecting," put on a small annual show, Lancecon, for friends and diehard collectors at his Oregon home. On a larger scale, and still held, is the Los Angeles Vintage Paperback Collectors Show, commonly called Lessercon, after Tom Lesser, who organized it in 1980 and held it at his home for the first two years. It has been held at various locations in the L.A. area, most recently in Glendale. The NYC Collectible Paperback and Pulp Fiction Expo in Manhattan was organized by Gary Lovisi in 1989, and he held it for twenty-five years until 2013. Doug Ellis sponsored the 2004 Windy City Pulp & Paperback Convention in Chicago, and it has been held ever since. There were four hundred in attendance in 2017 and over a hundred sales tables.

Fans of old-time-radio (OTR) are often mystery fans because

some of the great fictional sleuths, including Ellery Queen, Nero Wolfe, Mr. and Mrs. North, and Sam Spade, had radio programs. There were also such popular non-detective shows as *Suspense* and *Escape*. There are still old-time radio groups, and SPERDVAC (The Society to Preserve and Encourage Radio Drama Variety and Comedy, Inc.) still holds meetings and an annual convention. An important group, Friends of Old Time Radio, held its last convention in 2011 at a hotel near the Newark airport after thirty-six years, citing sparse attendance, likely due to aging of those interested. However, many still listen to old time mysteries via such new electronic devices as the MP3.

Fans of mysteries are often movie fans, and rare mystery films are part of the programs at conventions. Cinefest was held each winter for thirty-five years in Syracuse, New York, until 2015, ceasing when it became difficult to get the films people wanted to see.

However, there is still Cinevent, held for over forty years in Columbus, Ohio, and Cinecon, a Labor Day Weekend film festival held for over fifty years in Hollywood. Especially mystery-related are film noir festivals. The oldest of these is probably the one held at the Seattle Art Museum since 1977. Similar events are held in New York, Palm Springs, Los Angeles, San Francisco, Austin, Albuquerque, and Santa Fe, among other locations.

James Bond Clubs (1972–)

The popularity of Ian Fleming's character led in 1972 to the James Bond 007 Fan Club, founded by two high school students, Richard Schenkman and Bob Forlini of Yonkers, NY. Forlini dropped out, leaving Schenkman to run the club, which grew in the 1980s to 1,600 members, mostly males in their twenties. An article about the club in *Playboy* had helped swell the membership. In the summer of 1974, it began to publish *Bondage*. Planned as a semiannual journal, though it sometimes missed a year or two of publication, it emphasized interviews with those connected with Bond films. The magazine, published until 1989, carried considerable advertising of movie posters, pins, T-shirts, etc.

The James Bond International Fan Club (JBIFC), founded in 1979, is still alive and published on its website, though there had been rumors the club might fold. David Black is its chairman. At its peak, it had members in forty countries and operated many websites, including unusual ones such as *Roger Moore, a Polish Fan Site*. Its headquarters is in England. Like its predecessor, the emphasis is on the screen versions of Fleming's work. Its magazine is now called *Kiss Kiss Bang Bang,* which is also the title of Mike Ripley's book about Bond.

The Ian Fleming Foundation was formed about 1990, dedicated to study and preservation of material regarding Fleming. One of their objectives is to preserve the cars used in making James Bond films. They have at least thirty-four of these. Their publication is *Goldeneye,* named after Fleming's retreat in Jamaica.

***Current Crime* (1973–1980); *Bloodhound* (1987–1988)**

Mystery fans who like to read reviews had every reason to be pleased with this magazine. Each issue contained dozens of reviews, mostly written by its editor Nigel Morland, a prolific British writer. (No one else's name appeared in the magazine.) Morland said that *Current Crime* had nearly 12,000 "direct subscribers." He also optimistically reported "a franchise system where organizations such as libraries or universities can receive the pages of *Current Crime* prepared for litho-printing and produce their own copies." According to Morland, "it has been calculated…that world distribution of each issue…must be well over 100,000 copies."

Morland said that *Current Crime* has always been non-profit and his "only desire is to help his colleagues to sell as many of their books as possible." A fire, after the last issue, December 1980, destroyed *Current Crime*'s premises. Ill health prevented Morland from resuming publication. Years later, *Bloodhound,* a review magazine, edited by Simon Wood, incorporated *Current Crime* and was published bimonthly from March 1987 to March 1988. It contained many reviews, the occasional article, and lists of "personal favorites." Margaret Thatcher was quoted as being a fan of Frederick Forsyth, Dick Francis, and P.D. James, and "all the Agatha Christies long ago." No reason was given as to why *Bloodhound* ceased publication.

*Mystery*File* (1974–)

No other fan magazine has risen, phoenix-like, from self-imposed ashes more often than Steve Lewis's *Mystery*File.* Lewis, a retired mathematics professor at Central Connecticut State College, started it in the spring of 1974 as "a combination fanzine and sales list." After seven issues, it had its first hiatus but soon reappeared, though not always as an independent magazine. It was part of Don Miller's *Mystery Nook,* where Lewis was briefly Associate Editor, and then in *The Mystery FANcier* (*TMF*) preview issue of November 1976, continuing for *TMF*'s first six years. Sporadically, it was Lewis's magazine in *DAPA-EM*. Sometimes, his magazine would be called *Fatal Kiss,* and occasionally *Fatal Kiss* would be the title of the review portion of his magazine.

Steve Lewis, founder of *Mystery*File*, and one of his columnists, *DAPA-EM* "den mother" Ellen Nehr

Lewis resumed publishing *Mystery*File* as his own magazine with issue #26 in December 1990. Ten of twenty-four pages consisted of Lewis's mystery and movie reviews. Another five of the pages were "*Fatal Kiss*: A Letter Column." However, he also had reviews by Dorothy Nathan, Kathi Maio, and Sue Feder, plus Ellen Nehr's column "Murder Ad Lib," consisting of reviews and interviews. Beginning with #29, Maryell Cleary wrote a column

"Vintage Crime" in which she discussed classic writers such as Mary Roberts Rinehart, and H.C Bailey.

There was another hiatus after issue #34 in 1991, and when *Deadly Pleasures* began in 1993, Lewis was part of it with a review column under the punny title "Fatal Quiche" in the second and third issues. The latter column was numbered *Mystery*File* #35. Lewis then did mystery reviews as *Mystery*File* #36–38 in the next three issues and again in the twelfth issue of *Deadly Pleasures*, with what was apparently intended as #39, though it was not numbered.

In December 2003 Lewis began his most ambitious iteration of *Mystery*File* with issue #40. He said it was "not to be an up-to-date newsletter for the field, but a place where old and new works co-exist, where older mysteries can be brought up and discussed as well as those by the most recent hot authors, and where the careers of writers can be looked at in perspective. *Mystery*File* will be for those fans who love to read and talk about mysteries and series characters, and those who love to make checklists, and those who love to have them, and if you can assist in accomplishing any of these goals, then so much the better."

Lewis attracted knowledgeable fans who liked writing about mystery's past because most other current American fan magazines were specializing in reviews of new books. *Mystery*File* printed Al Hubin's "Addenda to Crime Fiction IV," his correction and updating of his bibliography which had gone through the year 2000. Bill Crider wrote about (and reviewed) legendary paperback originals in "The Gold Medal Corner." Mike Nevins had a column of autobiographical mystery commentary called "First You Read, Then You Write." I had a column of reviews and miscellanea called "The Crime of My Life." Lewis encouraged my penchant for puns by naming his letter's column, at my suggestion, "Scarlet Letters," and not complaining when I called my film review section "Déjà View."

In line with Lewis's plan to cover past writers in depth, much of *Mystery*File* #42 was devoted to Robert Wade, best known as co-author of the Wade Miller mysteries of the 1940s and 1950s. There were five articles about him and an interview with him. #45 had Ed Lynskey's article on Ed Lacy, probably the best writing ever on that almost forgotten writer. #46 had an article, interview, and bibliography of Jonathan Latimer. In February 2005 Lewis added *The Crime Fiction Research Journal* to *Mystery*File*'s title to reflect the direction in which his readers had taken it. He has welcomed questions and tried to answer them.

After November 2004, *Mystery*File* joined other fan magazines on the internet as *M*F Online*. By the end of 2006 Lewis was too busy to continue this, but it morphed into one of the best blogs. It included "Ed Gorman Rambles" or "Gormania," along with articles by Nevins and Crider, and others. There were also reviews from some of the now-defunct journals of the past.

A project that is taking much of Lewis's time is helping Al Hubin on his bibliography. Hubin kept accumulating and correcting data, especially in the form of additional titles, birth and death dates, and new series characters. Lewis publishes this information online.

Xenophile (1974–1980)

Nils Hardin of St. Louis started *Xenophile* in March 1974 as "a monthly advertiser and journal devoted to fantastic and imaginative literature." The advertising was especially important because for much of the time *Xenophile* was a full time-job for Hardin. In 1978 he reported he had only earned $324 the previous year. Though some issues consisted primarily of ads, and others were mainly about science fiction, Hardin also published mystery-related issues, including one in June 1975 devoted to Ellery Queen. Several other issues were devoted to pulp detectives and included bibliographies. *Xenophile* lasted forty-five issues, until March 1980.

Baker Street Miscellanea (1975–1995)

Interest in Sherlock Holmes has never flagged, but it increased in the mid-1970s. This journal, whose first issue was April 1975, was founded in Chicago by longtime Sherlockians John Nieminski and William D. Goodrich. In the first issue Nieminski stated that the motivation of the founders of this quarterly was "an abiding interest in the great detective and his life and works; a desire to share our enthusiasm through the medium of a self-wrought amateur publication which, hopefully, will open yet another channel for speculation and creative expression for ourselves and others; and not the least, the making of a few new friends along the way."

Beginning with the fourth issue in December 1975, the magazine obtained the sponsorship of Northeastern Illinois University, thanks to another noted Sherlockian, Professor Ely Liebow, chairman of its English Department. This helped its finances and permitted it to reach a circulation of 430 by 1981. Among its features were Goodrich's lengthy series, "The Sherlock Holmes Reference Guide," Sherlockian parodies, comments by Dame Jean Conan Doyle regarding Charles Higham's biography of her father, and an article on Sherlock Holmes and Tarzan by Philip José Farmer.

Photo by Phoebe Liebow

Professor Ely Liebow, co-publisher of *Baker Street Miscellanea*

Baker Street Miscellanea survived the death of Nieminski in 1986 and, under the stewardship of Goodrich and Liebow, lasted until the first issue of 1995, when, after twenty years, it ceased publication.

The Mystery Nook (1975–1981)

Don Miller of Wheaton, Maryland, also a longtime science fiction fan, founded *The Mystery Nook* in July 1975; it was designed to give mystery fans another forum. The first two issues consisted mainly of comments by the editor, along with reviews and sales lists. However, by the third issue mystery fans were sending letters and articles, and *The Mystery Nook* had several outstanding issues during its relatively short life.

Though *The Mystery Nook* came out fairly regularly in 1975, thereafter Miller's ill health (he had two bouts of cancer) caused long delays between issues. For example, there were eight months between No. 8 and No. 9 and nine months between No. 9 and No. 10. Nos. 10 and 11 appeared only a month apart, but then there was another eight months before No. 12, and over three years before the final issue in July 1981. Guy Townsend joked that *The Mystery Nook* was the only quarterly in the business that comes out every other year. Its subscribers knew about Miller's health problems and were forgiving. Early in 1982 Townsend learned of Miller's death when Miller's copy of *The Mystery FANcier* was returned by the Postal Service marked "deceased." The May/June 1982 issue of *The Mystery FANcier* was dedicated to Miller.

Most of those involved in other fan magazines of the 1970s also wrote articles for Miller and letters for the section he called "Things That Go Bump in the Night." A Rex Stout memorial issue in August 1976 drew articles from leading Nero Wolfe scholars, including Townsend, John J. McAleer, Judson C. Sapp, and Art Scott. A Ruth Rendell issue in 1977 contained eleven pieces about her, including a bibliography. The final issue of *The Mystery Nook* had a dozen pieces about Georgette Heyer, a writer often ignored in mystery fan magazines.

Nero Wolfe Fandom (1975–)

So popular is Nero Wolfe that Rex Stout is one of the few Golden Age authors whose work remains available in reprint in the United States. An early start in Wolfe fandom was the *Nero Wolfe and Archie Goodwin Fans Newsletter*, edited and published by Lee

E. Poleske of Seward, Alaska, beginning in 1975. After three issues, its title changed to *Lone Wolfe*. It discontinued publication after its sixth issue, January 1976. It contained reviews, quizzes, biographies of Wolfe's favorite chefs, and even a diagram of the structure of a cattleya orchid.

In 1977, inspired by Carol Brener, owner of the Murder Ink bookstore, Ellen Krieger founded The Wolfe Pack, and it soon had over a thousand members. Its quarterly publication, *The Gazette* commenced with the Winter 1979 issue. The consulting editor was John McAleer, Stout's Edgar-winning biographer. In 1984 McAleer started *The Rex Stout Journal*, which had five issues before ending in 1988. *The Gazette* includes a variety of scholarly articles about the Wolfe corpus, including such perennially popular topics as Wolfe's parentage, early life, and the actual address of his West Thirty-Fifth Street brownstone. (Unlike Sherlockians who use "canon," Wolfe fans use "corpus" for the Nero Wolfe body of work.) Regional Chapters of the Wolfe Pack, unlike Sherlockian scions, are called "racemes," using a flower-bearing term. Now semi-annual, *The Gazette* lists as editor "Lon Cohen," the name of the reporter on the fictional newspaper, *The Gazette*, who often helped Wolfe and Archie.

Since December 2, 1978, when 127 persons gathered at the Gramercy Park Hotel. The Wolfe Pack has held an annual Black Orchid Banquet in New York on the first weekend in December—to correspond with Stout's birthday. It was an evening of food (prepared by a European chef following recipes in *The Nero Wolfe Cook Book*), songs, speeches, quizzes, and even a fake murder. At the dinner in 1979, the Pack first awarded the Nero Award to a mystery novel "meeting Stout's Criteria for Excellence." Lawrence Block won for *The Burglar Who Liked to Quote Kipling* (1979). The 40th Banquet was held in 2017 in Toronto as part of Bouchercon. In addition, beginning in 1979 the Pack has held a Shad Roe dinner in the spring, honoring one of Wolfe's favorite fish dishes. The Wolfe Pack meets on other social occasions. In 2017 members went to St. Paul, Minnesota, to attend the premiere of Joseph Goodrich's second Nero Wolfe play, based on the novel *Might As Well Be Dead* (1956). Unlike some fan organizations, the Wolfe Pack remains healthy today with about five hundred members. It arranged to have a plaque placed at 454 W. Thirty-Fifth Street (Wolfe's address according to their scholarship) by New York City's Park Commissioner. Beginning in 2008, *Alfred Hitchcock Mystery Magazine*, in conjunction with the Wolfe Pack, has sponsored the Black Orchid Novella Award for a story that meets the criteria of Wolfe's work: detection, and humor, without gratuitous sex and violence.

The Thorndyke File (1976–1988) and _John Thorndyke's Journal_ (1991–1998)

In Spring 1976, Philip T. Asdell of Maryland started *The Thorndyke File*, a journal devoted to R. Austin Freeman and his series detective, the medico-legal expert Dr. John Thorndyke. In addition to publishing scholarship, the journal, led by reader Frank Archibald of Needham, Massachusetts, waged a successful campaign to have a stone placed at Freeman's unmarked grave in England. When other commitments forced Asdell to relinquish editorship of *The Thorndyke File*, John McAleer took over in 1980 and soon doubled the subscribers to 156, half of whom were medical doctors. Though *The Thorndyke File* is no longer published (the last issue was in 1988), another fan magazine, *John Thorndyke's Journal*, was published in England from 1991 until 1998 by David Ian Chapman of Aldershot, Hampshire. Chapman also published, as a supplement, a bibliography of the works of Freeman.

Georges Simenon Organizations (1976–)

Though most of his mysteries, especially his Inspector Maigret series, are set in France, Georges Simenon was Belgian. Among several Simenon organizations in Belgium is *Le Centre D'études Georges Simenon* in Liège. It was established in 1976 "for the development and dissemination of Simenon's work." They sponsor a colloquium every two years and publish an annual review, *Traces*. Scholarly information can also be found in Liège at a foundation, *Le Fonds Simenon de l'Université de Liège*, which provides access to over seven thousand works by or about Simenon. About four hundred fans, readers and scholars belong to *Les Amis de Georges Simenon*, in Beigem, Belgium, which was founded in 1986. They publish *Les Cahiers Simenon* annually.

The Dorothy L. Sayers Society (1976–)

The popularity of Lord Peter Wimsey on British and American television, beginning in the 1970s, led to renewed interest in Dorothy L. Sayers. Biographies and collections of her letters have been published. The Dorothy L. Sayers Society was established in 1976. Located in West Sussex, England, it sponsors regular meetings, an annual conference, and a bimonthly newsletter. Their archives are open to members. The Dorothy L. Sayers Centre in Essex, England, has a collection of works by and about Sayers.

Mohonk Mountain House Mystery Weekend (1977–)

Because it started in 1977, the annual Mohonk Mystery Weekend at the Mountain House at Lake Mohonk, in New York State's Catskill Mountains, was probably the first non-Bouchercon general mystery meeting. It was originally organized by Dilys Winn and Carol Brener of the Murder Ink Bookstore in Manhattan. When first held as a "Dead of Winter" weekend, January 27–30, 1977, there were panels about the mystery, famous authors such as Phyllis Whitney and Isaac Asimov, and people knowledgeable about mystery fiction, including Otto Penzler and Chris Steinbrunner. The setting was an atmospheric 108-year-old hotel, and the event quickly proved popular, selling out each year within two hours of the hotel accepting reservations. Whitney set her novel *The Stone Bull* (1977) at Mohonk, though she called the resort "Laurel Mountain House."

The first Mohonk weekend was not entirely a learned discussion of mysteries. There was a ghoulish cooking lesson by Winn, a talk by a safecracker, a ski tour, and a demonstration with raptors called, inevitably, "Maltese Falconry." Increasingly, murder games have predominated at these weekends. For a while, Mohonk continued to draw noted authors, but they often were there to participate in contests in which "murder" is committed, and attendees try to solve it, often in teams. These murder events have proven popular at other hotels, on cruise ships, as corporate events, and even at an occasional Bouchercon.

Max Allan Collins was invited to be the "killer" at one of these weekends, and a few years later returned the favor with *Nice Weekend for a Murder* (1986) set there, with his detective, Mallory, playing "suspect." A fortieth anniversary Mohonk weekend celebration was held March 3–5, 2017. The next weekend is scheduled for February 28-March 1, 2020.

The August Derleth Society (1977–)

In 1977, a Connecticut school administrator, Richard Fawcett, came upon *Walden West* by August Derleth, a book that so impressed him he called it "the heartbeat of middle America preserved in amber." This was a non-mystery by the author of the Solar Pons pastiches and the Judge Peck mysteries. Fawcett was determined to find other fans of this prolific author and founded the August Derleth Society later that year, becoming editor-publisher of *The August Derleth Newsletter*, which includes material regarding Derleth's mysteries but also about his other fiction. The society, with several hundred members, has annual meetings in Sauk City, Wisconsin, the Midwestern city where Derleth lived and about which he wrote, calling it "Sac Prairie."

***The Poisoned Pen* (1977–1987)**

Jeff Meyerson began *The Poisoned Pen* (*TPP*), his mimeographed magazine for *DAPA-EM*, in February 1977. The first issue was only six pages, but by the second, the page count increased to sixteen, and Meyerson, sending copies to a wider audience than *DAPA-EM*, received letters from non-members such as Al Hubin, Mike Nevins, and Bill Pronzini. He even received articles and checklists.

The Poisoned Pen became a bimonthly, general-circulation fan magazine in January 1978 and eventually reached a circulation of about 250. In his first editorial, "The Pen Rambles," Meyerson said the direction of the magazine was in the hands of its readers, depending on what they submitted to be published. He did not want *TPP* to be merely a forum for the current mystery scene, saying, "Reviews can be of any mystery, new or old, though I'd especially like the older, out-of-print titles, obscure or otherwise." The contents of *TPP* were similar to its contemporary *The Mystery FANcier*, though the editorial voice of Meyerson was more relaxed and less contentious than Guy Townsend's.

The first issue contained "All Too True" by Mary Groff, starting her long series about fiction that was suggested by true crime. Mary Ann Grochowski contributed a Sherlockian parody, set in Poland. Also in the first issue was Neville Wood's article on "The Golden Age," based on a speech he gave to the Cambridge Old Boys Book Club.

R. Jeff Banks began "Mystery Plus," his series on books (usually Westerns, science fiction, or horror) with a crime element. In the second issue I began a series called "Department of Unknown Mystery Writers," about those who have written at least one good mystery and yet have either received little attention or are almost forgotten now. I started with an article on William Krasner, who had not published a mystery in twenty years. A couple of years after my article, he published two new novels, though I doubt there was a connection.

In another example of material in *TPP* seeming to take on a life of its own, I included South African writer Peter Godfrey as one of my "Unknown Writers." Bob Adey, searching for a possible

Godfrey short story collection published in South Africa, wrote to him and received three letters (reprinted in *TPP*) that provided considerable additional information about him. In 2001, Godfrey became less "unknown" when Crippen & Landru published the first American collection of his stories.

Other articles in the early issues included Howard Waterhouse on Roy Vickers, Maryell Cleary on Elizabeth Daly, Steve Lewis on old-time radio programs, and Barry Pike regarding David Williams. There were checklists of the Mercury, Bestseller, and Jonathan Press digest-sized books, the short stories of John Lutz, and the contents of *Mystery League*.

It wasn't all serious. Philip Asdell wrote about E.C. Bentley's humorous poetry, the clerihews. After giving some examples, Asdell contributed his own. Ola Strom of Norway also included a few, saying "Too many people are taking mystery fiction much too seriously these day—a more balanced view is sorely needed." Gary Crew, punning that he was "fairly well-versed in crime," submitted some, and Jane Gottschalk provided ten poems.

I wrote one of my speculative articles, "The Detective Who Would Be King," in which I drew "evidence" from Margery Allingham's Albert Campion series "proving" that Campion was really a fictionalized version of British King Edward VIII, who abdicated the throne in 1936. I received three letters disagreeing, including one from Barry Pike in England in which he said George VI was Campion's more likely source.

The dissents regarding Campion were in good humor, unlike what greeted the article I wrote regarding Elizabeth Linington's Luis Mendoza. I said that her intrusive right-wing politics was spoiling the series. I gave examples of her reactionary views, including her saying that women who wear miniskirts invite rape. Rinehart Potts, who published the *Linington Lineup*, asserted that I was against freedom of speech for Linington. Jon L. Breen and Bob Briney, in letters to *TPP*, defended me. Breen was unable to understand how Potts could consider me "some kind of a wild-eyed left-wing revolutionary," since I am generally considered rather conservative (I usually wear a tie).

Another series was Pike's "Pen Profiles," brief biographies and bibliographies of English writers. He eventually published thirty-four of these in *TPP*. In "First Appearances," Cleary wrote of the first mysteries in which well-known series characters appear. Waterhouse, one of the earliest contributors, died of a heart attack early in 1980. Ironically, he had just purchased the mystery collection of Don Miller of *Mystery Nook*, when the latter was seriously ill with cancer. Miller outlived Waterhouse by two years.

The contents of *TPP* were lively, and Joe R. Lansdale favorably compared it to *TAD*, which he considered "stuffy." Jim McCahery said *TPP* "exemplifies the best in serious scholarship without undue erudition; it is clearly a vehicle by mystery lovers for mystery lovers." Reviews were often negative, warning people away from books. Three decades later, almost all reviews in U.S. fan magazines are favorable.

By the start of Volume 5, dated July 1982, *TPP* become a quarterly. The pressures of putting out a regular fanzine had led to a six-month delay between the last issue of Volume 4 and the first of Volume 5. Other delays followed, and Meyerson announced in Volume 6, No. 3 (Fall 1985), that *TPP* would be "irregularly published," something already apparent. Letters were fewer due to irregular publication, and *TPP* was suspended indefinitely after Volume 7, No. 1 (Fall/Winter 1987) finally appeared—one year following the previous issue. Meyerson announced that he was no longer accepting subscriptions but would publish on an issue-by-issue basis. To date, it has not reappeared.

Notes for the Curious: A John Dickson Carr Memorial Journal (1978); _Notes for the Curious_ (1995)

A chapbook was published and edited by Larry L. French in 1978 to commemorate Carr's 1977 death. In addition to bibliographic material and a chronology of Carr's life, there were comments about him from most of the important names in fandom, including Hubin, Penzler, Breen, Nevins, Shibuk, and Briney. French was at work on a book about Carr, tentatively titled *The Grand Master of Mystery,* when ironically this journal became a memorial to French, who died in an auto accident.

Tony Medawar also produced a magazine devoted to Carr, also titled *Notes for the Curious.* In its only issue, dated Autumn 1995, Medawar said it was "published by the Noughts-and-Crosses Club." That is the name of a fictional club that Carr had used in at least one novel and two short stories. Medawar also said that purchase of that issue "entitles the reader to Club membership which, at the moment, has as yet no significance whatsoever other than providing a convenient peg on which enthusiasts are warmly invited to hang their hats and coats." Neither club nor the magazine went further.

The Holmesian Federation (1978–1991)

Surely the strangest Sherlockian publication of the 1970s was *The Holmesian Federation,* which began in November 1978. This "admittedly weird hybrid," as editor-publisher Signe Landon of Oregon called it, attempted to combine two of her favorite universes: Sherlock Holmes and the TV series *Star Trek.* It was partly nonfiction with such articles as "A Study in Harlots" by Frankie Jemison, purporting to be "a shocking account of the real circumstances surrounding the meeting of Holmes and Dr. Watson," and "Holmes was a Vulcan," a study by Priscilla Polner. The fiction either transferred *Star Trek* characters into Victorian times or placed Holmes and Watson in the future. A second issue did not appear until October 1980. The eighth and last issue was published in 1991. In 2001, some of the short stories from this magazine, parody-pastiches of Sherlock Holmes and Captain Kirk, were collected in hardcover as *The Federation Holmes.*

***The Not So Private Eye* (1978–1984)**

Andy Jaysnovitch of New Jersey, a fan of private eye fiction and early television series, and a collector of almost everything, started *The Not So Private Eye* in 1978. His goal was to promote the private detective story, which seemed to have fallen on hard times. (This was before the popularity of books by Marcia Muller, Sue Grafton and Sara Paretsky and the founding of the Private Eye Writers of America.) His illustrated magazine containing features such as "Series Spotlight" by Jim McCahery, who wrote about great private detectives of the past. Paul Bishop contributed articles on current private eyes. There were also interviews. In 1980 Jaysnovitch announced the demise of his magazine, but it resumed in 1982. It has not appeared since 1984.

***Paperback Quarterly* (1978–1982)**

In 1978 Charlotte Laughlin and Billy Lee of Brownwood, Texas, launched *Paperback Quarterly,* calling it the "Journal of Mass-Market Paperback History." The first magazine devoted to collectible paperbacks, it ceased publication suddenly after Volume V No. 2 (Summer 1982). At least half of the articles in it were mystery-related, including "Dashiell Hammett in the Dell Mapbacks" by William Lyles, "Skeleton Covers" by Bill Crider, "The Paperback Dr. John Thorndyke" by Daniel G. Roberts, and "Avon Classic Crime Collection" by Don Hensley.

***813: Les Amis de la Littèrature Policière* (1979–)**

Over 800 French writers and fans belong to *813: Les Amis de la Littèrature Policière,* founded in Paris in 1979. Their quarterly journal is also called *813,* the title of a 1910 Arsène Lupin novel by Maurice Leblanc. The organization is still active.

The John Buchan Society (1979–)

It was founded by Eileen Stewart of Edinburgh University on March

3, 1979 "to promote a wider understanding and appreciation of the life and works of this author and statesman." They publish *The John Buchan Journal* which combines scholarly work with lighter observation and comment.

Buchan was Baron Tweedsmuir and became Governor-General of Canada. He was also the author of thrillers, including *The 39 Steps,* which was adapted into a movie by Alfred Hitchcock in 1935 and a popular stage play in 2005. The membership of this group of devotees of Buchan is about three hundred.

Mystery (1979–1982)

Mystery, a slick-paper fan magazine published in Los Angeles, made its appearance with the November-December 1979 issue. Few of the articles about the mystery contained much depth, and up to a third of each issue was fiction. The first issue began a continuing story, "Ace Carpenter, Detective," by Hamilton T. Caine, a pseudonym of *Mystery*'s editor-publisher Stephen L. Smoke.

Though supposedly professionally produced, *Mystery*'s schedule was as erratic as many amateur fan journals. In 1982 it was converted, without explanation, into a digest-sized magazine and then ceased publication in July. Unused subscriptions were transferred, without permission, to *The West Coast Review of Books.* The final issue of *Mystery* included an ad for a book by Smoke, raising questions as to whether the magazine had only been a means of promoting his writing career.

Chapter Eleven

BOUCHERCONS: 1980S

1980: Washington, DC

Bouchercon XI, October 10–12, proclaimed that it was in "Washington, DC, Where Crime Is Your Government's Business." Some thought there would be echoes of Watergate, but the panels on true crime emphasized law enforcement. One was about a successful "sting" operation, and another, "Support Your Local FBI," featured two FBI agents, but also author Al Nussbaum, once on the FBI "Wanted" list for bank robbery.

There was a Cold War panel on spying, with an FBI agent who worked in intelligence operations and a retired CIA agent. One of Bouchercon's Co-Chairmen, Jon L. Lellenberg, who moderated the panel, described himself as "a strategic analyst at a Washington, DC, national security research organization." The other Co-Chairman, Peter E. Blau, a geologist and journalist, is, like Lellenberg, a member of the Baker Street Irregulars.

At the Bouchercon site, the National Press Club, about 280 people attended, more than three times the 1970 figure. John Nieminski said that the original California organizers must be pleased because "...Bouchercon has flourished, blooming annually for over a decade now, and sprouting up in locales as removed from its West Coast birthplace as Boston, Chicago, and New York."

On Friday night, in addition to the get-acquainted party, there was a panel on screen adaptations, with horror stories by Brian Garfield, James Grady, and Michael Hardwick on what was done to their work.

Phyllis White explained on Saturday morning why her late husband, born William Anthony Parker White, adopted his Boucher pseudonym. Realizing how many authors were named William White, he decided a fledgling writer needed a less common name, so he chose Boucher, the name of a relative on the maternal side of his family.

Because of my interest in regional mysteries, I was chosen to lead a panel on mysteries set in Washington. Since there were six writers on the stage, my job was more traffic manager than moderator. I still regret that I did not reduce the panel by one when Warren Adler objected to being introduced as a "mystery writer," claiming he was a "novelist." I should have ushered him off the stage. In introducing another panelist, Patricia McGerr, I called her *Pick Your Victim* one of the best and most unusual mysteries ever written. (It tells who the killer is but leaves it to the detective and the reader to identify the victim.) Later, a member of the audience showed me a used copy of the book, which she had purchased in the bookroom for $5. She hoped she would find it worth the price.

We had disagreement Saturday during a panel called "The Care and Feeding of Mystery Fans." Otto Penzler, on his way to being a successful publisher and bookseller, opined that the mystery was in good shape, pointing to the emergence of mysteries on bestseller lists. Editor Michael Seidman had a different viewpoint, complaining about the corporate mentality in publishing. Seidman's telling the audience they should support writers by buying books brought a response from the third panel member,

Art Scott, that there were enough good mysteries already in print that fans did not have to purchase for that reason alone.

Saturday evening there was a live performance of William Gillette's one-act play *The Painful Predicament of Sherlock Holmes*, which originally played in New York in 1905 with Ethel Barrymore. Gillette had played Holmes, as he did for many years. Sunday morning was partly devoted to Holmes, with a panel led by Blau commemorating the fiftieth anniversary of Doyle's death. Panelists worried that pastiches written to cash in on the success of *The Seven-Per-Cent Solution* might damage the reputation of the great detective.

On Sunday morning, William Ryan presented, albeit in a monotone, the interesting theory that Edgar Allen Poe had been murdered. Then, Guest of Honor Gregory McDonald, author of the Fletch series, spoke. He had harsh words for critics but was also amusing, telling how he was almost arrested for eating ice cream on Washington's food-free subway.

1981: Milwaukee

Mary Ann Grochowski, a child psychologist, ran this Milwaukee Bouchercon with the help of librarians Beverly De Weese and Gary Warren Niebuhr. It was held October 9–11 at the Marc Plaza and drew attendance of 212 people. Registration for the weekend was only fifteen dollars per person, a bargain compared to later Bouchercons.

Seventy-seven-year-old Helen McCloy was Guest of Honor, the first female selected. Frail physically, but mentally acute, she had many anecdotes to tell, including some regarding her stormy marriage to the late Davis Dresser who, as Brett Halliday, created the Mike Shayne series. For the first time Bouchercon had a Fan Guest of Honor, and the choice was obvious: Allen J. Hubin, whose founding of *The Armchair Detective* led to mystery fandom as we now know it.

Grochowski realized that Bouchercon's chances for success

would be improved if it also had a "name" bigger than McCloy or Hubin. With the help of the Miller Brewing Company, she secured one of the best-selling writers of all time, Mickey Spillane. Spillane had acquired further celebrity by being featured in humorous television beer commercials. He proved friendly and not conceited, and his interview by Max Allan Collins was a highlight of this Bouchercon, which was called "Beer City Capers."

Another wise move was inviting William Campbell Gault, a former Milwaukee writer who now lived in Southern California. Gault had given up writing mysteries in 1963 to write juvenile sports stories because he could make more money from them. He thought no one would remember his mysteries and was reluctant to come, finally agreeing to "patch up the holes in my topcoat" so that he could journey from his warm home to Wisconsin in the fall. Gault was considering writing mysteries again, and the reception he received encouraged him to do so. To his surprise, fans not only remembered and missed him, but also could discuss books he had written thirty years before. Autographing books was becoming an important part of Bouchercon, and Gault and other authors were asking fans that presented old books to be signed, "Where did you find this one?"

Gary Warren Niebuhr and Mary Ann Grochowski

Another Bouchercon highlight was the first of many slide shows by Art Scott, a leader in the branch of mystery fandom specializing in paperback cover art. On Saturday night I joined a congenial group at a restaurant called The Safe House. Its decorations: espionage paraphernalia. When I left on Sunday, I found that Milwaukee had a used bookstore at the airport. I bought an old mystery to read on the plane.

1982: San Francisco

"Bouchercon-by-the-Bay" at the Jack Tar Hotel in San Francisco, October 8–10, used that city for much of its programming, as well as for activities outside the convention site. There were two mystery-related walks: one following Anthony Boucher's footsteps in Berkeley, the other locations about which Dashiell Hammett wrote. Boucher, who never drove a car, walked all over Berkeley—and San Francisco when he crossed the Bay. Ever the reader, Boucher read while he walked the Berkeley streets, leading one to marvel that he survived. I took the Hammett walk myself on a hot day (October is San Francisco's "summer"), and ended up meeting other fans for beer at the S. Holmes, Esq. Pub, where there is an excellent recreation of 221B Baker Street, including the sounds one might have heard in London during Holmes's time.

Don Herron, who leads the Hammett tour, chaired this Bouchercon, aided by local bookseller Bruce Taylor and the Maltese Falcon Societies of San Francisco and San Jose. Attendance was about six hundred. The committee reached three thousand miles for its guest of honor, bringing in Robert B. Parker of Boston.

Friday night included, appropriately, an Anthony Boucher panel, with his sons Lawrence and James White among the speakers. Saturday, for the first time, there was two-track programming, which included Hammett and Holmes panels, another Art Scott slide show called "The Babe on the Paperback Cover," and a panel on California mystery writers. Private Eye Writers of American (PWA), founded by Robert Randisi, presented its first Shamus Awards.

Other topics for the weekend panels included collecting, pulp magazines, and "The Current State of the Mystery." At a panel on reference books, Walter Albert, author of the definitive book on secondary sources about the mystery, declared himself "a passionate bibliographer."

This Bouchercon had an especially good selection of mystery films. They included the two film versions of *The Maltese Falcon* that preceded the 1941 Bogart movie, and *Charlie Chan at Treasure Island,* with its background of the San Francisco area.

Despite the appeal of panels and movies, much that was enjoyable occurred outside the meeting rooms. Friday night dinner for many was at The Shadows, a restaurant near landmark Coit Tower, where they served an unlikely, but delicious, green clam chowder. There were the usual parties held by the *DAPA-EM* group, at one of which I called *The Maltese Falcon* "a good, not great, book." It's a line *DAPA-EM*ers never allowed me to forget. After Bouchercon was over, Art Scott invited a group to his home in Livermore, where people drooled over his collection of vintage paperbacks.

1983: New York City

Bouchercon returned to New York, courtesy of Co-Chairmen Otto Penzler and Chris Steinbrunner, to the Barbizon-Plaza Hotel, on Central Park South, October 21–23, and was successful, with about 450 in attendance, despite having to abandon Columbus Day because hotels were not available. Advance publicity was good; in an article in the *New York Times* Eric Pace pretended he was a private eye investigating Bouchercon.

John D. MacDonald was the Guest of Honor. At the Sunday banquet luncheon, MacDonald revealed that his famous series character was originally named "Dallas McGee," but he changed the first name to "Travis" after John F. Kennedy's 1963 assassination in Dallas.

Various media were used, beginning with a Friday night radio mystery *Kiss My Face with Bullets,* performed by a group associated with Bogies, a Manhattan restaurant that attracted mystery fans and put on special events, such as cruises and tours. There was a panel on the "Golden Age of Television," with excerpts from several crime shows. A Saturday night tribute was paid to recently deceased Jonathan Latimer with two films featuring Preston Foster as his series detective Bill Crane. Walter Gibson performed one of his popular magic shows. Also "performing" were two NYPD dogs. Police dogs proved a popular attraction at later Bouchercons.

Donald E. Westlake read a paper in which he suggested that the private eye novel was dead, and that writers of hardboiled novels were now merely following past greats and needed to set out in new directions. His talk was followed by panels about hardboiled mysteries at which there was agreement and disagreement with what he said. One of those agreeing was James Ellroy, who showed up wearing the baggy knickers favored by golfers in the 1920s. Another panelist, William Campbell Gault, agreed with Westlake about the overuse of metaphor by the late Ross Macdonald. Gault used a metaphor of his own when he said mysteries were minor league writing compared to the major leagues of Ernest Hemingway and F. Scott Fitzgerald. However, he seemed pleased to be in the minors in his resurrected career, because he told me happily that he had sold two new mystery novels to Walker. Later, there would be much discussion of Westlake's opinions in fan magazines.

Saturday night there was the usual noisy *DAPA-EM* party. During this one a German runner came to the door and begged for quiet because, "I have to run twenty-six miles tomorrow." He was entered in Sunday's New York City Marathon. After the convention, many attendees boarded subway trains for Brooklyn and a Bouchercon party at the home of Jeff and Jackie Meyerson.

1984: Chicago

It's hard to be objective about Chicago's third Bouchercon, called "Second City Skullduggery," since I was Fan Guest of Honor, only the second person so honored. On October 26–28, 430 people attended at the Americana Congress Hotel. Three friends, Mary Craig, Ely Liebow, and John Nieminski, produced this especially well-run Bouchercon. Bill Pronzini was Guest of Honor, and he made himself readily available to fans. At Sunday's luncheon-banquet he read more examples of "alternate classics," bad mystery writing like that in his hilarious book *Gun in Cheek*.

For the first time Phyllis White couldn't attend Bouchercon; she was hospitalized with a severe case of shingles. Instead of her opening remarks on Friday night, Bob Briney read some of Boucher's reviews and other writing as tribute to him. The other Friday highlight, in a convention with single-track programming was "Make a Mystery: An Improvisation Workshop" put on by two Chicago-area actors.

In order to ensure good attendance at the first Saturday session (8:30 a.m.), "The State of the Mystery—1984," free paperbacks were given to early arrivals. The panel included an agent and an editor. It was clear the publishing world was beginning to notice Bouchercon. Other noteworthy Saturday sessions included Bill Crider's interview with Pronzini and what would become an annual event, a panel on short stories that included that form's most prolific writer, Edward D. Hoch.

As Fan Guest of Honor, I was interviewed by Nieminski. He elicited the story of the coincidences that happened to me in 1980. I had just published an article about fictional mysteries with operatic backgrounds, "Murder at the Opera," in the July issue of *Opera News* when a week later a violinist was murdered in the Metropolitan Opera House. *The New York Times* mentioned my article and the coincidence of the Met's first murder shortly after my article about crime and opera. But the coincidences were not over. Five weeks later, the police arrested a suspect, and he was someone who lived on the same floor of the Bronx apartment building in which I had resided until eighteen months before the murder. I had often said good morning to him while waiting for the elevator. He was found guilty of felony murder. And I am the fan who decries coincidences in my mystery reading!

There was another coincidence to go with this Bouchercon, the publication of *Kill Your Darlings*, a mystery novel by Max Allan Collins, set at a Chicago Bouchercon. Collins said he started it before he knew that Bouchercon would be held in Chicago in 1984.

Sunday's schedule included a panel on collecting, moderated by Otto Penzler. It included Allen J. Hubin, who amassed a collection of twenty-five thousand mysteries before he had to sell them to fund his children's college educations. There was suspense at the closing session as attendees chose between two California locations, Berkeley and Los Angeles, as the site of the 1985 Bouchercon. Berkeley won. The convention approved Bouchercon's first bylaws, as drafted by Len and June Moffatt.

1985: San Francisco

The sixteenth Bouchercon was supposed to be held in Berkeley, but the convention committee had problems with the Claremont Hotel, and the convention was moved to San Francisco's Sir Francis Drake Hotel, October 25–27. Advance registration was only twenty-five dollars, and a single room at the Drake could be had for seventy dollars per night. A new record was set for Bouchercon attendance: 875 people. Bookseller Bryan Barrett was chairman, with help from Bruce Taylor and a large committee. Advertising referred to Bouchercon for the first time as "The World Mystery Convention."

Cornell Woolrich fans Marv Lachman and Don Yates

Bouchercon honored the California Crime Novel as "Guest

of Honor," though it singled out Joe Gores, Joseph Hansen, and Collin Wilcox as examples of that subgenre. Fan Guests of Honor were June and Len Moffatt, who had been so important in founding Bouchercon.

There was dual-track programming, plus a third track devoted to almost continuous showing of crime films. Two panels were devoted to the California Crime Novel. Other panel topics included humor, cops, pulps, and Sherlock Holmes. Don Yates and I discussed Cornell Woolrich. A first was the hotly contested trivia contest, with prizes awarded to the winning team: Steve Stilwell, Bob Samoian, John L. Breen, and me. Stilwell's identification of Carter Dickson's 1944 novel *He Wouldn't Kill Patience*, cinched the victory.

The Saturday night banquet was held in an extremely crowded room with only one exit, and the peace of mind of those attending was not helped by a fire alarm going off and wailing for ten minutes. Fortunately, it was a false alarm. Meal service was poor, leading a frustrated author, J.J. Lamb, to let out an ear-shattering whistle when he had not received his entrée. There was another funny talk by Toastmaster Tony Hillerman about inept criminals and police officers in New Mexico.

1986: Baltimore

Attendance dropped to about 450 at the seventeenth Bouchercon at Baltimore's Sheraton Inner Harbor, despite a return to Columbus Day weekend, October 10–12. Lack of adequate publicity kept the attendance relatively low at 450, but for many that was perfect. In *TAD*, Edward D. Hoch reflected, "Perhaps that was about the right size for a Bouchercon after all. A decade from now, when they do attract thousands of delegates, I have a feeling we'll look back on these smaller gatherings with fond recollection." Hoch proved prescient.

Gail M. Larson of The Butler Did It bookstore in Columbia, Maryland, was chairwoman, and unlike San Francisco, which had twenty-two people on its committee, she had one person, Bill Deeck, who did a superb job of programming. Larson didn't seem to feel any pressure. In the program book she described herself as "the short blonde who can probably be found with a cigarette in one hand and a drink in the other asking, 'Are we having fun now?'"

Donald E. Westlake was Guest of Honor, and Chris Steinbrunner was Fan Guest of Honor. A film and television producer, and occasional professional writer, Chris said he preferred to think of himself as a "mystery activist," rather than a fan. He did not appear to enjoy himself, perhaps because he was already suffering from the depression and ill health that plagued him until his death in 1993. He certainly deserved recognition for many reasons, including bringing the films that were so important to early Bouchercons.

Another notable attendee was Richard S. Prather, the creator of private eye Shell Scott. Prather had not published in about ten years while he fought a lawsuit against his publisher. Successfully concluding it, he had just published a new hardcover mystery. He was doubly pleased in Baltimore because PWA gave him The Eye, their lifetime achievement award, and he was remembered by many fans who brought his books, especially the Gold Medal paperback originals, to be autographed. PWA, in conjunction with St. Martin's Press, imaginatively scheduled their annual Shamus luncheon to take place on a harbor cruise.

Though there was only one track of programming Friday night and Sunday morning, there were three tracks on Saturday. All panel titles were cleverly taken by Deeck from books or stories by Westlake. Thus, the opening panel, during which Patricia Moyes, Francis M. Nevins, Robert E. Briney, and I discussed Boucher's career, was called "The Busy Body." When Douglas Greene discussed John Dickson Carr, Deeck called it "Lock Your Room," after a Westlake short story. Publishers donated free books, but they were placed in the rooms of attendees, causing concern by some about who had entered their rooms.

This Bouchercon had a mystery award, the Anthony, named

after Boucher. About 200 people voted for the first Anthonys, which were presented at the Sunday luncheon. Some fans don't approve of the Anthonys, considering them popularity contests, unlike the Edgars, in which a committee is charged with reading all the books or stories in a category before voting.

There was a coda to the Baltimore Bouchercon that left a bad taste in the mouths of those who read about it and those who chaired prior and future Bouchercons. There were precedents and a bylaw requirement that profits of one Bouchercon be turned over to future Bouchercons. *MDM* published an open letter to Larson from Barrett, Taylor, and Donna Rankin of the 1985 Bouchercon committee and Steve Stilwell and Becky Reineke who were co-chairing in 1987. They said they were troubled that, despite Baltimore having been profitable, "we are at a loss to explain how you managed to pass on to Bouchercon XVIII less money than was passed on to you from Bouchercon XVI." Having sought an accounting of funds for almost a year they wrote, "Your failure to respond to what we felt is a reasonable request for an accounting has forced us to make this a public matter." Stilwell and Taylor told me they never received a response.

1987: Minneapolis

To some, the 18th Bouchercon, held in Minneapolis's Ritz Hotel, October 9–11 will always be remembered as "the Convention with the Magician." The convention was well run by Steve Stilwell, in charge of programming, and Becky Reineke, handling hotel and registration arrangements. Well, there was another problem, and that had to do with the Guest of Honor.

Lawrence Block had the writing credentials; he was author of the popular Matt Scudder and Bernie Rhodenbarr series. Still, the Guest of Honor should interact with fans. Stilwell had reservations about him for in *MDM*, announcing Block's selection, he wrote, "I think he is a good choice. Bright, witty, articulate, well known, and he should be accessible and easy to work with. We shall see."

Before anyone could evaluate Block's "performance" in Minneapolis, the choice of a male Guest of Honor brought the committee grief. There was a letter from Carol Brener of New York's Murder Ink in which she jokingly (I assume) threatened to bash Stilwell's head in with a copy of Hubin's heavy bibliography. Brener said that if it weren't for the insult to Block, "I would urge fans to boycott Bouchercons until women are given at least token equal representation."

Block seemed uncooperative during his Bouchercon interview, giving one-word answers to many of Sandra Scoppettone's questions. The following year, when Block published a very "New Age" novel, *Random Walk*, many wondered whether his behavior at Bouchercon wasn't due to a new philosophy. He wasn't much more outgoing at the banquet, claiming he didn't know he was supposed to give a speech and thus gave one that was very brief. It should be noted that at conventions during the 1990s Block was far more outgoing.

Many attendees wished the Fan Guest of Honor could have been there because John Nieminski, who died the previous December, was honored posthumously. No one enjoyed Bouchercons more than Nieminski, and his friends never felt the convention was under way until they saw him. Because many considered him the best writer in mystery fandom, a chapbook of his writings, *John Nieminski: Somewhere a Roscoe*, was distributed to all registrants.

Friday night opened with panels regarding Minnesota and Midwestern mystery writers. On Saturday when there were two tracks, plus movies, there were panels on the British and Canadian crime scenes, one on hard-boiled female writers, and four Sherlockian panels in honor of the one-hundredth anniversary of *A Study in Scarlet*. The first auction to benefit a charity was held, raising $1,500 for the Minnesota Literacy Council. Otto Penzler and Bruce Taylor were auctioneers, and an "item" auctioned off by authors, due to become standard at Bouchercon auctions, was the opportunity to have one used as a character in a mystery.

As toastmasters, Mary Craig and Max Allan Collins did everything to keep the Saturday banquet moving. The amateur magician brought things to a grinding halt. Not only was he boring, but he was inept and could not even do simple card tricks. Yet he was unwilling to leave the stage. Richard Moore said that the year he served in Vietnam was shorter and more fun than the magician's act. Many people walked out. Stilwell has had to put up with many years of kidding because of his role in scheduling the magician. Stilwell later wrote, "Two years of my life went into planning this convention and what will people remember about it? The magician [sic] at the banquet."

Another occasion marked during this Bouchercon was the twentieth anniversary of *TAD*. A Sunday morning panel, moderated by its founder, Al Hubin, had panelists who were early contributors. On sale at the convention was *TAD Schrift: Twenty Years of Mystery Fandom* in *The Armchair Detective*, edited by Randy Cox.

It was clear, despite Baltimore's drop in attendance, that Bouchercons were going to get bigger; six hundred-fifty attended Minneapolis. Bouchercon was becoming more international as well as more commercial. There were nineteen booksellers, two from England. Longtime Bouchercon attendees, while enjoying themselves, felt its flavor was changing. John Apostolou summed up the feeling of many when he wrote in *MDM*, "Bouchercon was more fun when it was a smaller event."

Some fans felt that Bouchercon was becoming designed more for writers and editors than fans. Stilwell said that most "fans" coming to the convention want to hear writers, not other "fans." It was clear from attendance at presentations by "name" authors and increasingly long autographing lines that many attended because of these authors. On the other hand, panels regarding the past or fannish activities, such as the *TAD* panel, drew fewer people.

A Sunday panel, "The Writer as Critic," moderated by William L. De Andrea, gave Gary Warren Niebuhr the impression that "some authors claimed they are the best reviewers because their understanding of the craft would make them more sensitive to their fellow authors." He wondered whether, as reviewers, they have the interest of book buyers at heart. Ann Williams said that unless the issue of writers reviewing other writers is raised, "nobody will ever believe a review or jacket blurb by another writer."

Some might think Bouchercon was becoming too writers' business oriented, but it was still an event to which fans looked forward. Ellen Nehr summed it up in *MDM* when she wrote, "I go to these affairs for conviviality. I've made friends at these conventions that I wouldn't trade for blood relatives, have met authors whose works have entertained me for years and could say to their faces, 'Thank you for the hours of pleasure you have given me.'" After Minneapolis, Williams expressed the view of first-time attendees. "I'm still reeling from my first Bouchercon, and I expect that it will take me at least a week to get back to 'normal,' assuming that I ever do."

1988: San Diego

"Murder Sunny Side Up" was the title of Bouchercon 19 (October 7–9) at San Diego's U.S. Grant Hotel, and the weather cooperated. Initially, the committee, chaired by Phyllis Brown of Grounds for Murder Mystery Bookstore and Ray Hardy, announced membership would be limited to eight hundred, but they relented and eventually almost nine hundred attended, a Bouchercon record.

Charlotte MacLeod was Guest of Honor, and Robert Barnard of England Toastmaster. Considering the mysteries they write, it was only logical that each moderated a panel called "The Mystery as Social Satire and Comedy of Manners." Bruce Taylor was Fan Guest of Honor.

There were three, at times four, tracks, but they were not enough to accommodate the number of professional writers (more than two hundred) who attended and wanted exposure. The presence of so many professionals again led to a perception by some that author dominance at Bouchercons was increasing. They pointed to the failure to acknowledge fans at the opening ceremony or to introduce Boucher's widow, Phyllis White, either then or at the banquet dinner. Along with name badges, attendees were given ribbons to attach based on their status as Author, Bookseller, Reviewer, Editor, or Panelist. Otto Penzler had so many ribbons that, according to Richard Moore, he "looked like a commodore in the Prussian Navy." There were no ribbons for fans, leading Moore to wonder, "Why create this class distinction at an event historically free of them?"

Two Maryland fans, Bill Deeck and Kerry Littler, better known for her alter ego, "Sherlock Hound"

The most controversial panel had the longest title: "Fans, Readers, Aficionados: What Is the Difference? Is There a Difference? Who is Making 'Fan' a Dirty Word and Why?" Panelist Michael Seidman said that those who write and review for fan magazines do not affect the sale of mysteries. Unanswered was my question from the audience as to whether fans had not done much good for professionals by founding Bouchercon and reviewing thousands of books since 1967, most favorably.

Seidman and moderator Robert Randisi told tales of fans bothering writers, including a story of one fan who allegedly trailed an author into the rest room to get an autograph. There was also no response to Art Scott's point from the audience that it was schizophrenic for writers to come to conventions to court fans while at the same time wanting to be left alone.

There were four private eye panels, including one asking, "The Traditional Private Eye: Is He Dead or Alive and Well?" There was also a panel, led by Sara Paretsky, called "The Mystery Writer as the Conscience of Society."

One of the memorable people at the San Diego Bouchercon (and other conventions) was Kerry Littler, a tiny woman from Annapolis, Maryland, who dressed in a deerstalker and carried "Sherlock Hound," a stuffed dog, also in a deerstalker. For the most part she only talked to people through the dog. She had the disconcerting habit of barging into private parties. In San Diego, though not a subscriber to *MDM,* she crashed the Saturday party that its editor, Bob Napier, gave. In the early 1990s people noticed she had stopped appearing at Bouchercon. Don Sandstrom, whose daughter lives in Annapolis, did detective work to track her and found she had died of cancer in 1991. That news made some of us feel guilty that we had not tried to be kinder to her since she obviously had trouble with interpersonal relations.

There were late parties on Saturday night, but early Sunday morning people at the U.S. Grant were awakened at dawn by helicopters flying over the roof. Vice President George Bush was in San Diego to campaign for President, and helicopters were providing security. He moved into the hotel, and Mary Higgins Clark had to give up her suite to him.

The 1990 Bouchercon bid got much attention because London was bidding against Omaha which, as a Midwestern city, was next in rotation. London won, leaving some Americans annoyed that there would not be a U.S. Bouchercon. There was a feeling that the Midwest was being denied its year since a California bid for 1991 had already been approved. Sandstrom wondered, "Why did the Midwest have to lose its turn at bat?" However, many supported an international Bouchercon; it was now regularly calling itself the World Mystery Convention. Bruce Taylor and Steve Stilwell, who had put on U.S. conventions, were among the strongest supporters of London, promising to help. Stilwell asked in *MDM,* "Why shouldn't British fandom have a shot at enjoying what we've enjoyed all these years?"

1989: Philadelphia

The twentieth Bouchercon reached a milestone when over a thousand people attended, October 6–8, at Philadelphia's Society Hill Sheraton. Deen and Jay Kogan, a Philadelphia couple, also active in local theatre, chaired the convention. "Give Me Liberty or Give Me...Death" was the convention slogan, and it was used on T-shirts and sweatshirts for sale. There were also bumper stickers, one of which my wife bought and placed on her car because it said, "Take Pity on Me; My Spouse Collects Books." In1990 the Kogans applied for and obtained a trademark for Bouchercon.

Simon Brett, the British mystery writer, was Guest of Honor. Not only did he give an amusing speech, much of which was in the form of a poem, but he wrote a witty article for the program, as if by his series character, Charles Paris, explaining why he couldn't attend. Beginning a trend toward multiple honorees, Philadelphia also honored Dorothy Salisbury Davis with a Lifetime Achievement Award, editor Joan Kahn for "Distinguished Contributions to the Field," and William Link, co-creator of *Mannix, Columbo,* and *Murder, She Wrote,* with a performance award.

There were two Fan Guests of Honor: Linda Toole, of Rochester, New York, an ardent fan of Rex Stout, and witty William F. Deeck of College Park, Maryland. When toastmaster Bruce Taylor introduced Deeck at the banquet, he joked about the latter's affinity for the unintentionally funny books of James Corbett. Deeck's reply, "But he doesn't mind selling me the books," drew many laughs.

In the past, Bouchercon started on Friday evening, allowing people to travel on that day. With authors so anxious to be on panels, a full third day was deemed necessary. Philadelphia started at 9:30 a.m. Friday. There were four tracks, with videotapes also shown. In response to requests, Friday's programming included three fan-oriented panels: a retrospective on twenty years of fandom that I moderated; one on fan magazines, led by Deeck; and collecting from the fan perspective, moderated by Toole. People spent much time (and money) in the booksellers' room. Many attendees wanted to purchase the books of authors at Bouchercon and have them autographed. Carl Melton, attending his first Bouchercon, set a two hundred-dollar limit for book purchases but found the book room so tempting that he spent that amount in his first hour, leaving him unhappy on future trips when he saw more books he wanted.

At a panel called "After Equality What?" Sandra Scoppettone "outed" herself, revealing she had written three mysteries under the pseudonym "Jack Early" because she found it easier to get published using a man's name. She also revealed she would be using her own name hereafter and was writing a private eye novel with a lesbian protagonist.

Another notable panel was booked as an interview of writer Michael Avallone by Mike Nevins. Those who attended wondered what to expect because of Avallone's vituperative letters in *MDM*. It was a mellow, charming "Avo" in Philadelphia, but he hardly allowed Nevins to get a word in. Bruce Taylor described Nevins's efforts to conduct the interview as "like trying to hold fifty pounds of water in a thirty-pound sack." It was amusing to see Nevins almost speechless as Avallone talked enthusiastically, but without stop, about movies and his books.

The Kogans scheduled innovative activities. Charlotte MacLeod was hostess for "Tea and Bloody Marys," at the Edgar Allan Poe House, where Poe lived when he wrote what is generally recognized as the first detective story. Two short stories by members of Sisters in Crime, a new organization formed to promote female writers, were dramatized at the Kogans' Society Hill Playhouse. "Boucher's Corner" was a room where times were scheduled for fans to meet and talk to the writers.

The banquet, for the first time, had assigned seating. Some were upset at not being able to sit with friends. However, others liked the practice because the randomness allowed them to meet people they might not have met otherwise. For example, we sat next to a new novelist, Anita Zelman, and her husband, and became friends.

The controversy regarding the selection of London resumed in 1989 with rumors that there would be attempts in Philadelphia to overturn the vote. In *MDM* (see a later chapter regarding this magazine), Max Allan Collins called the selection of London "elitist." He said, "I sincerely hope London can be voted down or that an alternate con (perhaps sponsored by PWA) will offer the continental United States an option.

Fortunately, the advice of Taylor, Stilwell, et al, was heeded, and there was no attempt to derail the London Bouchercon. For those choosing not to go to London, there would be 1990 convention choices not conflicting with Bouchercon.

No report on Philadelphia is complete without mention of its large lobby. For the first time, fans, especially those who wrote to each other in *MDM*, gathered in one place and talked for hours. A relatively young fan, Gary Warren Niebuhr, reported that he "sat at the feet of" Charles Shibuk, Bill Deeck, and myself. He generously said, "So much information was flying through the air I felt like someone should be making an oral history of the conversation." One of the most active fans during late-hour lobby discussions was Orietta Hardy-Sayles, who could have been speaking for many in Philadelphia when she wrote, "I had a terrific time at Bouchercon. I didn't get any sleep."

Observant Linda Toole reported that a month after Bouchercon, on November 19, an episode of *Murder, She Wrote* was set at a San Francisco "Boucheron [sic]." Television not only misspelled the convention's name but also gave it a French pronunciation, whereas Anthony Boucher pronounced his pseudonym to rhyme with "voucher."

Chapter Twelve

MYSTERY READERS INTERNATIONAL AND *MYSTERY READERS JOURNAL* (1981–)

In 1981 Janet Rudolph of Berkeley, California, started Mystery Readers International, an organization of fans, authors, booksellers, and others "dedicated to enriching the lives of mystery readers." It has grown into the largest mystery fan organization, with fifteen hundred members, located in all fifty U.S. states and at least fifteen foreign countries. Rudolph has edited and published her organization's journal since the Autumn of 1985. It has had several minor title changes and in 1989 assumed its present title, *Mystery Readers Journal (MRJ)*.

MRI Director
Janet A. Rudolph

Each issue since February 1986 has focused on a specific theme. Some topics: art, religion, medicine, gardening, sports, and legal mysteries, for example, are so popular they have been the subject on several occasions. Often, the response is so great Rudolph has to devote two issues to a theme. Because her readers are split between those wanting to receive *MRJ* in a hard copy and those happy with it online, Janet has continued to give them both.

Whatever the topic, Rudolph finds people willing to write reviews and articles about it. They include fiction writers who are not averse to a bit of self-promotion by writing articles when their books match that issue's theme. For example, for an issue on religious mysteries, Rochelle Krich wrote "Coming Out of the Orthodox Jewish Closet." Regarding music, John Harvey wrote on jazz, and Reginald Hill wrote, "Me, Music and Mahler."

Rudolph has gathered a group of columnists able to deliver material on almost any subject to meet her deadlines. Kate Derie, *MRJ*'s Associate Editor, is responsible for the magazine's pleasing design; she also writes "Crime Seen," reviews of movie and television mysteries. Gay Toltl Kinman writes "The Children's Hour," about children's and young adult mysteries. Jim Doherty, a police officer, writes about crime and police procedure in "Just the Facts." Though she uses different titles, Cathy Pickens, a lawyer, business professor, and mystery novelist, also writes about real crime. Since 1989 I have written a column, "In Short," covering short stories using the theme of a given issue.

In "From the Editor's Desk," Janet, besides providing important mystery information, gives her readers insight into their editor's life, discussing her hobbies and other work. She grows roses (she once had 125 bushes), has pet animals, and loves chocolate. Forever busy, she has a blog *Mystery Fanfare* with many features as well as current news and a listing of more than a hundred mystery discussion groups. In her other blog, *Dying for Chocolate,* she indulges herself (and her readers) in articles such as "How to Make the Best Brownies." Wearing her Murder on the Menu hat, she writes material for presentations at meetings of various groups. She and her husband Frank also prepare presentations for businesses interested in team building.

In 1985 Janet Rudolph started the Macavity Awards, which readers of *MRJ* vote on and then are presented at Bouchercon. Rudolph received the Ellery Queen Award from Mystery Writers of America in 2016 as one of the "outstanding people in the mystery publishing industry."

Chapter Thirteen

MYSTERY & DETECTION MONTHLY (1984–2003)

The passion seemed gone from the letters column of *The Armchair Detective.* Correspondents waited two or three issues to see their letters published, and there was little controversy. Fortunately, "Cap'n Bob" Napier, a former Army enlisted man who was given his "rank" as a nickname while on a gold-prospecting trip, filled the gap. He launched *Mystery & Detection Monthly (MDM)* in June 1984, with sixty-one subscribers, as a magazine for letters by fans. Napier said, "*MDM* was specifically designed so people who would never consider preparing an article for a fanzine could still find a forum for their ideas and opinions." He later punned in calling it "the magazine of great letterature." In the second issue, I called *MDM* "Bouchercon Through the Mails."

Jeff Smith wrote the valuable "New Releases" column, describing recent books, for most of the first fifty issues. Then, Bob Samoian wrote the column until No. 110 in the month of his death, February 1995. Napier took over in No. 112 and continued until Kelly Wolterman stepped in for issues 167 through 200.

MDM grew steadily. At first, Napier offered a free issue to anyone who contributed a letter of 100 words or more. By issue #13 he was receiving thirty letters, most more than 100 words, and it became an economic necessity that, with issue 15, he stopped giving free copies in return for letters. However, he did permit subscribers to run free ads. Though *MDM* occasionally had columnists, they did not last long. Ed Gorman had a column, "The Criminal Element," for only three issues, beginning with No. 14 (September 1985). Frank Denton's column, "D.O.A." began in No. 18 (January-February 1986) and ran until No. 41 (April 1988). *MDM* remained, except for "New Releases," primarily for letters and Napier's editorials ("My Word").

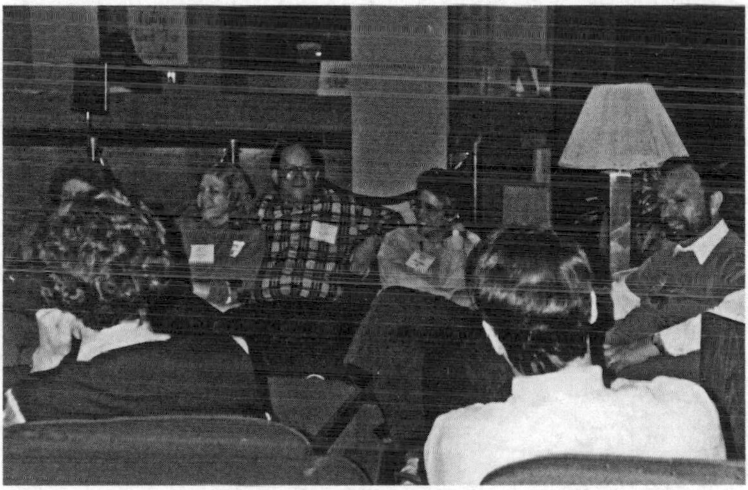

Photo by Len Moffatt

The infamous MDM takeover of the Omaha Holiday Inn lobby at the Midwest Mystery & Suspense Convention in 1990. Facing the camera (left to right): Ann Smith, Jeff Smith, Jo Ann Vicarel, Marv Lachman. With backs to camera (left to right): June Moffatt and Mike Nevins.

From the beginning, the letters (there were eleven in the first issue) were lively, controversial, and fun to read and answer. A feature from the start was a humorous heading above each letter. (June Moffat said he should be called "Caption Bob.") *MDM* attracted fans, but it also received letters from professional mystery writers.

MDM contained accounts of mystery conventions, opinions

on books, reports on correspondents' writing careers and personal lives, and stories of book hunting. Some opinions were well informed. For example, LAPD detective Paul Bishop wrote about the errors and lack of authenticity in Elizabeth Linington's police procedurals. Other opinions were outrageous, apparently meant to provoke debate. In issue No. 4 Robert Randisi said he "detested" English mystery writers. There were helpful letters, as when Art Scott wrote on how to catalogue one's collection, using a computer database. Even obscure questions, such as the identity of the dedicatee of an Aaron Marc Stein mystery, were usually answered.

An area of controversy involved fans of hardboiled mysteries versus those who preferred emphasis on detection. Joe R. Lansdale was popular with many *MDM* readers, but Samoian said of one of Lansdale's stories, "This kind of vulgar writing belongs, if anywhere, in an adult bookstore, or a garbage can, but not in my library." Lansdale's editor, Wayne Dundee, defended him and then attacked Barry Pike and Meredith Phillips, who had agreed with Samoian, calling them "cozy readers" with a contempt for hardboiled and "blue collar" writers.

Herb Resnicow was also involved in the *MDM* debate sometimes characterized in simplistic terms as cozy versus hardboiled. Resnicow, who wrote well-plotted detective puzzles, criticized what he termed "GEMSAV (Gratuitous Explicit Mindless Sex and Violence)."

Another debate concerned the balance in crime fiction between plot and character. I thought plot the most important part of a mystery, but Michael Seidman advocated emphasizing character development, saying, "Plots are for graves."

MDM regulars thought of themselves as part of a family, especially after the gathering in the Holiday Inn lobby at the first Omaha Midwest convention in 1990. The next year, Cap'n Bob was honored at that convention for his work on *MDM*, and his readers provided him with a special copy of *MDM*, numbered

72½. Inspired by Orietta Hardy-Sayles, it was a written "roast" of Napier.

On the night before the 1991 Pasadena Bouchercon, people who wrote letters for *MDM* were invited to Samoian's home and provided with food, drink, and a tour of his library of 23,000 mysteries. Also memorable was a hilarious informal dinner of *MDM* contributors at a Japanese restaurant at the 1992 Toronto convention. At the 1994 Seattle Bouchercon, Cap'n Bob arranged an *MDM* dinner on Bainbridge Island, following a scenic ferry ride.

Subscribers felt free to share life experiences, happy and sad. Josh Pachter wrote of his heartache during a custody fight over his infant daughter. Ann Williams told of her husband's terminal illness, but a few years later she shared the good news that her first novel was to be published. Arnold Marmor's widow sent a letter announcing his death, and telling how much reading *MDM* and writing for it meant to him. Paul Bishop described what it was like to be on duty on the streets of Los Angeles during the riots following the verdict in the trial of the policemen accused of beating Rodney King. When Bill Crider was wondering whether to retire, he shared his uncertainty with *MDM* readers. In one issue David McKean wrote why he was closing his bookstore, while Sue Feder reported she was buying one. Correspondents wrote of their illnesses so often George Kelley suggested that *MDM* stood for "Medical Diagnosis Monthly." Samoian said that *MDM* kept him going during his final illness.

As in all families, there were disagreements and misunderstandings in the *MDM* "family," making for lively reading. In 1985, Napier announced his editorial decision to ban mention of writer L.A. Morse from his pages. Morse had gone to Canada to avoid the draft during the Vietnam War. Napier opposed mentioning "the ones who deserted their country in a time of crisis, and who left other of their countrymen to take their place." Guy M. Townsend called Napier's position "reactionary" and canceled his subscription to *MDM*. The issue was debated in *TMF*, but not

MDM because of Napier's ban on mentioning Morse. By 1989 Napier was willing to let Morse's name appear. *MDM* had won an award from *Mystery Scene* as best fan magazine, and he felt, having "achieved a level of prominence," he must cater more to the views of his readers than his own feelings.

Some of Michael Avallone's letters were almost four pages long. He claimed he was cheated out of royalties by publishers and then blacklisted because he complained. Avallone sent long letters with complaints to individual fans, but *MDM* gave him a wider audience. Napier preferred not censoring letters, but possibly libelous material from Avallone, as well as the length of his diatribes, sorely tested his patience, and he occasionally was forced to use the editorial blue pencil until Avallone left on his own. Before he left, Avallone criticized Anthony Boucher and, in what seemed to be envy, currently successful writers Mary Higgins Clark, Lawrence Block, Sue Grafton, and Bill Pronzini. What was valuable in Avallone's letters were his personal reminiscences of mystery writers of the 1940s and 1950s, especially Cornell Woolrich.

Robert Randisi failed to appreciate Herb Resnicow's heavy-handed humor when he urged Randisi to return to MWA, "We need you. To hell with personal problems; a divorce you can always get. Or you can make an appointment to be home one night a month; if that doesn't satisfy Anna, she isn't fit to be the wife of a mystery writer." Randisi took offense and, denying that personal problems caused him to quit MWA, said, "I will never again write a letter to *MDM*, or any other fanzine."

Randy Russell wrote a letter that implied that he and Joan Hess had a personal relationship at an Omaha convention. Hess indignantly denied it and said she resented what "I perceived of as a snide attack on my reputation." Russell subsequently apologized in *MDM* for his attempt at humor. Later, Russell had "words" with Hal Blythe and Charlie Sweet, who write fiction as Hal Charles, but he soon disappeared from *MDM*'s pages and from the mystery scene.

When, in 1998, I questioned Mickey Spillane's influence on the mystery, Max Allan Collins responded by referring to my assertions as "absurd." Knowing that Collins feels strongly about Spillane, I chose not to take what he had written personally, responding that I wasn't referring to his impact on publishing but to the quality of his work, calling Spillane "a writer for the 16-year-old in the American male reader." There was little comment about our controversial remarks, an ominous sign for *MDM* and fandom.

Some correspondents who were professional writers and editors reacted to what they considered negative reviews of their work by fans. They thought writers should only be reviewed by their peers. Most strident in this regard was William Campbell Gault, who was cantankerous in print, though well liked personally. In No. 18 he wrote, "For those vitriolic fans with cast iron opinions, who rave on endlessly in your columns, may I suggest they spend their energies fruitfully by writing mysteries (or whatever) instead of opinions." Later, he wrote, "I don't need the support of amateurs to keep me going. Or fanzines." Gault was quick to criticize, but equally quick to apologize, as after he suggested that Paul Bishop needed a remedial reading course. He had a second feud with Paul Bishop when the latter criticized one of his stories. When a Canadian, Charles MacDonald, criticized his novels, Gault called him "that puke from British Columbia." His increasingly thin skin led Gault to stop writing for *MDM*, but urged by its readers, he returned. When he no longer could get published (his later novels were weak), he still wrote to *MDM*, saying "I have to write; that is the nature of this critter." He wrote of his felt need to "educate your opinionated readers." Sometimes he had two letters in an issue of *MDM*, also using one of his pseudonyms, Roney Scott or Dial Forest.

Randisi and Collins objected to criticism of Gault in the pages of *MDM*. Randisi belittled fan reviewers, saying "when it comes to commenting on writing—good or bad—they should leave that to the professional reviewers and critics." He distinguished between readers and fans, calling the latter "that breed of 'reader' who, when they don't like a book, write to a fanzine or go to a convention for the purpose of telling that writer how bad his book was, and what he should have done." Far less stridently, Carolyn G. Hart suggested why authors should review each other. "The point is not to protect poor writing, but to afford an author a thoughtful judgment by a peer."

Fans gave as good as they got, recommending that no writer be considered above criticism. Ann Williams objected to Randisi's premise that fans can't tell good writing from bad. Michael Reilly said, "Appreciation of good writing, and recognition of bad, comes from close and intelligent reading rather than from joining the 'professional reviewers' union." I paraphrased Clemenceau regarding generals in war when I said that mystery reviewing was too important to be left to the mystery writers alone. They could judge how difficult it is to *write* a mystery, but fans are best able to judge the final product. Randy Himmel pointed out that most reviews in fan journals were favorable and provided good publicity.

Bill Deeck used sarcasm, writing, "Still it's nice that Randisi accepts most of the fans despite their being unpleasant, opinionated, and wrongheaded." Jo Ann Vicarel feared "The danger here is that fan is becoming a dirty word and something that no right-thinking lover of mystery fiction wants tacked onto her name." Several fans writing to *MDM* reported a noticeable anti-fan bias at San Diego's 1988 Bouchercon.

Some *MDM* subscribers were bothered by the controversies. Maryell Cleary, a minister, announced that she would not resubscribe, partly because of the "feuds." She was told she would be missed and changed her mind. Through *MDM* she met Ellen Nehr, whose tastes in mysteries she shared, and Nehr loaned books to her.

Eventually 232 people contributed letters to *MDM*, but there was a small group of fans that wrote often. Bill Crider never missed an issue. Carolyn G. Hart described the plight of new readers to *MDM*: "It's like dropping into a cocktail party late and overhearing snatches about people you know." Using the same metaphor, Margaret Maron likened *MDM* to "a nicely raucous cocktail party where one may barge in on conversations." *MDM*'s regulars were welcoming, and newcomers quickly felt at home.

In September 1993, Napier raised the possibility that he might have to discontinue publication after that issue, No. 96. Many letters in No. 97 expressed dismay at the news, and Napier decided he could continue. He considered ending *MDM* in the year 2000 because, with job and family commitments, it was too time-consuming. However, Kelly Wolterman's agreeing to handle "New Releases" shifted enough of the burden to allow *MDM* to continue. In February 2001 Napier announced an irrevocable decision to cease publication, though not until after issue 200. By 2001 only about a dozen people wrote letters for each issue; in the late 1980s several issues had thirty-three letters. There were only ten letters in No. 190, but fourteen pages listing "New Releases."

Twenty-five people contributed to the final issue in October 2003, heaping praise on Napier. Art Scott pointed out that he was "the sole loony in mystery fandom" who had been putting out a publication (*DAPA-EM*) longer than Napier's almost twenty years. Beth Fedyn wrote, "Bob and *MDM* have introduced me to a lot of wonderful people. I treasure the friends I've made through these pages." Blythe and Sweet asked, "Where could you find a more knowledgeable, friendly group than we've encountered here over the years?" Bob Adey wondered where he would now get "this class of scuttlebutt" about the mystery. I wrote that, as part of my research for the book you are now reading, I reread *MDM* from the first issue and "many letters are just as interesting now as they were the first time."

In October 2003, at the Las Vegas Bouchercon, the final *MDM* gathering took place, a breakfast organized by Fedyn honoring Napier. He downplayed his own role, graciously repeating, in essence, what he had written in the last issue: "I've gotten back tenfold what I've put into *MDM*."

Chapter Fourteen

CADS: *CRIME AND DETECTIVE STORIES* (1985–)

In July 1985, five years after Ethel Lindsay discontinued the first general British fan magazine, Geoff Bradley, an Essex school teacher (now retired), launched CADS (*Crime and Detective Stories*). In his first editorial, Bradley described himself as a longtime reader of fanzines such as *The Armchair Detective* and *The Mystery Trader*, but he promised not to use "that horrible word fanzine" again. He decided not to offer subscriptions or follow a strict schedule, removing the pressure of deadlines. However, occasionally even he has seen fit to apologize for long delays.

In addition to encouraging articles on any subject related to crime fiction (he offered complimentary copies to those writing them), Bradley was especially anxious to receive letters, which he called "the life-blood of any magazine," and his readers responded, often disagreeing with each other, as well as supplying corrections and additional information. Because CADS was lively, readers, including Al Hubin, quickly compared it to the early issues of *The Armchair Detective.* American reader Myrtis Broset said in issue

No. 7 (December 1987) that "I get information I cannot find in any other publication here." Others noted "CADS' personal touch," something *TAD* had lost. By his third issue, Bradley had more articles than could be included in one issue, and that has generally continued.

Some writers appear in virtually every issue. Phillip L. Scowcroft of Yorkshire, since the second issue, has found mysteries about such unlikely subjects as Parliament, walking sticks, trams, and snow to discuss interestingly. His series on British regional mysteries cries for publication as a book. Peter Tyas had an article or letter in every issue of CADS, including No. 28 (May 1996), which, sadly, announced his death. Bill Deeck was one of CADS' best and most varied contributors. He wrote, with tongue in cheek, "The Genius of James Corbett" and "Further Gems from the Literature." Deeck also wrote "Mysteries with Magicians: A Mildly Annotated Checklist." He was a frequent reviewer and assumed the task, in the CADS column "Checking the References," of correcting the many mistakes in *Sleuths, Sidekicks and Stooges* (1997) by Joseph Green and Jim Finch.

British fans Bob Adey, impossible crime specialist, and Geoff Bradley, founder of CADS

Deeck compiled an index of CADS' first thirty issues. He had also indexed through issue No. 43 when he died. Christine R. Simpson picked up where Deeck left off, adding an index for issues 44 through 50 so that their joint index for Nos. 31 through 50 could be published. Then, in 2016, alone, Simpson did an index for issues 51 through 70.

Bob Adey was a frequent writer about his specialties: impossible crimes and locked room mysteries, and he also wrote reviews of obscure short story collections. He was one of CADS' literary detectives, reporting bibliographic discoveries, something done rarely, if at all, in other fan journals. Adey reported on his discovery of what was probably the second book *about* mystery fiction: *Masterpieces of Detective Fiction,* by C.A. Soorma. It was published in 1919 in Rangoon, Burma, by the American Baptist Press. Paul Moy was another of CADS' sleuths, discovering in No. 7 a lost John Dickson Carr novel, written under the pseudonym "Nicholas Wood."

Chief literary sleuth for CADS, writing under the title "Serendip's Detections," is Tony Medawar, who has discovered a new Roger Sheringham story by Anthony Berkeley, a Nigel Strangeways radio play by Nicholas Blake, a new Agatha Christie short story as well as information regarding a Christie play that was destroyed, a Carr short story, a John Rhode radio play, and another pseudonym for Major Cecil Street, who wrote as Rhode and Miles Burton. In No. 37 (May 2000), another CADS' detective, Thea Clayton, wrote engagingly of her research into the life (and death) of Herbert Adams, the leading author of golf mysteries. She traveled to interview Adams's nephew (age 88) just a few days before *his* death.

Other scholars who have contributed to CADS include Barry Pike, Ian Godden, and Malcolm Turnbull, as well as the two leading scholars about John Dickson Carr: Douglas Greene and James Keirans. Many leading British fiction writers, such as H.R.F. Keating, Martin Edwards, Peter Lovesey, and David Williams, have also written articles or letters.

When *The Mystery FANcier* ceased publication in 1992, several features from it moved to CADS. William A.S. Sarjeant continued his series "Crime Novelists As Writers of Children's Fiction," with articles on Patricia Moyes, Gladys Mitchell, J.S. Fletcher, and Frances and Richard Lockridge, among others. In March 1993 my obituary column, "Death of a Mystery Writer," began to appear in CADS, where it is still published. It includes critics, reviewers, actors, directors, and others with a relationship to the mystery. I have help from many fans, especially CADS readers, people I have dubbed "Lachman's Obituarians," coining the latter word because it flows more easily than the correct word "Obituarists."

My column inadvertently started a political controversy in

CADS. In writing of the deaths of people who worked in movies or television, I mention, if factual and important to their careers, whether they had been "blacklisted" in the McCarthy era. Rinehart Potts, with whom I had clashed in *The Poisoned Pen*, took exception to the use of "blacklist" and pointed out that many of these people denied employment had been members of the Communist Party. He compared them to spies who had worked for the Soviet Union, but in response to requests by Bradley and myself, failed to "name names" of any in the arts who had been Soviet agents. Potts decided not to read CADS anymore; he had been getting it from Bradley in exchange for his *Linington Lineup*.

Since the ninth issue, Bob Cornwell has contributed good artwork on the front cover of every issue of CADS. He also conducts "The Questionnaire," an interview column. One of the questions he asks all writers he interviews is: "Are you in favour of the death penalty for murder?" All he interviewed are against it, with the exception of Dick Francis who suspected Cornwell's motives when he replied, "Is this the real question to be answered camouflaged amongst all the others? The answer is 'Yes,' but not as a mandatory sentence for all murder as it was prior to 1965. Particularly brutal crimes demand brutal punishment."

In 2006, to celebrate the fiftieth issue of CADS, Cornwell had 84 readers and contributors pick the mysteries that are their "Private Passions" and "Guilty Pleasures." Devoting much time to this project, Cornwell compiled and edited the responses he received, and they were published as a Supplement to CADS.

A non-political controversy was sparked by John Hogan's letter in No. 19 (October 1992) in which he objected to obscene language in Robert B. Parker's Spenser series. Most who wrote letters disagreed with Hogan, who then replied in rather intemperate fashion, questioning their moral values. Hogan died in September 1993; the announcement of his death appeared along with a reasonable response from Barry Gardner who said that many accepted Parker's language in their reading without routinely using such language themselves.

Though CADS devotes more space to Golden Age writers than other journals, it also discusses recent mysteries. Cornwell wrote in No. 26 (September 1995) that he wanted "more realism, blood, sex and violence" in the mystery. Before printing John Boyles's "The Drift to Realism," an article about James Crumley in No. 36 (November 1999), Bradley wrote in advance that the language might offend some readers.

CADS is important in establishing ties between mystery fans on both sides of the Atlantic, with Americans significant contributors to it. Americans visiting England have met with Bradley, Adey, Pike, and other English fans. CADS has also helped to publicize British mystery conventions.

In the fourteen years since the first edition of this book, CADS has continued to publish much that is of interest. One example was Josef Hoffmann's articles in issues Nos. 44 and 48 about the eminent philosopher Ludwig Wittgenstein and his interest in mysteries.

Many fans can remember when and where they bought some mysteries, especially if they were impressed by them. In Mike Ripley's "Bargain Hunt" column in CADS he discusses acquiring mysteries that are "crime novels found in unusual circumstances," not in a conventional book store.

Tony Medawar has continued to play the role of bibliographic detective, recently unearthing talks by Dorothy L. Sayers and Anthony Berkeley, and forgotten articles by Freeman Wills Crofts and Agatha Christie.

There may be disagreement as to the exact years of the Golden Age, but it is clear that the readers (and writers) of CADS are its fans. Martin Edwards is most knowledgeable about it as he proved in *The Golden Age of Murder* (2015), a book that won almost all of the major mystery awards, and his speech "Trending: Why Is the Golden Age Fashionable Again?" given at St. Hilda's Crime and Mystery Weekend and reprinted in CADS No. 74 (January 2017). Curtis Evans, a relatively new voice in CADS, who first appeared in No. 60, writes of Golden Age writers with knowledge and enthusiasm in his books and articles.

CADS circulation was about 250 in 2017. I have no data to prove it, but I suspect that theaverage age of CADS readers is greater than that of other fan journals. Too often, Geoff Bradley has the sad duty of starting his "CADS Comments" by reporting the deaths of CADS' subscribers and contributors.

Chapter Fifteen

MYSTERY SCENE (1985–)

Though containing material of interest to fans, *Mystery Scene* was started by professional writers Ed Gorman and Robert J. Randisi and once devoted much space to the business of publishing. In the first issue (four pages), dated 1985 and mailed with *MDM,* Randisi stated its goal was "to entertain and inform mystery writers and readers as fully and completely as possible with publishing news, stories and, when necessary, rumors, as well as book reviews, articles, and interviews." Publishing news made up most of the first issue, which included an article by Ray Puechner, "Finding an Agent."

Mystery Scene, looking to increase its subscriber base, in the second issue (twenty-four pages) added "The Horror Scene" and reported on the World Fantasy Convention. Still, there were profiles of mystery writers and Ellen Nehr's column "Murder Ad Lib," containing news and reviews, mostly of "cozy" books, providing contrast in a magazine that seemed to tilt in favor of hardboiled material. Michael Seidman and William Campbell Gault began columns in the second issue.

By the third issue in 1986, *Mystery Scene* had almost 200

subscribers and was fifty-two pages. A new columnist was Warren B. Murphy, writing "Curmudgeon's Corner," giving them two curmudgeons because Gault fit that description too. The magazine continued expanding its definition of the mystery scene with Kevin Randle's article on "The World of Action Adventure." More mystery-related was Josh Pachter's short story column "The Short Sheet." In Issue #16, Bill Pronzini showed that he was a fan as well as a writer with his article on forgotten short story writer Bryce Walton.

I was not alone in perceiving an early bias against fans in *Mystery Scene*, though it never extended to refusing our subscription payments. I criticized the inclusion of horror and fantasy in a magazine titled *Mystery Scene*. Michael Seidman responded, taking umbrage, especially at my calling him "Mike," which I had heard people do at Bouchercons. He also objected to my characterizing as "whining and doomsday forecasting" the remarks he made at Bouchercons about the state of the mystery, when he admonished fans to support writers by buying their books. In the January 1987 issue, he launched his strongest attacks on fans, saying the majority were negative and that "Ultimately, those who label themselves fans do not have the power to create. They are vampires, sucking the very essence of life from those and that which they adulate."

Not willing to let Seidman have the last word, I wrote a letter for the eighth issue about his artificial distinction between "aficionados," whom he regarded favorably, and "fans," whom he denigrated. I said he was ignoring the time and money fans had put into writing for fan magazines and putting on Bouchercons, activities that benefit writers. I also mentioned a gratuitous dig by Gault at fan magazines in *Mystery Scene*.

It was difficult to keep up with the changes in format of *Mystery Scene*. What started as a four-page first issue had grown to a ninety-eight-page publication, with a slick cover, by the fourth issue. Then, the fifth issue morphed into a tabloid newspaper without issue number, date, or table of contents, but the sixth issue was a magazine again, now with a comic book section, as well as an original short story. In January 1987 it was a tabloid again, and had added eight pages about Westerns. Then, in March 1987 the eighth issue was called *Mystery Scene Newsletter,* and it was in the form of a magazine. Randisi described it as containing "forty-eight pages of information about the mystery and horror publishing scene, essays, columns, interviews and reviews." He promised eight issues a year. The fiction was omitted, to be included in a new quarterly magazine to be called *Mystery Scene Reader*. Fiction occasionally returned, as with a 20,000-word story by Dean Koontz in 1999, followed by two issues in which *Mystery Scene,* in its promotional mode, included first chapters of many novels.

The newsletter concept did not last long, nor did the *Mystery Scene* Reader. By the 13th issue, it was back to simply *Mystery Scene,* and it still did not give the month of the issue. The fans versus writers "feud" was apparently over, but *Mystery Scene* was, in the words of Jon L. Breen, "a lightning rod for controversy." Warren Murphy in his column criticized Harlan Ellison, drawing a heated response followed by an apology from Murphy for what he admitted was a "gratuitous cheapshot." Other early feuds included Seidman versus MWA and Joe Lansdale versus Jo Ann Vicarel on the subject of Elizabeth George. Barbara Mertz, Linda Grant, and Laurie R. King wrote of their perceptions of male sexism.

Jon L. Breen, frequent contributor to *Mystery Scene* and *EQMM* reviewer

In No.15, *Mystery Scene* was soliciting votes from their readers for "The American Mystery Awards." One category was for "Best Fan Publication," and *Mystery Scene* got the most votes for 1987. They decided not to accept the award, but it was apparently due to modesty, not because it wasn't a fan magazine; at the 1986 Bouchercon Randisi claimed that *Mystery Scene* is not a fan magazine. Editing was casual, and they admitted they could improve their proofreading; they reported the death of Elizabeth "Lennington" [sic].

Anthologist Martin H. Greenberg replaced Randisi as publisher, with Ed Gorman soon sharing editorial duties with his son Joe. Ed referred in issue No. 31 (October 1991) to "the new, improved *Mystery Scene*," which would be published seven times yearly. (In his 2002 article on the history of the magazine, Breen found there had been an average of 4.4 issues per year.) Gorman said he was incorporating suggestions from Scott Winnette, who had experience with the science-fiction magazine *Locus*, and who felt "*Mystery Scene* wasn't so much a magazine as a grab bag of pieces that happened to interest Ed Gorman." The amount of non-mystery material was reduced. Still, contributors came and went from the pages of *Mystery Scene*. As Breen said, "*Mystery Scene* would pick up and lay down reviewers and columnists in numbers too dizzying to keep track of." My short story column was a casualty in 1993.

Whatever the problems of *Mystery Scene*, perhaps in tribute to Gorman's flexibility, it continued being published for seventeen years under his aegis. With health problems in 2002, Gorman decided to cut back on his work and sold the magazine to Kate Stine, former editor of *The Armchair Detective*, and her husband, computer-expert Brian Skupin. Their first issue (No. 76) was dedicated to Gorman and included tributes by many writers, most of whom had never met him. Something of a recluse, Gorman seldom left his home in Cedar Rapids, Iowa. However, Dean Koontz had been there, and he wrote humorously about his visit. Gorman was popular with other writers, many of whom he had helped.

The cover of No. 76 proclaimed "See Our New Look!" and it was an attractive, well-illustrated ninety-four pages. *Mystery Scene*'s columnists remain important to it. Breen has continued writing "What About Murder," and Dick Lochte reviews audiobooks in the column "Sounds of Suspense." More recent are the reviews by Betty Webb of small presses and Ben Boulden's reviews of short stories in the column "Short and Sweet." Until 2015 Roberta Rogow reviewed children's mysteries in "Child's Play." Hank Wagner reviews paperback originals. An unusual column that has not appeared recently was "What's Happening With..." by Skupin. He would select a writer who had once been highly thought of but hadn't had a mystery published recently. He would find out why they weren't being published and what their current plans were.

Gorman remained till his death with a column called "Gormania," which was part of a large section, "The Writing Life." It showed *Mystery Scene* was still more focused on publishing than other fan journals, as did articles by James Grippando and Adam Meyer on their writing lives.

Louis Phillips is still writing a column like one he started in Volume 21 No. 1 (Winter 1988) of *The Armchair Detective.* Once called "Dial N for Nonsense," but now "Mystery Miscellany," it combines humor with odd bits of information about crime, both fiction and nonfiction. *Mystery Scene* occasionally included material about a neglected area of the mystery, the crime play.

Articles in *Mystery Scene* are a combination of the new (important current novelists and screen adaptations, often of noir films) and important writers of an earlier era. Mike Nevins wrote of Harry Stephen Keeler, whom he called "Nut King of the Universe." Elizabeth Foxwell had an article on Metta Fuller Victor, who, as "Seeley Regester," wrote *The Dead Letter* (1866), generally considered the first American detective novel. In 2017 Michael Mallory wrote of Raffles, who was created in 1899. In 2018 Mallory wrote of *The Whistler,* the popular radio mystery of the 1940s and 1950s.

The magazine is especially well-illustrated with pictures in color of authors, dust jackets, and material from movies and television shows. *Mystery Scene* has the largest readership of any magazine about the mystery, with a circulation of approximately 23,000 copies in late 2017. In addition, about three hundred libraries subscribe to it.

Chapter Sixteen

MALICE DOMESTIC (1989–)

By the mid-1980s, the success of Bouchercon led fans to consider starting conventions closer to their homes. The idea of smaller, more intimate conventions was also attractive. Convinced that MWA and Bouchercon were dominated by male writers and hardboiled books, some wanted a convention devoted to what they called the "traditional" mystery, which was defined as those "without explicit sex or excessive gore or violence." Mary Morman was the one who brought the idea to life. However, she gave credit to Barbara Mertz (better known under the pseudonyms "Elizabeth Peters" and "Barbara Michaels") as the focal point around whom Malice Domestic was built. Morman published a newsletter called *The Friends of Barbara Mertz* and held a small (twenty-person) meeting called "Mertzcon" in 1986. It was there that the idea for Malice Domestic took root, with planning beginning in the fall of 1987. Morman said Malice would never have succeeded without Mertz's hard work, especially in attracting famous writers.

The first Malice Domestic, chaired by Morman, was advertised as taking place in Washington, DC, though it was held

April 21–23, 1989, at the Sheraton Northwest in Silver Springs, Maryland, close to downtown Washington. It had been decided that Malice would remain in the Washington area, rather than moving each year as Bouchercon does. Phyllis Whitney was announced as Guest of Honor, but she could not appear due to illness, and Mertz took her place.

Ellen Nehr was the Fan Guest of Honor. Tough-talking, she was, nonetheless, a great fan of cozier fiction, especially novels involving detectives she called "little old ladies" and "little old men." From the first, Malice Domestic initiated the practice of honoring a dead writer from the past; Agatha Christie was "Ghost of Honor." Later, references to deceased writers and fans were changed to "Malice Remembers," possibly more respectful than calling someone a "Ghost."

About three hundred fifty people attended; Morman said seventeen were males. Most people enjoyed themselves, though there were complaints. Regarding hotel food and service, Bill Deeck said, "The dining room was actually a waiting room, and when the food did arrive you wished you were still waiting." The rest of the hotel was just as bad with, according to Morman, rooms without hot water, a meeting space that needed cleaning, and maids who left notes in the rooms asking guests to leave the rooms "as clean as possible." Some who attended in 1989 formed an unofficial Silver Springs Survivors' Club.

At the banquet, Toastmaster Robert Barnard praised Christie, joking that anyone who disliked her could not be his friend. Perhaps reacting to those who dubbed Malice Domestic "Biddycon," Barnard poked fun at PWA and its lengthy award ceremony the year before in San Diego, wondering why critics refer to "the laconic American private eye."

Beginning in 1989, Malice Domestic awarded the Agatha Award for the best traditional work in various categories. Nominees were selected by those who had registered and then voted on by those attending. Carolyn G. Hart won the first

Agatha; it was in the form of a teapot with a skull and crossbones on it, for Best Novel. Editor Ruth Cavin announced that in 1990 St. Martin's Press would award a ten-thousand-dollar advance against royalties for the Best First Traditional Mystery Novel in a contest jointly sponsored with Malice Domestic.

Malice Domestic moved to the Hyatt Regency in Bethesda, Maryland, for 1990, and it proved to be a popular location, with its large atrium-lobby and glass elevators. About 400 people attended. Malice was made more affordable, with Ellen Nehr functioning as "Roommate Coordinator," so those who wished could share the cost of a room. Patricia Moyes was Guest of Honor. Malice "Remembered" Dorothy L. Sayers. Phyllis Whitney, at age eighty-six, was now well enough to attend and received a Lifetime Achievement Award. Sharyn McCrumb was Toastmistress. Mary Morman was again Chair. Phyllis Brown, owner of the Grounds for Murder bookstore in San Diego, was Fan Guest of Honor.

In 1991 Charlotte MacLeod was Guest of Honor. "Malice Remembered" Mary Roberts Rinehart. Gerry Letteney was Chair that year and again in 1992. Janet Rudolph, founder of Mystery Readers International, was Fan Guest of Honor.

Sue Feder, originator of the Ellis Peters Appreciation Society, appeared in a monk's cowl similar to that worn by Peters's Brother Cadfael. A most unusual panel was "Warning: Endings Revealed!" in which Margaret Maron, Barbara D'Amato, and Bill Deeck deliberately disclosed the endings of mysteries in order to discuss the craft of writers in resolving plots.

So recognizable had "Malice Domestic" become that in 1992 the first of a series of original short story anthologies using that title was published. No editor was shown; it was "presented by" Elizabeth Peters. In her introduction, Peters called Malice Domestic an "Idea Whose Time Had Come" and attempted to define "traditional" mysteries. She felt the kinds of murders in books she called "cozy" involved the personal and private aspects of crime, as opposed to the public and impersonal found in books about serial killers, terrorists, assassins, and hit men.

Many understood what the term "Malice Domestic" meant as far as mysteries, even if they didn't know its origin in Shakespeare's *Macbeth*. The words have been used as the titles of at least six mystery novels and a prize-winning short story in *Ellery Queen's Mystery Magazine* by Philip MacDonald, one that was televised on *Alfred Hitchcock Presents* in 1957.

More men were attending Malice. In 1992 Aaron Elkins was Guest of Honor, and Deeck was Fan Guest of Honor, delivering a hilarious speech about his favorite "bad" writer, James Corbett, who penned such lines as, "He was galvanized into immobility." In *The Armchair Detective*, editor Kathy Daniel said, "Why don't we just name Bill 'King of the Fans' once and for all?" Mary Higgins Clark was Toastmistress. Margery Allingham was "Remembered." There was an imaginative panel in which Ellen Nehr and her good friend Joan Hess pretended to argue, with Joan "murdering" her. They acted so well that some in the audience grew uncomfortable, not realizing it was scripted.

Reporting in *TAD*, Janet Rudolph mentioned "the special touches at Malice which make it stand out head and shoulders above the rest—including giving panelists Godiva chocolates and flowers for their rooms and serving champagne at the opening night reception." In 1992 Malice incorporated, establishing bylaws and a board of directors. It even has its own archivist.

By mid-January 1993, three months before its opening date, Malice was sold out. 535 people attended. It coincided with the Gay Rights March in Washington, and Marlys Millhiser said wearing her Sisters in Crime sweatshirt on the plane didn't stand out among sweatshirts proclaiming "Dyke." Other passengers thought Millhiser was just making a statement. She was seated next to a young actor who said he wished there were more mysteries with gay or lesbian characters.

Anne Perry was Guest of Honor. Mary Morman was Fan Guest

of Honor. The unusual selection for Malice "Remembrance" was Shakespeare, whose plays are, after all, replete with murders. Nancy Pickard was Toastmistress. Ron McMillen was Chair, as he would be in 1994 and 1995. A highlight was a luncheon hosted by Phyllis Whitney, who was almost ninety. In summation, Millhiser described Malice as "a gathering where readers have their say in person, and authors, critics, booksellers, and even editors must listen."

In October 1993 Malice Domestic, founded the Malice Domestic Grants for Unpublished Writers "to...encourage the next generation of Malice authors." The first grant was awarded to Jeffrey Marks in 1994. Since then, the grants have gone to forty writers, including Sujata Massey, Marcia Talley, Gigi Pandian, and G.M. Malliet. In 2004, in honor of his advocacy of aspiring mystery writers, the grant program was named for Bill Deeck.

Attendance at the sixth Malice Domestic closed shortly after January 1, 1994 with over 500 registrants, including 140 first-time attendees. In a letter to *MDM*, Deeck, one of the organizers, had defined its purpose as "to celebrate what was felt to be a neglected aspect of the mystery...Malice Domestic is a fan—some would prefer to say, a readers' convention, not an authors' convention. Certainly flogging books is not frowned on, but our primary purpose is not to increase book sales." Malice Domestic had now fixed its dates as the weekend after the Thursday night MWA Edgar ceremony in New York, allowing those attending that to also come to Malice for the weekend.

Many attendees wore large hats, a throwback to fashions during the Golden Age between the World Wars. British writer Sarah J. Mason recalled that someone gave her a hat in the elevator, and she was so surprised that she had gotten off at her floor before she could identify the donor, whom she called "Anonyma." Steve Stilwell, a frequenter of the bars at Bouchercons, attended in 1994 and was amazed to find "no one in the bar at a mystery convention." That appears to have changed later, and some echo the line, "All roads at Malice lead to the bar."

Dorothy Salisbury Davis was Guest of Honor. Edgar Allen Poe, often credited with inventing the detective story, was "Remembered." A Lifetime Achievement Award went to Mignon G. Eberhart. Dorothy Cannell was Toastmistress. Jim Huang, publisher of *The Drood Review*, was Fan Guest of Honor.

There was great disappointment that ill health prevented Guest of Honor Edith Pargeter, who wrote as Ellis Peters, from attending in 1995, though there was a taped audio interview with her. In the centennial of her birth, Ngaio Marsh was "Remembered," and B.J. Rahn, America's leading fan and scholar of Marsh's work, portrayed her during an interview by Simon Brett. Rahn also scripted a Friday night event in which Toastmaster Edward Marston played the part of Roderick Alleyn, Marsh's sleuth. Dean James, manager of Murder by the Book, a Houston bookstore, was Fan Guest of Honor. He also won, with Jean Swanson, an Agatha for Best Non-Fiction for *By a Woman's Hand: A Guide to Mystery Fiction by Women*. James gave a touching speech on how important mysteries had been in his life. The Agatha Awards were announced by Sue Feder, wearing her Brother Cadfael monk's habit.

There was occasional disagreement about the definition of the type of book celebrated at Malice, and at one 1995 panel Stephen White and Frances Fyfield said that though their books were darker than many "cozies," they qualified. Panels also introduced fans to Sisters in Crime's official email server and to DorothyL, a popular internet chat service for fans.

Proving again that males were welcome, Jeff Abbott (he also won an Agatha for Best First Novel) was presented with the "Cozy-Boy Fan Club Award," with female attendees interrupting his panel to give him the award and then display T-shirts with the name of their club, whose purpose apparently was to honor male pulchritude.

The popularity of Malice was growing, and more than seven

hundred people attended in 1996. Peter Lovesey was Guest of Honor. Margaret Maron was Toastmistress, and Josephine Tey was "Remembered." Mary Stewart received a Lifetime Achievement Award. Beth Foxwell, editor of fan journals, was chair for this Malice and also the next. The program book contained a tribute to Malice's first Fan Guest of Honor, Ellen Nehr, who had died the previous December. 1996 Fan Guest of Honor was Shirley Beaird. Since then almost every Fan Guest of Honor at Malice has been one of its hardworking board members or volunteers.

Attendance was about 725 in 1997. At the opening ceremony Malice founder Mary Morman was "murdered," and one panel was devoted to solving the killing. Carolyn G. Hart was Guest of Honor. Mary Latsis and Martha Henissart, the women writing as "Emma Lathen," received Lifetime Achievement Awards. In accepting it, Henissart said about attending this, their first convention, "If we had known it was going to be this much fun, we might have come to one of these affairs sooner." She also mused that "It seems a small step from Lifetime Achievement Award Winner to Ghost of Honor."

Frances and Richard Lockridge were "Remembered." The Agatha Awards were presented by Carole Nelson Douglas and Parnell Hall, acting as the Lockridges series characters Pam and Jerry North. Joan Hess was Toastmistress. Jack and Judy Cater were Fan Guests of Honor. They had attended every Malice Domestic and continue to do so.

Don Sandstrom, longtime Malice Domestic participant

The tenth Malice Domestic in 1998 had poignant moments. Longtime attendee Don Sandstrom had died the previous October. Kate Ross's *The Devil in Music* won the Agatha as best novel, but she, too, had died. Her father accepted the award for her in a moving speech. Robert Barnard was Guest of Honor. Katherine Hall Page was Toastmistress. Ellery Queen was "Remembered." Charlotte MacLeod received a Lifetime Achievement Award. Carol Whitney chaired Malice that year and the next. Maureen Collins, president of the Chesapeake Chapter of Sisters in Crime, was Fan Guest of Honor.

With attendance now over 800, Malice had outgrown Bethesda and moved to the Renaissance Hotel in Washington. That site proved unpopular with many who felt it was in an unsafe, remote area.

In 1998, those who had attended all ten Malice Domestics were given a special gold numeral 10 on a chain. Malice had its first stalker when someone followed Leslie Slaasted, a fan and member of the convention staff, and called her room at 1:30 a.m. When the stalker did not follow hotel security's instructions to stay away, an implied threat to knock his teeth down his throat by Richard Moore, one of those with a perfect Malice attendance record, succeeded.

In 1999, Mary Higgins Clark was Guest of Honor. M.D. Lake (pseudonym of James Allen Simpson) was Toastmaster. John Dickson Carr was "Remembered." Patricia Moyes received a Lifetime Achievement Award. The Fan Guest of Honor, Carol Harper, Associate Editor of *Mystery Readers Journal,* came all the way from Saudi Arabia, where she was living, to be honored. Patricia Moyes received a Lifetime Achievement Award.

Simon Brett, a frequent Malice attendee, was Guest of Honor in 2000. Eileen Dreyer was Toastmistress. Sir Arthur Conan Doyle was "Remembered." Dick Francis received a Lifetime Achievement Award, which was accepted for him by his son. Cindy Silberblatt chaired Malice, as she would in 2001 and 2002. Sheila Martin, a longtime volunteer, was the Fan Guest of Honor.

Malice Domestic's move to the Crystal Gateway Marriott in Arlington, Virginia, in 2001 was a popular one. Margaret Maron was Guest of Honor and Rita Mae Brown Toastmistress. Rex

Stout was "Remembered." A Lifetime Achievement Award was given to Mildred Wirt Benson, who wrote many books in the Nancy Drew series, the first mysteries read by many people who attend Malice. Patti Ruoco, a librarian in Illinois, was Fan Guest of Honor.

In 2002 Edward Marston was Guest of Honor and Tony Hillerman received a Lifetime Achievement Award. Annette and Martin Meyers were joint Toastmasters. G.K. Chesterton was "Remembered." Gerry Letteney, former Malice Chair, was Fan Guest of Honor. He had received a similar award at the World Science Fiction Convention.

The 2003 Malice Domestic was treated as a special event, with a separate section in the program book, "Memories of Malice: 15 Years Celebrating the Traditional Mystery." It was largely the work of Tom O'Day, Chair of that Malice. Agatha Christie was "Remembered" for a second time. Malice gave out its first Hercule Poirot Award, designed for those who made significant contributions to the mystery through other than writing. David Suchet, who acted Poirot on television, was the recipient. Barbara Mertz was a popular choice for the Lifetime Achievement Award. Donna Beatley was Fan Guest of Honor. She had attended every Malice. During the Agatha presentations, Guest of Honor Barbara D'Amato and Toastmaster Parnell Hall engaged in a funny pie-throwing sketch.

Malice Domestic stayed in Arlington in 2004 but moved to the Sheraton National. Dorothy Cannell was Guest of Honor. Marian Babson was given a Lifetime Achievement Award, Jan Burke was Toastmistress. Erle Stanley Gardner was "Remembered." The second Poirot Award went to Ruth Cavin and Thomas Dunne of St. Martin's Press. Tom O'Day continued as Chair, as he would in 2005. Linda Pletzke was Fan Guest of Honor, but Carole Ann Nelson, recently deceased, was selected as a "Fan Malice Remembers."

Still in Arlington in 2005, Malice Domestic returned to the popular and convenient Crystal Gateway Marriott. It is less than a mile from Reagan Airport, and there is a stop there on Washington's Metro line. The Guest of Honor was Joan Hess.

H. R. F. Keating of England received a Lifetime Achievement Award for his forty-plus years of writing fiction and non-fiction about the mystery. Carole Nelson Douglas was Toastmistress. Ellis Peters was "Remembered." Angela Lansbury, whose television show *Murder, She Wrote* introduced so many viewers to the mystery, was give the Poirot Award. Anne Reece was the Fan Guest of Honor; she had attended every Malice Domestic.

One of the most popular fans at Malice Domestic had been Bill Deeck who died in August 2004 and was sorely missed. Bill's dry sense of humor was matchless. His brother-in-law Gene Wood spent time with Bill during his last days. At one point Bill said to him, "It may be time, but I cannot be certain as I do not have any direct experience with this sort of thing."

Malice Domestic 2006 returned to Arlington, with attendance of about 800. The Guest of Honor was Katherine Hall Page, whose series about caterer Beth Fairchild includes much regarding food. At the reception, desserts from recipes in her books were featured. Douglas Greene was the Poirot Award Honoree. Kate Grilley was Toastmistress. Robert Barnard received a Lifetime Achievement Award. Receiving it, he joked that he hoped that his next award would not be as "Ghost of Honor." Kay McCarty was Fan Guest of Honor.

The writer "Remembered" at this Malice was Craig Rice and on the first evening the Malice Theatre of the Air did a radio play based on Rice's most famous short story, "His Heart Could Break," dramatized by Hal Glatzer. Panels of uncommon interest during the weekend included "Tea and Strumpets," "Mr. Monk, Meet Mr. Poirot," "Chick Lit Mysteries," and "Cozy Taboos." More serious was a panel on confronting social issues in the mystery.

Verena Rose assumed the time-consuming position of Chair of Malice and keeps that to the present, missing only one year, 2009, when Louise Leftwich took over.

Malice Domestic 2007 was still in Arlington. Rochelle Majer Krich was Guest of Honor. Carolyn G. Hart received a Lifetime Achievement Award. Georgette Heyer was "Remembered." She had been a well-regarded author of detective novels before achieving impressive sales with her Regency romances. Kate Grilley was Toastmistress. Lee Mewshaw, another fan who had never missed a Malice, was Fan Guest of Honor. She was also active in the Chesapeake Branch of Sisters in Crime.

Georgina "Gigi" Pandian, who won a grant in 2007 for *Artifact*, credits the Deeck Malice Domestic Grant program and "the whole traditional mystery community" for convincing her she could be a writer and having her first book published.

One of the 2007 highlights was the presentation of Lucy Zahray, aka "The Poison Lady," discussing popular poisons that can be used in mysteries.

Malice Domestic 2008 in Arlington had Charlaine Harris, who writes mysteries and an even more popular vampire series, as Guest of Honor. Lindsey Davis of England was International Guest of Honor. Peter Lovesey, also of England, received a Lifetime Achievement Award. Toastmaster was Daniel Stashower. The Poirot Award went to Janet Hutchings and Linda Landrigan, respectively the editors of *Ellery Queen's Mystery Magazine* and *Alfred Hitchcock Mystery Magazine*. Malice Remembered "All Previously Honored."

Fan Guests of Honor were Elizabeth Foxwell and Ron and Jean McMillan. Foxwell is Managing Editor of *Clues: A Journal of Detection*. Ron McMillen had been Chair of Malice from 1993 to 1995.

Malice Domestic 2009 had Nancy Pickard as Guest of Honor. Elaine Viets was Toastmistress. Anne Perry of England won a Lifetime Achievement Award. Charlotte MacLeod was "Remembered." Again, two people shared the Poirot Award, but they represent the same magazine: Kate Stine and Brian Skupin of *Mystery Scene*. Fan Guest of Honor was Laura Hyzy.

Does anyone outside of Malice attendees still wear a hat? In 2009 a contest for most creative hat at Malice was won by Liz Zelvin with one featuring a bobblehead of Poe, a bat, and a rose on top.

The Poison Lady was back in 2009 with her ever-popular talk on how to do people in. Another unusual panel posited that Jane Austen, if she were alive today, would be a mystery writer.

In 2010 Malice Domestic moved to Betheda, and though they had crossed state lines from Virginia to Maryland, it was still in the same general Washington, DC, area. Parnell Hall was a familiar figure at the banquets, but this year in addition to singing his humorous songs about books, he was the Guest of Honor. Rhys Bowen was Toastmistress. Malice "Remembered" Edward D. Hoch. Mary Higgins Clark received the Lifetime Achievement Award. William Link, television writer and producer of shows such as *Columbo* and *Murder, She Wrote,* received the Poirot. Tom and Marie O'Day were Fan Guests of Honor.

Barb Goffman, Program Chair, explained that naming a writer of private eye stories, such as Parnell Hall (though he also writes cozy crossword mysteries) was not unusual, as she described Malice as a big tent under which many subgenres could fit. All of the panels were moderated by fans.

There were twenty-one tables at the Malice-go-Round, an annual event at which writers go from table to table to describe their books to potential readers/buyers. Each author had only ninety seconds per "pitch." Twenty-six writers celebrated their first novels at the New Authors Breakfast. One of many popular panels was "Into the Wild," with authors telling of their experiences in the "Great Outdoors" as they researched mysteries with nature as background.

Malice Domestic 2011 had Carole Nelson Douglas as Guest of Honor. Sue Grafton received a Lifetime Achievement Award for her Kinsey Millhone private detective series, a further indication that Malice was flexible in what they considered a "traditional" mystery. Grafton was a gracious honoree, even when she was, according to author Sarah Parshall, accosted by a fan in the ladies' room. Frequently asked why she would not allow a movie to be made based on her Millhone series, Grafton cited her own negative experience in Hollywood as a screenwriter. She said she'd rather roll naked on glass.

Donna Andrews was the humorous Toastmistress. The Poirot "for contributions to the traditional mystery" went to Janet Rudolph who had been publishing *Mystery Readers Journal* and heading Mystery Readers International for thirty years. Louise Penny interviewed Rudolph and drew laughs when she asked her why she'd never been invited to one of Rudolph's famous mystery soirées in Berkeley. Malice "Remembered" Lynn Hamilton. Anne Murphy, Coordinator of Volunteers at Malice, was Fan Guest of Honor.

Mystery Scene again sponsored a New Authors Breakfast. Two popular panels were "Private Eyes and Thrillers, Oh My!" and "Funny Gals, Dark Books: An Intellectual Look at Humor in Mysteries."

Malice Domestic returned to Bethesda in 2012. Jan Burke was the Guest of Honor. The Lifetime Achievement Award went to Simon Brett. Toastmistress was Dana Cameron. Malice "Remembered" Tony Hillerman. His daughter Anne, who is continuing his Navajo detectives series, accepted for him. Lee Goldberg, who wrote the *Monk* television series about the obsessive-compulsive detective, received the Poirot Award. The Fan Guest of Honor was Ruth Sickafus, a longtime member of the Malice Board, a past secretary, treasurer, and archivist.

A new award, the Amelia, went to Barbara Mertz, who had been so important in the early days of Malice. This award was designed "to be given to individuals the Board determined had contributed to the Malice Domestic community and exemplify what Malice Domestic represented." The "Amelia" is named after Amelia Peabody, Mertz's anthropologist series detective under her Elizabeth Peters pseudonym.

Jan Burke spoke about a subject dear to her heart, the Crime Lab Project designed to raise public awareness of the challenges facing underfunded forensic science agencies. There are cases in which the innocence or guilt of those accused of crime depends on evidence issues being resolved.

Malice Domestic 2013, in Bethesda again, had Laurie R. King as American Guest of Honor. Peter Robinson of Canada was the International Guest of Honor. Carolyn G. Hart won the Amelia Award. Aaron Elkins won a Lifetime Achievement Award. Laura Lippman was Toastmistress. Malice "Remembered" Dick Francis, with his son there to tell anecdotes about him. Malice also "Remembered" fan-reviewer Sally Fellows who had died the previous September.

Fan Guest of Honor was Cindy Silberblatt who after twenty years in the U.S. Navy "enlisted" in Malice and at various times was Program Chair, Publicity Chair, Auction Chair, and Chair of the Board of Directors of Malice Domestic.

Popular panels at Malice 2013 included "You've Got Fan Mail," "Here Comes the Corpse: Wedding-Themed Mysteries," "Kids Love a Mystery," "Shot Through the Heart: The Role of Romance in Mysteries," and "First, Let's Kill All the Lawyers." Luci Zahray, "The Poison Lady," did another well-liked presentation on famous poisons and poisoners. She said that 90 percent of those who administer poison never get caught.

A book, *Not Everyone's Cup of Tea: An Interesting and Entertaining History of Malice Domestic's First 25 Years,* edited by Verena Rose and Rita Owen, was published in 2013. It included reminiscences, essays, speeches, and program notes of fans and writers who had attended.

Malice Domestic 2014, was again at the Grand Hyatt in Bethesda. Kathy Lynn Emerson, author of historical mysteries, was Guest of Honor. Earline Fowler was Toastmistress. Lifetime Achievement was split three ways, with Margaret Maron, Joan Hess, and Dorothy Cannell being recognized. Malice "Remembered" Reginald Hill, with Martin Edwards representing him. The Poirot Award went to Tom Schantz who reprinted and sold "traditional" mysteries and chaired several conventions.

The Fan Guest of Honor was Audrey Reiths, a Malice volunteer for over ten years. Her husband died shortly before the convention, but Audrey showed up. When people seemed surprised she was there, she said, "Malice is my family."

Malice-go-Round, the convention equivalent of speed dating, continued, but now authors were also giving out candy and bookmarks.

Malice Domestic 2015 had Charles Todd as American Guest of Honor. Todd is the name used by Charles and his mother Caroline for several series of mysteries. Ann Cleeves of England was International Guest of Honor. Sara Paretsky got the Lifetime Achievement Award, another example of Malice flexibility, though one could say that she writes "traditional" private eye mysteries.

Patricia Moyes was "Remembered." Toni L. P. Kelner was Toastmistress. No Poirot Award was given. William L. Starck was Fan Guest of Honor. He had been Co-Chair of the 2001 Bouchercon, held in Washington in the difficult days after 9/11.

Increasingly, those who attended Malice would send blogs about it on returning home. Often, they referred to being exhausted due to sleep deprivation. They had stayed up late and gotten up early so as not to miss early morning events like the Sisters in Crime breakfast. They invariably said it was worth it. In addition to fans pleased at meeting other fans, authors were gratified to meet the people reading their books.

At Malice in 2016 the Guest of Honor was Victoria Thompson, author of New York City historical mysteries. The Lifetime Achievement Award went to Katherine Hall Page. The Amelia Award went to Douglas Greene, whose Crippen & Landru Press reprints "traditional" mystery short stories. The Poirot Award went to Barbara Peters and Rob Rosenwald, whose Poisoned Pen Press publishes mysteries that Malice fans like. Toastmistress was Hank Phillippi Ryan. Malice "Remembered" (still referred to as the "Ghost of Honor" by many) Sarah Caudwell. Martin Edwards was there to accept for her.

Fan Guest of Honor Linda Smith Rutledge had much experience, including being Volunteer Chair, Hotel Liaison, Chair of the Agatha Committee, and a member of the Malice Board for five years.

"Malice-go-Round" continued, and "You've Got Mail" came back again, allowing the honorees to discuss the reactions of some of their fans. Becoming traditional at Malice (and other conventions) was "101," in this case "Malice 101," telling those attending for the first time what to expect and how to get maximum enjoyment of their experience.

Malice Domestic 2017 had Elaine Viets as Guest of Honor. The Lifetime Achievement Award went to Charlaine Harris. Martin Edwards, who had accepted awards for other writers, got his own when he was given the Poirot. Malice "Remembered" Bill Deeck, so important to the convention in many ways. Toastmistress was Marcia Talley.

Luci Zahray was Fan Guest of Honor. Known for her popular talks about poison, she is a pharmacist who holds a master's degree in Toxicology. She has often helped fiction writers who are using poison in their plots. She is also a Sherlockian, member of the South Downers' Scion.

Attending Malice was Dru Ann Love, who has been called "a legendary blogger." In 2015 she was nominated for an Anthony at Bouchercon as a blog editor. In 2017 MWA recognized her with the Raven, which she then named "Koko." After the MWA banquet she (and "Koko") came to Malice.

Malice Domestic 30 (April 27–29, 2018) was held at the Bethesda North Marriott Hotel and Conference Center. Louise Penny of Canada was Guest of Honor. Nancy Pickard received a Lifetime Achievement Award. David Suchet who has long acted Hercule Poirot on television was given the Amelia Award. The

Poirot Award went to Brenda Blethyn, who plays Vera Stanhope on the popular British television series based on the novels of Ann Cleeves. Toastmistress was Catriona McPherson, a Scotswoman now living in the United States. She had performed similar duties at Left Coast Crime. Malice Remembered Robin Hathaway, a novelist who frequently attended Malice. Fan Guest of Honor was Janet Blizard, Secretary of the Malice Board and a retired attorney who said that the only way she survived law school was by reading mysteries.

Tea may be the symbol of Malice Domestic; the Agatha Awards are in the shape of a teapot. However, several who attended write of their love of hanging out at the bar there, "...because that is where people tend to congregate and either catch up with old friends or make new ones." In her recap of 2018 Malice, Dru Ann Love describes Malice thusly: "You walk a few steps, see a friend, hug a friend, chat with a friend and then repeat these steps over and over."

About 190 authors attended Malice in 2018, and most of them wanted the exposure that being on a panel provides to their books. Some of these authors had their books published by "vanity" presses, with the financial help of the authors. Some were upset when the Malice Board decided, "In order to provide the best possible experience to the fans for whom the convention was created, panel assignments would be limited to authors whose books were published by traditional publishers or those who had been nominated for an established award." Malice Domestic published another anthology, this one titled *Malice Domestic 13: Mystery Most Geographical* and featuring thirty regional short stories.

Luci Zahray, the popular "Poison Lady," gave another presentation. P. J. Coldren, 2019's Fan Guest of Honor who often travels to Malice with Zahray says that Luci collects poisons, and they stop at garage sales where they occasionally find some. Another popular panel was "Murder at the Improv," at which the panelist were tasked with making up a mystery on the fly, using suggestions from the audience.

Author Sybil Johnson referred to differences some make about the categories of mysteries at other conventions. She said that at other conventions, "…I almost feel I have to apologize for writing the lighter side of mystery. Not so at Malice."

Sometimes derided by those who use "cozy" in the pejorative sense, Malice Domestic has proven for thirty years that it and the mysteries it celebrates provide superior escape for many. Though not averse to including writers, Malice Domestic remains, in the words of Katherine Hall Page, "a readers' con."

Chapter Seventeen

OTHER FAN MAGAZINES, ORGANIZATIONS, AND CONVENTIONS: 1980S

Clues: A Journal of Detection **(1980–)**

Though fans wrote for and subscribed to *Clues,* it was a scholarly publication, originally edited by Pat Browne and published by Bowling Green State University of Ohio. *Clues* began with the Spring/Summer 1980 issue and maintained a semiannual schedule until it halted publication in 2002. In his bibliography of secondary sources, Professor Walter Albert said, "*Clues* is criticized by fans for being too academic and by academics for not belonging to that unstable list of 'prestige' journals beloved of university tenure and review committees." Some of the articles may have been written under "publish or perish" strictures. However, the contents included articles not out of place in strictly fan journals, for example Martha Alderson's "Death at the Stage Door" about the theatre mysteries of Anne Morice and Simon Brett.

After a brief hiatus, *Clues* returned in 2004. It is now published by McFarland and Company, with Janice M. Allan of England as

Executive Editor and Elizabeth Foxwell of Virginia as Managing Editor. The members of the eleven-person Editorial Board all have academic affiliations.

Some issues were devoted to a single famous author, for example Margery Allingham, Dashiell Hammett, or Sara Paretsky. In 2017 the lineup was more varied. Volume 35 Number 1 included articles on Conan Doyle and Sherlock Holmes, Baroness Orczy, Gladys Mitchell, Geoffrey Household, Nancy Drew, and Joyce Carol Oates.

The Wilkie Collins Society; *The Wilkie Collins Journal* (1980–)

In 1980 this group—still active—was founded in London to promote interest in the life and work of this author of nineteenth-century novels, including mysteries such as *The Moonstone and The Woman in White*. It publishes *The Wilkie Collins Journal*, "an academic peer-reviewed resource," edited by Joanne Parsons of Bath Spa University.

***Cloak and Pistol* (1981)**

1981 saw the start of another magazine devoted to appreciation of the pulps, produced by Joseph Lewandowski of San Juan Capistrano, California. *Cloak and Pistol* was professionally produced and well-illustrated, with cover art by Frank Hamilton. The first and only issue included articles about The Shadow, Secret Agent X, and The Phantom.

***The Bony Bulletin* (1981–1990)**

Having left *The Thorndyke File* in the early 1980s, Philip Asdell started another fan journal, "published at irregular intervals for Bony and Upfield enthusiasts." Asdell's audience, of course, knew that he referred to Australian writer Arthur W. Upfield and his series detective, the part-aborigine Napoleon "Bony" Bonaparte. Asdell dedicated his twenty-fifth issue (July 1988) to Bony fan Betty Donaldson, who had encouraged him.

The last issue, No. 33, was in 1990. In 2005, Claudia Stone

scanned the complete run and created *The Complete Bony Bulletin* with the permission and encouragement of Asdell. It is for sale on the internet, and there is a copy in the National Library of Australia.

Maltese Falcon Societies (1981–) and *The Maltese Falcon Flier* (1982–)

The Maltese Falcon Society was organized by Don Herron and others in San Francisco. It had its first meeting on May 20, 1981. At its peak, it had between 100 and 150 members. Originally it met monthly, but after about a year, as the initial enthusiasm tapered off, its meeting schedule was irregular. Speakers included Charles Willeford, Bill Pronzini, as well as two of Dashiell Hammett biographers: William F. Nolan and Diane Johnson. Its last meeting, May 27, 1986, coincided with Hammett's ninety-second birthday. His daughter, Josephine Marshall, spoke.

Jiro Kimura, arguably Japan's leading fan, founded the Maltese Falcon Society of Japan in 1982, and it still is active, though he is no longer in charge. It issues *The Maltese Falcon Flier* ten times yearly.

The Crime File (1982–1991)

The Crime File was born in June 1982 as the monthly newsletter of The Mystery Club, a group sponsored by the Grounds for Murder Mystery Bookstore in San Diego. Annual dues of six dollars included the newsletter and attendance at twice-monthly meetings. Laurie Mansfield Gore, the club's secretary-treasurer, published it, at first for members only. By August 1987, *The Crime File* was described as "an independent newsletter." Most of the material was written by Gore at first, though in October 1987, Tom

Don Herron,
Dashiell Hammett fan

Nolan wrote of the old radio show *Yours Truly, Johnny Dollar*. Gore did interviews, wrote reviews, and reports of Bouchercons she attended.

I transferred my column "The Short Stop" in January/February 1989 (*The Crime File* had gone bimonthly) and continued until it ceased publication. With the undated first number of Vol. 10 (apparently in 1991), *The Crime File* had become a quarterly. Beginning in that issue, George Easter conducted the "Future Investigations" column, listing and reviewing new books. *The Crime File*'s publishing life was marked by frequent delays. At one point, Gore asked readers to excuse her "apparent disappearance." Most issues were sixteen pages, though some were shorter. Unspecified problems, the bane of existence of fan magazine publishers, beset Gore. An undated "Special Double Issue," copyright 1991, ended *The Crime File*'s run.

The Thieftaker Journals (c. 1981–1985)

Paul Bishop, the often-decorated Los Angeles police detective had more energy than any person should have. He was a marathon runner and a mystery fan. He published *The Thieftaker Journals* as his *DAPA-EM* magazine and then, after leaving that group, he published it independently in the early 1980s, using distinctive green paper. Bishop was a great fan of horse racing mysteries, and his May 1983 issue was dedicated to that subject, with articles by him and Jon L. Breen, who is equally knowledgeable in that small subgenre. Bishop went on to become reviewer for *Mike Shayne's Mystery Magazine* and later a successful writer of fiction, but he kept his hand in fandom, especially with an article on *HuffPost* regarding *DAPA-EM*.

Echoes (1982–2004)

The time, effort, and expense of publishing cause many fan magazines to come to a quick end. An exception was *Echoes*, the fanzine started by Tom and Ginger Johnson of Texas in June 1982; it lasted until December 2004. That it lasted was due to the efforts of the Johnsons, not because they grew wealthy. In an editorial they said, "The magazine must break even if it is to survive." At one time they drove 424 miles to get it printed at a price they could afford. Still, they lost five-hundred dollars their first year.

This was a nostalgia magazine, and though it was mostly about the pulps, there was also material for fans of old films, old-time-radio, and collectors of juvenile series. About half of each issue involved crime fiction, often about *Doc Savage, Operator #5,* and *The Spider.* There were also articles on such unusual crime-related pulp magazines as *Gun Molls* and *Underworld Romances.* I wrote an article on *Dime Detective* which, because it was regarded as the second best mystery pulp magazine after *Black Mask,* I called "The Avis of Detective Pulps." *Echoes* attracted the people who wrote for other pulp fan magazines, including Robert Sampson, Will Murray, Nick Carr (a cousin of John Dickson Carr), Link Hullar, and Rex Ward.

At its peak, *Echoes* had almost 300 readers, including two in France and one in Australia. Controversy, largely absent from its pages, surfaced with issue No. 96 (December 1997) after a few readers complained about sexy covers drawn by Ron Wilber. Many liked Wilber's work, and Tom Johnson defended publishing it. In No. 97 he expressed his dismay at the "infighting" and announced he would stop *Echoes* after No. 100, turning it into a smaller advertising/news magazine. Later he said that it was not only the "infighting" that caused him to cease publication; there were also health reasons. Despite this, Johnson continued *Echoes* as an eight-page monthly newsletter for pulp fans for over six more years.

Mystery News (1982–2009)

By the 1980s, as mysteries grew increasingly popular, the fan revolution led to new journals that did not emphasize articles and letters. Established magazines were providing the scholarship, as were new reference books. With more mysteries published, many readers said they most needed reviews. Once, Boucher's column was the "gold standard" for recommendations. By 1980 there was no single person who carried his critical stature, though Allen J. Hubin and Jon L. Breen were especially well regarded. 1982 saw the birth of two journals consisting mainly of reviews.

The purpose of *Mystery News*, as stated by editor-publisher Patricia Shnell (and her husband Jack) of Sparks, Nevada, in its first issue (January–February 1982) was to inform readers "about as many new mystery books, those recently published and those about to be published, as possible." Despite changes of ownership, *Mystery News* remained consistent in fulfilling this goal, though it also provided information about mystery conventions and awards as well as doing interviews.

In 1988 Harriet Stay, a U.S. Postmaster from Port Townsend, Washington, and her husband, Larry, took over *Mystery News* as editor and publisher respectively. Harriet conducted interviews and wrote reviews and editorials. An important feature was "Previews," which in some issues occupied almost half of the space with brief plot synopses of forthcoming books.

With the July-August 1997 issue Lynn Kaczmarek of Illinois and Chris Aldrich of New York, operating as Black Raven Press, took over *Mystery News*, which had not been published for a year. They changed little about it but increased the number of pages, sometimes to forty. Kaczmarek wrote editorials under the heading "Quoth the Raven," while Aldrich provided a Mystery Calendar and other important news in her "Mysterious Stuff" page.

They added new columns. I wrote about books and authors of yesteryear in a column called "Out of the Past." Starting in the March-April 1999 issue, Stephen Miller interviewed authors of first novels under the heading "In the Beginning…" Later, in a column called "The Sound of Mystery," Dave Magayna reviewed books on tape and DVD. Roger M. Sobin wrote of mystery films in his "Real to Reel."

Mystery News's stock in trade remained its reviews and previews, with such excellent reviewers over the years as Frank Denton, Virginia R. Knight, Sally Fellows, Barry Gardner, Don Sandstrom, Barbara Peters and Gary Warren Niebuhr. Interviews, usually conducted by Kaczmarek, were also important. In 2001, *Mystery News* won an Anthony as best fan journal; it was later nominated three times for the Anthony. As of 2009, it had more than a thousand readers.

After twelve years and over seventy issues, *Mystery News* ceased publication. As Chris and Lynn said, "We were both working day jobs that were more than full time for most of those years, traveling for work much of the time, and it just became too much."

Some fan journals ceased operations without notice and without reimbursing subscribers for issues not received. Unlike them, *Mystery News* remained a classy operation to the end, treating its subscribers fairly when it ceased publication with the November/December 2009 issue by arranging subscriptions for them to *Mystery Scene*.

The Drood Review of Mystery (1982–2005)

The other review journal that began in 1982 was *The Drood Review of Mystery*, founded by Jim Huang. From 1977 through 1980, when he lived in New Jersey, Huang had published *Cloak and Dagger*, which was primarily, according to him, "a mystery news 'zine.'" It had fewer than a hundred subscribers.

In 1982 Huang, then living in Boston, began to publish *Drood* as a "partnership owned and managed" by him and eight other individuals. For most issues there were at least six editors listed. It always consisted mostly of reviews and one of the most complete listings of forthcoming mysteries. Their leading reviewers included Jeanne M. Jacobson, Ted Fitzgerald, and Susan Oleksiw. Articles were relatively few, though in 1987 I wrote a four-part series on the "Nameless Detective" books of Bill Pronzini. I called it "the mystery fan's detective" because Pronzini and his protagonist are diehard collectors, and pulp magazines and paperback mysteries have sometimes been plot devices in Pronzini's stories.

Drood has been accused of political correctness. Huang once called himself "the last bastion of liberalism." Sexism and racism were mentioned in his editorials. For example, he said in April 1985 that he finds sexism in a disproportionate number of reviews by men.

***Drood Review* editor Jim Huang**

Social issues found their way into *Drood* reviews, for example in Ed Blachman's "Mysteries with a Conscience: Social Problems in Today's Crime Fiction" in October 1990. In that issue, Kevin R. James in "Voodoo Social Policy" cautioned crime writers to be aware of the potential social message of their work.

Drood eventually moved with Huang from Boston to Ann Arbor, Michigan, and then to Carmel, Indiana, where he sold books as The Mystery Company and published as Crum Creek Press. In 1990 *Drood* was honored as a fan magazine at the first Midwest Mystery & Suspense Convention. Its circulation was 1,440 at the end of 2004.

Since *Drood* ceased publication in 2005, Huang has remained important to the mystery field, editing books about the mystery that have won awards and co-chairing the 2009 Bouchercon.

The Elizabeth Linington Society and *Linington Lineup* (1984–2004)

In 1984 Rinehart S. Potts, of Glassboro State College in New Jersey, began this group and *Linington Lineup*, the quarterly newsletter devoted to study and discussion of Elizabeth Linington, the author of police procedurals who was equally famous under her Lesley Egan and Dell Shannon pseudonyms. Potts seemed to share the right-wing political views that Linington held, and this led him into disputes that I wrote about in connection with *The Poisoned Pen* and CADS. The society remained active long after Linington's death in 1988, thanks to the efforts of Potts. However, Vol. 21, No. 6 (November/December 2004) was his last issue, due to his advancing years and declining health. He said he would reimburse unfulfilled subscriptions.

I Love a Mystery (1984–2014)

Sally Powers was casting director for the successful television program *Hill Street Blues* and also a mystery fan. In February 1984, she started a fan magazine with the catchy title *I Love a Mystery*, once the name of a popular radio show. At first, she wrote mainly about the Southern California scene, but she began to go farther afield visiting, writing about, and photographing Bouchercons and MWA Edgar banquets.

Using the title of my *DAPA-EM* magazine, *Just in Crime*, I started a review column for *I Love a Mystery* in May 1985. My column included "Doom with a View," my reviews of television and film mysteries, and also the mystery obituaries that I still write for CADS. Powers stopped publishing *I Love a Mystery* as a magazine after May 1986, though she brought it back as a review newsletter for at least nine issues in the early 1990s. It later became an online-only newsletter and remained so until 2014.

Stephen Wright's Mystery Notebook and *Whitechapel Journal* (1984–2000)

The Mystery Notebook was one of the more personal journals. Its premiere in Winter 1984 coincided with W. Somerset Maugham's birth date in January, and the issue was devoted to Maugham and James M. Cain, two of Wright's favorite writers. Most of the next issue (ten of twelve pages) was devoted to Dashiell Hammett, another favorite of the eponymous editor-publisher. More than half of Vol. 2, No. 3's eight pages were devoted to Wright's article

"The Gay Detective Story." In Vol. 3, Wright began publishing his own novel, *The Adventures of Sandy West.* This novel about a private eye, which Wright eventually self-published as a book, was billed as featuring the first bisexual detective.

After a hiatus, Wright returned, now calling his magazine *Mystery Notebook,* saying he removed his name due to "modesty." He continued to run material about Maugham and also had an article about Oscar Wilde. Increasingly, non-mystery related material, often about gays, appeared and by his twenty-fourth issue the magazine was called *The Notebook.*

Another interest of Wright's was Jack the Ripper, and he devoted space to the Ripper's crimes. By the fall of 1996, *The Notebook* was gone, and Wright published the first issue of his new magazine, *Whitechapel Journal,* a newsletter devoted to Jack the Ripper and true crime. It was last published in mid-2000, and mail to Wright was returned as "undeliverable."

***Hardboiled* and *Detective Story Magazine* (1985–2014)**

Hardboiled was started in the summer of 1985 as a fiction magazine by Wayne Dundee of Belvidere, Illinois. However, there were occasional articles about mystery fiction, for example, on Jim Thompson and Robert J. Randisi in the first issue. Hardboiled fiction is also a great love of Gary Lovisi of Brooklyn. He started a magazine of hardboiled fiction in May 1988, using the name *Detective Story Magazine.* After the twelfth and final issue of Dundee's *Hardboiled* in 1990, it was combined with Lovisi's magazine as *Hardboiled Detective* for three issues. By March 1992, Lovisi was publishing it with the less restrictive title *Hardboiled.* For the first twenty issues of Lovisi's magazines, I wrote a column, "That's the Story," about short stories. I was given freedom to write anything I wanted, including my view that the generally accepted definition of "hardboiled" is far too narrow since, by my lights, Miss Marple with her cynical and realistic view of human nature, is hardboiled. Many issues have contained other nonfiction about the mystery, for example, Art Hackathorn's article on Frank Gruber in issue #9, introducing a Gruber story never previously published.

Hardboiled ceased publication in August 2014.

Paperback Parade (1986–)

Lovisi, as part of his publishing line called Gryphon Books, started *Paperback Parade* in 1986. It followed the pattern of *Paperback Quarterly*, and while there were issues devoted to science fiction, gay and lesbian art, Westerns, and juvenile delinquent paperbacks, much of its content was mystery-related. The first issue had "The Mystery and Detective Paperback" by Jon White. Later issues included "Cornell Woolrich in Paperback," "Collecting Jim Thompson," a "Richard Prather and Shell Scott Special Issue," a "Mickey Spillane Special Issue," and "The Earl Norman Spy Series." *Paperback Parade* is still being published and had issue No. 101 in the Spring of 2018.

The Criminal Record (1986–1996)

The Criminal Record was a one-woman operation of Ann M. Williams of Denver. She called her pocket-sized, bimonthly magazine "A Newsletter for and by fans of Mystery/Detective Fiction." It consisted mainly of reviews written by Bill Deeck, Mary Helen Becker, Sue Feder, Don Sandstrom, and Barry Gardner, among others. Williams wrote editorials, punny headings for the reviews, and Bouchercon reports. Though she occasionally had computer and printing problems, it was usually on time and a bargain at $1 (later $1.25) an issue.

There were times when Williams included personal material. During the third year of *The Criminal Record*, her husband Bob was stricken with cancer, and she continued the magazine but occasionally told of his struggle with the disease and chemotherapy. He died shortly before the 1989 Bouchercon, but Ann went to Philadelphia, keeping her commitment to be on a panel about fan magazines. Though ill, Williams finished ten complete years of publishing with issue No. 60 in November 1996, before dying that month of a severe liver ailment.

Agatha Christie Fandom (1986–2003)

In 1986 Amy Lubelski of New York edited and published *Woman of Mystery*, a short-lived magazine described as a "compendium of ideas devoted to Agatha Christie." *The Christie Chronicle*, which began in 1993, lasted longer. It was the journal of the Agatha Christie Society, whose chairman was Mathew Prichard, Christie's grandson; the president was Christie's daughter, Rosalind Hicks. Kate Stine edited the newsletter and acted as the society's U.S. director. It included an article, "Teaching Agatha Christie," by Gordon Clark Ramsey, who in 1967 wrote the first book about Christie's work. (There have been at least a dozen since then.) Other articles told of Christie celebrations, including the society's annual trip to see *The Mousetrap* in London, and the yearly gathering of the society in Torquay, Christie's hometown.

By 2003, the Society (and its magazine) had been disbanded and replaced by an English website, *AgathaChristie.com*, called "The Official Online Home of Agatha Christie." Agatha Christie, Ltd., which runs the website, is a business company. Their newsletter, issued irregularly, is a marketing tool, with links to products, books, adaptations, and events related to Christie.

One person who is helping to keep interest in Christie alive with fans is John Curran of Ireland, *the* expert on Christie's life and works. He was once editor of the *Christie Society Newsletter*. His *Agatha Christie's Secret Notebooks* (2009) and *Murder in the Making* (2011) are the definitive books about Christie's writing. Curran investigated over seventy notebooks that Christie used in plotting her detective stories. John O'Connell, in *The Guardian*, said that Curran was "too much of a fan to be an objective critic" of Christie's work. That opinion is debatable, and it may be just the reason why Curran's books are so popular with other fans and mystery awards committees.

Crime Fiction Catalogue (1987–1988)

The American interest in journals that were heavy on reviews was replicated in England. In the first issue of *Crime Fiction Catalogue*, dated January 1987, editor-publisher R. K. Taylor said that his magazine aimed to give a "comprehensive list of all detective and police stories, mysteries, thrillers and any other kind [of] crime fiction published in the U.K. during January." In its short life, it reviewed many books in addition to listing more. None of the reviews (averaging about two hundred words each) were signed, so Taylor may have written them. After twelve issues, it ceased publication with the Winter 1988 issue, referring to other commitments and mentioning a possible return that never materialized.

The Short Sheet (1987–1988)

Josh Pachter's column, "The Short Sheet," in *Mystery Scene* outgrew the space it was allowed, so in April 1987 Pachter, a fan as well as a writer and editor of short story collections, started *The Short Sheet*. Though Edward D. Hoch had written a column about the short story for *TAD*, Pachter's publication was the first fan magazine devoted to the mystery short story.

News of the short story and information about anthologies and magazines was an important part of Pachter's magazine. He interviewed authors known for their short fiction, for example Brendan DuBois. An interesting feature was "Critic's Choice," which contained reviews of favorite past anthologies. Morris Hershman reviewed Ellery Queen's anthology *101 Years Entertainment* (1941), and I reviewed *The Pocket Mystery Reader* (1942), edited by Lee Wright.

In December 1987, Pachter wrote an "obituary" for *Espionage*, a digest-sized magazine started in 1984 that, after a promising beginning, failed to attract enough subscribers to continue. Ironically, the next issue, January-February 1988, was the last for *The Short Sheet.*

The Margery Allingham Society and *The Bottle Street Gazette* (1988–)

This was a society that started in England but once had an American branch. It began in 1988 "to celebrate the life and work of a great "Queen of Crime." Barry Pike, author of *Campion's Career: A Study of the Novels of Margery Allingham* (1987) and Pat Watt were co-editors of the society's newsletter, *The Bottle Street Gazette,* which Pike now edits alone. Its title comes from the location of Campion's London flat: 17a Bottle Street. It has included biographical material about Allingham, candid photographs of her, and copies of her correspondence. In America, Maryell Cleary was editor of the U.S. newsletter. The final issue of the U.S. edition was Fall 1995, but the society remains active in England, with an annual dinner, trips, and publication of the semiannual newsletter. In 2004, the society celebrated the centenary of Allingham's birth with a traveling exhibition of visual and literary material from the Allingham archives, publication of a volume of articles and essays about her, and the unveiling of a commemorative plaque at her former London home.

Pulp Vault (1988–1996)

Pulp Vault, one of the best pulp fan magazines, was started in February 1988 by Doug Ellis of Chicago. In addition to reprinting pulp stories, each issue had articles by knowledgeable fans and by pulp writers themselves. For example, there was a series by Hugh B. Cave, "Magazines I Remember," and Theodore Roscoe's Depression memoir "By Writing I Could Eat."

A poignant feature of issue No. 11 in 1993 was Michael Avallone's obituary for Robert Sampson (1928–1992), perhaps the leading fan writing about pulps. Sampson had written for virtually every magazine, usually about crime stories, and he also wrote seven books about pulps for Popular Press, including six in the "Yesterday's Faces" series. Like some fans, Sampson had turned to fiction; he won MWA's Edgar for Best Short Story of 1986.

Pulp Vault promised it would be published "irregularly," and it lived up to its word; no issues have appeared since 1996.

Historical Mystery Fandom (1988–2002)

Sue Feder of Maryland, a one-woman advocate for the historical mystery, founded the Ellis Peters Appreciation Society in December 1988 because of her love of the work of Edith Pargeter, better known as Ellis Peters, the pseudonym she used for mysteries, including her series about Brother Cadfael. Shortly after the death of Pargeter in 1995, Feder suspended publication of *Most Loving Mere Folly: The Journal of the Ellis Peters Appreciation Society* after thirty-one issues. The title was taken from a Shakespearean quote that was also the title of a Pargeter novel.

Sue Feder, outstanding fan of historical mysteries, in 1999

In the spring of 1998, Feder founded a more general organization: The Historical Mystery Appreciation Society. Its magazine, offering news and reviews of historical mysteries, was *Murder, Past Tense*. The society presented the Herodotus Awards, honoring the best in historical mysteries, at Bouchercon. The magazine and the awards were suspended in 2002 when Feder's illness forced her to take "a long sabbatical." She died in 2005. The Sue Feder Historical Mystery Award is now voted on each year by the readers of *Mystery Readers Journal* and presented at Bouchercon.

With the exception of Malice Domestic, there were no new conventions during the 1980s and only a few organizations holding meetings. However, the future decades would see a great increase in the number of mystery conventions.

Chapter Eighteen

BOUCHERCONS: 1990S

1990: London

Bouchercon's London site, King's College in The Strand, was not a hotel. Some attendees stayed at nearby hotels, most of which were expensive, while others stayed in college dormitories for under £30 a night. People came from the United States, France, Finland, West Germany, Canada, Iceland, Greece, Japan, and Belgium. There were twenty-four booksellers, eight from the U.S.

There were complaints about the college as a convention site due to unavailability of water and coffee, a scarcity of bathrooms, and the need to climb stairs from one meeting room to another. There was a hospitality suite a block away at the Waldorf Hotel, but it was poorly publicized, and many didn't know it existed.

Controversy, an increasing part of Bouchercons, began before the convention officially opened on Friday, September 21st. Booksellers Marion and Robin Richmond, who were chairing Bouchercon, scheduled a pre-convention dinner at the Sherlock Holmes Pub in Northumberland Street. The Richmonds were upset that Maxim Jakubowski, owner of Murder One bookstore, had scheduled an open house at his store at the same time. Harsh words and threats of legal action were exchanged.

If there were problems with the site of Bouchercon 21, there was general agreement that the three-track programming arranged by British fan and scholar Barry Pike was excellent. Panels included one on legal mysteries; another called Scotland Yard—Past and Present; a centenary tribute to Agatha Christie, who was born in 1890; The Detection Club: Then and Now; and a talk on Sherlock Holmes's foil, Inspector Lestrade. The convention program book, edited by Robert Richardson, was highly praised.

Guest of Honor was bestselling British author P.D. James. Bob Adey, British expert on "impossible crimes," was Fan Guest of Honor. A Lifetime Achievement Anthony was given to Michael Gilbert. American Sue Grafton was Toastmistress. The sold-out awards banquet at the Waldorf started one hour and forty-five minutes late, with no announcement why to those waiting. It was later reported that the delay was caused by security checking rumors of an Irish Republican Army bomb.

In his report on Bouchercon in TAD, Ric Meyers used Dickensian language to assess it, saying, "It was the best of Bouchercons; it was the worst of Bouchercons." He praised the varied program and opportunity to meet authors new to him. However, he wrote of the college site's shortcomings and the absence of a central location where fans could gather as they had at American Bouchercons and regional conventions. He wrote of missing what he called "Lobbycon."

1991: Pasadena

Well before Bouchercon .22 (its number the caliber of a bullet) began October 11 at the Pasadena Hilton, the Co-Chairs, Len and June Moffat, were getting flak over the guests selected. All—Guest of Honor: Edward D. Hoch; Lifetime Achievement Award: William Campbell Gault; Fan Guest of Honor: Bruce Pelz; Toastmaster Bill Crider—were male.

Ronnie Klaskin and Sandra Scoppettone complained in *MDM*. Len Moffatt replied that the honorees were picked by a gender-split committee. "We are hurt that you would think that June and I would be part of a plan to deliberately exclude women from Bouchercon honors." Not placated, Scoppettone said, "I think the people who run Bouchercons must make a conscious effort to include women at this time in history." Calling her point "too much like tokenism," the Moffatts pointed out that one of the original guests invited was female, but she turned the committee down.

There were also complaints about Bouchercon having accepted a bid for 1994 from Austin, Texas, which most did not consider the Pacific Coast region. (That region was entitled to put on the 1994 convention.) As the Moffatts pointed out, at the time Austin was the only bidder. Not to accept their bid meant no 1994 Bouchercon. Furthermore, the rules had "no set boundaries" for the three regions: Pacific Coast, East Coast, and Midwest.

Bob Napier of Tacoma, Washington, was insistent that Austin's bid was inappropriate since he felt it could not be considered part of the Pacific Coast. On the other hand, James Reasoner of Texas felt that the current three-region rotation was unfair to people in the South and Southwest who had considerable distances to travel to *all* Bouchercons. Eventually, Seattle, Washington bid for 1994 just before the deadline. Later changes in Bouchercon bylaws would assign each of the fifty states and parts of Canada to one of the three regions.

Bouchercon .22 was put on by the Southern California Institute for Fan Interests, a nonprofit corporation which had previously sponsored science fiction conventions. Thirteen hundred attended, with the Hilton sold out and the overflow at nearby hotels. The weather, out of the committee's control, was close to 100 degrees and smoggy.

The program book was outstanding, including a reproduction of the entire program for the first Bouchercon. For the first time, there was a listing of writers and fans who had died recently. As mystery's unofficial "obituarian," I provided that. The program also included a copy of the Bouchercon bylaws, much needed in view of contention regarding location and finances. The first American publication of a short story by Guest of Honor Hoch was also included. Part of the registration package was a bibliography of the complete works of Hoch, compiled by June Moffatt and Francis M. Nevins.

There were three full days of programming, with three tracks. A highlight, called "The Panel from Hell," was scheduled for the hellish time of 9:00 a.m. Saturday. Sharyn McCrumb moderated, and she and her panelists, Joan Hess, Wendy Hornsby, Ann and Evan Maxwell, and Conrad Hayes, prepared skits and other hilarious material out of the lives of mystery authors publicizing their books. Hornsby displayed a sign: "Will Sign Books for Food."

Another outstanding panel, on Sunday, was about true crime as told through the viewpoints of Bob Samoian, an Assistant District Attorney in Los Angeles, Paul Bishop, a police detective, and Leila Dobscha, a police dispatcher.

The fiftieth anniversary of *Ellery Queen's Mystery Magazine* was in 1991 and a panel celebrated it. Editor Eleanor Sullivan had just died; there was a tribute to her by Hoch in the program. Janet Hutchings, the new editor, was introduced as one of the panelists.

My interview with Hoch went smoothly, though we hoped for larger attendance. Perhaps a relatively small crowd was inevitable since it was scheduled for noon and was in competition with lunch and two panels and a reading. It was immediately followed by Richard Moore's interview of Gault, which was embarrassing because Gault's memory was failing. Moore did his best to prompt Gault, but he was unsuccessful. Moore called it "one of the worst experiences I've ever had."

The lobby was a good one, spacious enough for fans to gather for conversation. Some people remained in their rooms to watch the Supreme Court nomination hearing of Clarence Thomas, with questioning of him and Anita Hill. Paul Bishop arranged a tour of the LAPD that included their police academy and firing range.

The Moffatts had asked for a financial report from the London Bouchercon and, according to them, "received an unsatisfactory reply—to say the least." They only received money from the San Diego and Philadelphia Bouchercons. Because of the committee's experience in budgeting and running conventions, Pasadena turned a profit of twenty thousand dollars, fifteen thousand of which they turned over as "seed money" to the next three Bouchercons. They gave five thousand dollars to the two Bouchercons following those. This profit was despite reimbursing panelists for their registration fees once it was determined that Bouchercon .22 would be profitable. Napier summarized the majority opinion about Bouchercon .22 when he wrote in *MDM* "Hats off to the Moffatts and their group for their honest and responsible work."

1992: Toronto

Fifteen hundred people, more than at any previous Bouchercon, attended October 8–11 at Toronto's Royal York Hotel. The chairman was Al Navis, a native-born Torontonian. Peter Sellers, Canadian short story writer and anthologist, did the programming.

Visitors arrived early for sightseeing in Toronto. They found a clean and safe city, though it had its share of homeless people. There were good restaurants, underground malls, and live theatre. I finally saw *The Mousetrap* and *The Phantom of the Opera*. The local baseball team, the Blue Jays, was in the World Series.

Registration did not go smoothly, and there were long lines before attendees received their packets. There were even longer lines for people to sign up for tables at the banquet. At Thursday night's opening cocktail party, a free copy of *Cold Blood II*, an anthology of Canadian short stories, edited by Sellers, was given out. Beginning Friday morning there were three (four on Saturday) tracks of programming.

The program did not have pictures or biographies of the participants, but it did have a good history of the short story by Edward D. Hoch, a short story set at the 1991 Bouchercon by English-born writer Peter Robinson, who lives in Toronto, and an article on Canadian crime fiction by David Skene-Melvin.

Panels included a slideshow of covers of Doubleday Crime Club mysteries, the subject of a forthcoming book by Ellen Nehr. Art Scott did another of his slide shows on sexy paperback mystery covers.

Some people who had attended many Bouchercons said that panel subjects were becoming "old hat," and seemed to brag about how many panels they did *not* attend. "Done to Death" was different. It was a panel with Gary Warren Niebuhr, Bob Samoian, Orietta Hardy-Sayles, Don Sandstrom, and me describing some of the worst clichés in the mystery. This was the funniest and most popular panel in Toronto. A crowd of 125 people filled a small room, some even sitting on the floor and others standing in back and outside the open door. (The panels were taped and this one sold more copies than any other.) The microphone was one step below the dais, and I tripped over that step and fell when returning to my chair. There was so much laughter during the panel that some were convinced I had taken the pratfall deliberately.

Two other unusual events were a panel on "Murder in Traditional Folk Music," with two folk singers giving examples, and an afternoon tea party and hat contest with Professor B.J. Rahn winning with her mystery-decorated chapeau.

Mystery fans were increasingly referring to themselves as part of a "family," and Toronto provided a perfect example. Naomi Hoida of Japan attended though she did not speak English well and did not know anyone there, except through correspondence in *MDM*. She was welcomed warmly, and when she returned home she wrote, "Now I am. . .truly missing Bouchercon XXIII and *MDM* family I met. I heartily enjoyed my first Bouchercon for their warm friendliness. *MDM* members are my great family."

Guest of Honor Margaret Millar, born in Canada though living in Santa Barbara, California, broke her hip shortly before Bouchercon and was unable to attend. Dorothy Salisbury Davis succinctly summed up Millar's contributions. Also succinct—and humorous—were Otto Penzler as Toastmaster and Lifetime Achievement Awardee Charlotte MacLeod, another Canadian living in the U.S. For the first time since 1983, there was no Fan Guest of Honor.

Chairman Navis decided to create suspense at the banquet regarding the vote for the 1995 Bouchercon. Nottingham, England was competing with two American cities: Miami and Washington, DC. Navis kept postponing the announcement until Ric Meyers, who reported on Bouchercon for TAD, threatened to come up on stage and force the issue. Finally, Navis announced that Nottingham had won, with almost twice the votes of its competitors combined.

1993: Omaha

Omaha, Nebraska, may seem an unlikely spot for Bouchercon, but not to fans who attended enjoyable Midwest Mystery & Suspense conventions there from 1990 through 1992. About a thousand people attended the 24th Bouchercon October 1–3 at the Holiday Inn Central, the hotel that had become infamous at those gatherings because of its maze of corridors.

Charles "Chuck" Levitt, responsible for the regional Omaha conventions, was chairman, and almost everyone had a great time, though an unusual number of mistakes caused some to label it "Botchercon." The PWA Shamus Awards were given out at the same time as the auction was held. Attendees were not given up-to-date information about which authors would attend, so some brought books for signing by authors not there and failed to bring books for those attending. Some panelists were unaware they had been scheduled. The program book had so many errors that Bob Napier nicknamed the convention "Typocon."

Don Sandstrom was Fan Guest of Honor. On Friday morning

his fellow correspondents in *MDM* had a breakfast honoring him. He was pleased and then shocked when he saw several dozen people performing what appeared to be a strip tease. It was merely to show that they were all wearing T-shirts proclaiming, "I'm a Fan of the Fan Guest of Honor." In keeping with the weekend's "typos," the convention's name on the shirts was spelled "Boucheron." At that breakfast, there was also the release of *Farewell, My Lobby*, the second book of parodies by mystery fans. Typically, the final paragraph of one story, by Bob Samoian, had been omitted.

The Guest of Honor was Evan Hunter, better known under his Ed McBain pseudonym. Also honored with Lifetime Achievement Awards were Hammond Innes, the British thriller writer, and Ralph McInerny.

Panels included one called "The British Are Coming," evidence that more British writers were coming to American Bouchercons. Two panels, "How to Get Published" and "Promotions," were geared toward the increasing number of new or hopeful writers attending. Wisely, Levitt continued his regional convention practice of scheduling panels so that there was one half-hour between panels for fans to obtain autographs.

The Saturday night banquet was brief, which to some was a plus. However, not allowing the winners of the Anthonys to make acceptance speeches, a major reason for brevity, was insufficient recognition of their achievements. Mistress of Ceremonies Ori Hardy-Sayles explained, "The dais was so narrow, with wires and uneven planking, it was best to keep the traffic down." Being one of the few to make it to the dais, to introduce Sandstrom, I can testify I had to be careful not to repeat my tumble in Toronto. The awards were handed out in front of the dais by Naomi Hoida, who again came from Japan. One Anthony, for Best Critical Work, went to fan Ellen Nehr, for her *Doubleday Crime Club Compendium*. Mystery writers who had died recently were recognized though, in an oral "typo," Levitt called the late creator of The Saint "Leslie Chartreuse."

After the banquet, music was provided by mystery writer,

Max Allan Collins and his "Cruisin' Band." In keeping with this convention, several dancers fell while jitterbugging.

To a veteran Bouchercon-goer, one of its joys is seeing the pleasure derived by first-time attendees. Gayle Lovett came from Australia. Barry W. Gardner, the retired Dallas Fire Department captain who became an outstanding fan reviewer, was thrilled when at Sunday breakfast I introduced him to Allen J. Hubin, whom he later confessed was "my idol."

1994: Seattle

The consensus was that the 25th Bouchercon, October 6–9 at Seattle's Stouffer Madison, was one of the best organized. Thom Walls was Chair, and he had an outstanding committee. Andi Shechter and Alan Rosenthal did especially good jobs of programming. 1,400 people attended and another hundred were turned away. Even the notorious Seattle weather cooperated; the entire weekend was sunny.

Thom Walls, chairman of the successful 1994 Seattle Bouchercon

The 140-page program was the best to date, thanks largely to Stu Shiffman, who also provided drawings. As one of several innovations, pocket programs were distributed, which attendees could easily carry to determine which panels to attend. This innovation has now become routine at conventions, and fans complain if pocket programs are not provided. The program made it clear that writers were welcome, but that Bouchercon was not a writers' conference or workshop. Longtime Bouchercon attendees had been noticing more writers, would-be writers, and editors promoting their own works. The program contained good articles on Anthony Boucher, Guest of Honor Marcia Muller, Fan Guest of Honor Art Scott, Lifetime Achievement Honoree Tony Hillerman, and Toastmaster George C. Chesbro.

Panels were enjoyable and occasionally innovative. For example, on the first morning, at "Bouchercon 101," Don Sandstrom tried to ease the way for new attendees awed at attending so large a convention. Another panel, "Women Who Love Cops Too Much," recognized the increase in mysteries with amateur detectives who have affairs with police detectives. The humor panel, with Donald E. Westlake and Parnell Hall, provided Bouchercon's first "pie-in-the-face," with Hall the gracious recipient.

A panel on forgotten writers produced arguably the greatest coincidence in Bouchercon history. In suggesting Thomas B. Dewey, who wrote about Chicago and was sympathetic to the young, I said "If you like Sara Paretsky, you'll like Dewey." At that exact moment, Paretsky walked into the room and wondered about the gasps of surprise that greeted her. I was asked if I had arranged that with her; I hadn't, barely having spoken to her at prior Bouchercons.

The last-named panel also showed the danger of political correctness carried too far. William DeAndrea, Jeff Marks, Maxim Jakubowski, and I recommended many forgotten writers, including Pat McGerr, Craig Rice, and Lee Thayer. A woman in the audience asked when we were going to suggest more female writers. It became clear that she didn't know enough history to realize that, despite androgynous first names, McGerr, Rice, and Thayer were women.

Because the banquet was sold out at five hundred attendees, the committee arranged to have it telecast by closed-circuit television to hotel rooms. The feature of the banquet was the best speech ever by a Fan Guest of Honor, one in which Art Scott delivered a tribute to fandom, recounting his twenty years as an active fan. He told of friends he had made and the enjoyment fandom had brought him. He concluded by recommending Bouchercon attendees become more involved, "There are all sorts of things you can do in fandom, interesting people you can get to know, 'zines you can write for, mystery events you can get involved in. Start to connect with people. I assure you that you will find yourselves sucked into it; it's almost impossible to resist, and it's my advice that you go with it; you'll be glad you did."

Even as near-perfect a Bouchercon as Seattle had a few negatives. The Stouffer Madison was too small a hotel to handle so many people, and there were crowds, especially waiting for elevators. Some meeting rooms were too small, shutting out people from panels they wanted to attend.

Another negative was one over which the committee had no control—an article in the British newspaper *The Independent* by crime writer Michael Dibdin. He gratuitously attacked fans at this Bouchercon, calling them "nerds" and claiming that fans are mainly interested in getting autographs for mercenary reasons. He quoted mystery authors, whom he said chose to remain anonymous, who claimed that authors have nothing in common with fans. Descending to his nadir, Dibdin quoted an anonymous publisher as to how the Fan Guest of Honor is chosen. "They look for the biggest nerd in the place." Andi Shechter was so angry and embarrassed that she responded to Dibdin for the Bouchercon committee, saying they were sorry they had invited him.

1995: Nottingham

Bouchercon returned to England, to Nottingham, where its chairman, Adrian Wootton, had successfully mounted "Shots in the Dark" conventions since 1991. As early as 1992, objections were raised to another Bouchercon in England so soon. The most valid argument was the expense for Americans. Geoff Bradley reminded those objecting that Bouchercon was the "World Mystery Convention" and that people different from the 1990s committee would be organizing it.

Nottingham "Criminal Masterminds" Martin Edwards, Sarah Mason, Ed Hoch, and Marv Lachman, who only appears to be asleep

Though Nottingham was considered by some to currently have a high crime rate, the Bouchercon committee emphasized the area's legendary past, especially Robin Hood. The convention was held September 28 through October 1 at the Broadway Media Centre, with events held at other locations. Because there was no hotel large enough for almost a thousand attendees, people were scattered at six hotels, but a shuttle bus service minimized inconvenience.

For the first time, brief cases were given with registration material. The program, in the form of a trade paperback, was the most unusual in Bouchercon history, including twenty-seven short stories, to be published later as the anthology *No Alibi,* edited by Maxim Jakubowski. Among the important writers in it, all of whom were attendees at Nottingham, were Edward D. Hoch, John Harvey (also in charge of programming), Peter Lovesey, and Val McDermid. It also reprinted an Anthony Boucher short story. Unfortunately, due to health reasons, Phyllis White missed this Bouchercon.

There was much discussion during Bouchercon about P.D. James, who had canceled her appearance. A few months before, she had been interviewed on BBC radio and made remarks some interpreted as her saying that only the middle class was educated enough to make moral choices that translate into good crime fiction. She drew protests in the media, and a flier for an upcoming anthology, *Fresh Blood,* edited by Jakubowski and Mike Ripley. The flier promised to "feature stories from most of the leading 'anti-establishment' British crime authors, who assert that in today's mystery writing, realism is far more important than outmoded questions of morality." James said later she was talking of an author's choice of fictional setting, and the detective novel "works best for me when the setting is orderly and law-abiding and the criminal is intelligent and capable of a moral choice."

There were two Guests of Honor. Colin Dexter, creator of Inspector Morse, proved to be congenial and likable. The American Guest of Honor, James Ellroy, using four-letter words often, seemed intent on shocking but only managed to bore. Ruth Rendell received a Lifetime Achievement Award. Reginald Hill was Toastmaster, and Geoff Bradley, publisher and editor of CADS, was Fan Guest of Honor. There was an international flavor at this Bouchercon, with attendees from the U.S., Japan, Australia, Finland, and Ireland. Twenty-four booksellers were there, unfortunately given a cramped area, but that did not deter many buyers.

Some of the panels showed considerable originality. Friday began with "How to Enjoy Bouchercon and Retain Your Sanity," a lighthearted introduction, like 1994's "Bouchercon 101" for newcomers. For "Two by Two" teams of writers discussed themselves and their work, while interacting. Among the combinations were Sue Grafton-Walter Mosley and Donald E. Westlake-Lawrence Block. Other panels discussed romance in crime fiction and "The Roots of Crime," with an interesting philosophical discussion of evil. Bill Deeck gave another of his hilarious dissections of the work of James Corbett.

Trivia quizzes from past Bouchercons were trivial indeed compared to the "Criminal Masterminds Quiz," based on a popular British television program, presented at the Royal Concert Hall. Edward D. Hoch and I represented the United States, and we could claim that we were awed by the surroundings and had trouble understanding British pronunciation, but the simple fact is that the team of Sarah J. Mason and Martin Edwards, two young English mystery writers who are also highly knowledgeable fans, was far too good for us.

For the banquet, attendees were bused to the East Midlands Conference Centre. In keeping with the Robin Hood motif, suitably dressed henchmen of the Sheriff boarded the buses, announcing that they were looking for "that villain Robin Hood." A sword fight was conducted during the banquet, and musicians played period music. Unfortunately, most of the winners of the Anthonys did not appear to receive their awards. There had been considerable lobbying by one member of the Sisters in Crime, apparently without that groups' approval, for Sharyn McCrumb, who won Anthonys for Best Short Story and Best Novel. As Geoff Bradley said, "the really sad aspect of the whole affair is that she will never know if she won fairly." The convention ended with an event that occurred at several mystery conventions. At 11:00 p.m. in my hotel, the fire alarms went off, forcing people in various stages of dishabille to tramp downstairs to the lobby, only to learn it had been a false alarm.

1996: Saint Paul, Minnesota

Bouchercon returned to the Twin Cities of Minnesota for a convention in St. Paul with its share of sadness. Ellen Nehr, the Fan Guest of Honor, died in December 1995. Barry Gardner, who had already written an article for the program, died in July 1996. William L. DeAndrea, a frequent Bouchercon attendee, died the day before it began.

This twenty-seventh Bouchercon almost never took place. As of 1993 there had been no firm bid, though Jimmie Butler talked of possibly holding it in Colorado Springs. MWA was not supportive, and there was also fear of a boycott. Due to a Legislative amendment perceived as anti-gay, other organizations had already canceled plans to meet in Colorado. It was reported that Atlanta was considering a bid, but they never submitted one. In 1994 Bruce Taylor and Thom Walls called Once Upon a Crime, a mystery bookstore in Minneapolis, to ask the owner, Steve Stilwell, and his employee Dennis Armstrong, whether either would be willing to chair the 1996 Bouchercon. Stilwell refused but ended up playing an important role by giving Armstrong the time off necessary to run it, paying his health insurance, giving advice, and handling the book dealers' room. Armstrong had the further assistance of Co-Chairman Bruce Southworth. Furthermore, Dennis Armstrong's mother, Jane Armstrong, edited the 160-page program book.

Sixteen hundred people attended, October 10–13, at the Radisson Hotel. One aspect of St. Paul emphasized throughout the conventions was its past as a "safe city" for the underworld, with gangsters of the 1930s, including John Dillinger and "Baby Face" Nelson, spending time there.

Booksellers and frequent convention hosts Steve Stilwell and Bruce Taylor

Most of Thursday was devoted to the "First Black Mystery Writers Symposium," with seven panels discussing topics pertaining to African-American writers and readers. A reception and fund-raiser followed, with Walter Mosley as keynote speaker at the Landmark Center. Bouchercon was co-sponsor.

The Bouchercon Welcome Reception was on Thursday night and the kindest word that can be applied to it is "unfortunate." It began with the playing of "The Star-Spangled Banner," which mystery writer Polly Whitney interrupted in a mock French accent, saying that since this was an international conference, the French

National Anthem should be sung. She proceeded to sing "Frere Jacques." She continued in this vein, much to the embarrassment of the emcee, Alan Russell. The acoustics were so bad that many people could not hear her, which may have been a blessing. Many left before Parnell Hall sang his hilarious "Signing in the Waldenbooks." Because of Whitney, Stilwell was pronounced "off the hook" for the 1987 magician.

A Friday breakfast sponsored by *Deadly Pleasures* magazine launched the third set of fan parodies, titled *The Lady in the 10,000 Lakes* to go with the Minnesota location. There were a dozen stories by contributors to *MDM*. Gary Warren Niebuhr published this booklet, which he called "A Deep But Still Meaningless Collection of Shallow Short Stories."

The Guest of Honor was Mary Higgins Clark, who spoke graciously at the banquet Friday night. Ellen Nehr's husband, Al, spoke about her, as did writer Joan Hess who was a good friend. The program book contained a touching article by Art Scott describing Ellen's diffident entry into fandom when she adopted the "I'm-just-an-ordinary-housewife-from-Ohio-who-likes-mysteries" guise. As Scott further said, "At her death she left behind a host of friends and a solid legacy of scholarship."

The Toastmaster was Jeremiah Healy, who didn't need a microphone to be heard. *The Armchair Detective* was recognized with an Anthony as Best Magazine. Though I had contributed to *The Armchair Detective Book of Lists,* I was surprised that it won the Anthony as "Best Critical Work" over outstanding biographies of John Dickson Carr and Jim Thompson by Douglas Greene and Robert Polito respectively. After the banquet, a Dixieland band played, and Sara Paretsky and Parnell Hall drew applause for their dancing skills.

In keeping with the opening symposium, there were two panels on minority writers. Several panels concerned the internet, then it its relatively early days. One called "To Boldly Go" was about the DorothyL email chat group. Having apparently found a niche, I was again on a "forgotten author" panel, this one called "The Best Author You've Never Heard Of." I selected *Whistle Up the Devil* (1953) by Derek Smith, a book published only in England, after which Smith apparently disappeared. It is an admirable detective story in which two seemingly impossible murders are solved ingeniously and fairly. To my surprise I was told after the panel by a Japanese fan that the type of Golden Age puzzle Smith wrote is still popular in Japan and that Smith's second book, *Come to Paddington Fair*, which he was never able to get published in England, would be published in Japan in 1997 in English!

There was a mass signing on Sunday morning by all the authors, so fans would not have difficulty getting books autographed. However, there were stories on DorothyL after Bouchercon of fans pursuing authors into rest rooms for autographs. Some wondered whether it was necessary to have "autograph-free zones" at Bouchercon, as they had in Seattle, but wiser heads suggested it was not possible to change human nature and that the few guilty parties were jerks, not fans.

1997: Monterey, California

There were complaints when the original site of this Bouchercon, co-chaired by Bruce Taylor and Bryan Barrett, was changed from San Francisco to Monterey. A few people questioned the extra travel and expense from the San Francisco or San Jose airport. However, the combination of perfect weather and the loveliest setting in Bouchercon history removed most objections. From October 30 through November 2, about 2,000 people, the largest attendance ever, were at the Monterey Conference Center, with the attendees (and some of the panels) spilling over into three nearby hotels. Programming consisted of seven simultaneous tracks, and there were fifty-one book dealers.

Sara Paretsky was Guest of Honor, and Bob Napier was Fan Guest of Honor. Donald E. Westlake received a Lifetime

Achievement Award. An additional honoree was Ross Thomas, who had died in 1995. Some of the people who regularly played poker with Thomas at Bouchercons (including Jan Grape, Jeremiah Healy, Gayle Lynds and Bob Randisi) played "The Ross Thomas Memorial Poker Game."

Another popular panel was on the "Hypermodern Mystery," those recent books that were so collectible their value had gone into four figures. Other panels were the opposite of "hypermodern." Burl Barer discussed The Saint, about whom he had written an Edgar-winning book, and Ted Hertel covered Ellery Queen, once the most popular American detective, but in 1997 largely forgotten.

My wife Carol and I presented a program that was new to Bouchercon: "Just in Crime, the Musical." Longtime fans of show music, we combined two interests by playing crime-related music from Broadway. Among the numbers were "The Ballad of Lizzie Borden," from *New Faces of 1952*, "All You Have to Do Is Wait" from the private eye musical *City of Angels*, and "Suppertime" from *As Thousands Cheer*. Carol sang a little, and I did my Monty Woolley impression, reciting "Miss Otis Regrets," Cole Porter's song about a lynching.

Don Sandstrom, probably the most popular of all mystery fans, had died of leukemia twelve days before Bouchercon. Because we knew he would not be able to attend, Carol and I had flown to Indianapolis where, with a few other friends and one of his daughters present, we performed "Just in Crime" for him at what someone called "DonCon." Gary Warren Niebuhr represented the mystery-fan aspect of Don's life at his funeral. In Monterey, Don was sorely missed, and people remarked that when they saw from a distance, a distinguished-looking gentleman with white hair they imagined they were seeing him. Don was honored at a special Bouchercon breakfast, and as tributes were paid to him, many a tear was shed.

A cocktail party honoring Paretsky and Napier at the Maritime

Museum was a success, though the line to greet them (and go inside for free wine) was long. Less successful was the banquet at which the Anthony winners were again asked not to give speeches, a mistake that many felt devalued their awards. Also, failing to seat Napier on the dais (or even at a table near the dais) was unfortunate.

Some attendees were distressed by the sheer size of this Bouchercon, and there was debate, especially in the pages of *MDM*, on the subject. Many fans, as Bill Deeck said, "wanted to make sure Bouchercon did not become a combined writers' conference and author-publisher business meeting." Yet, a proposed by-law change to call Bouchercon a "fan convention" failed to pass. Some fans, especially Lorraine Petty, complained that the Bouchercon business meeting, held at 10:00 p.m. on the day before the convention started, was perfunctory and not conducive to getting new people involved in putting on Bouchercons since people were tired, having traveled that day. Napier even proposed reserving the name Bouchercon for smaller, more fan-oriented conventions. However, Gary Warren Niebuhr, Co-Chairman of the forthcoming 1999 Milwaukee Bouchercon, was in favor of attracting as many people as possible. He said that fan-oriented panels were not what most attendees wanted. He gave as example no more than thirty people attending a panel on fan magazines, while four hundred to five hundred attended a panel on which published authors of first novels were interviewed. Apparently, there were more would-be writers who wanted to know how to get published than fans.

This Bouchercon was successful, with a net profit of $50,000. Money was passed on to future Bouchercons, though Deen Kogan, chairing Philadelphia in 1998, opted not to accept any and not to pass any along. Writing in *MDM*, Neibuhr said, "The time has come to abandon the concept that anyone can force the sharing of profits and seed money...Each committee should be left to disperse its funds as it sees fit."

1998: Philadelphia

There was difficulty getting a bidder for this year. Otto Penzler was willing to run a New York Bouchercon, provided he could keep any profits. He withdrew his proposal when Deen Kogan was willing, and she mounted a successful Bouchercon October 1–4 at the Wyndham Hotel in Philadelphia. The mayor of Philadelphia proclaimed "World Mystery Week." More than 1,650 people registered, and they came from sixteen countries, plus the United States. Testament to the popularity of mysteries was the presence of a record sixty-nine book dealers.

Bouchercon 1998 honored more people than past conventions. Janwillem van de Wetering, who was International Guest of Honor, attracted many by talking about his Zen Buddhist philosophy. The American Guest of Honor was Carl Hiassen of Florida, as amusing in person as in his environmental mysteries. Tom Fontana, writer-producer of television's *Homicide: Life on the Street,* was Media Guest of Honor. Hal and Sonya Rice were Fan Guests of Honor. Jonathan Gash was the Honorary Host for the Anthony Brunch; an additional honoree was Ruth Cavin, esteemed editor.

Deen Kogan put on two Bouchercons in Philadelphia and helped rescue later ones in Las Vegas and Chicago

There was an opening night reception at the Free Library of Philadelphia, plus other events away from the convention hotel, including a tour of a former penitentiary. The International Association of Crime Writers (IACW) played an important role. They had a reception, four panels, and the North American Branch presented their annual Hammett Prize. Mystery Readers International presented its Macavity Awards.

The program book was 128 pages, four of which were

devoted to the latest Bouchercon bylaws. They provided for bids in three U.S. regions, causing unhappiness in England. However, they were amended to permit an international bid every fourth year. There were also articles by writers titled "Why I Write Mysteries."

One of the first panels during three-and-one-half days of five-track programming was on "The History of the Mystery," and there was discussion of the Golden Age between the World Wars. It was not as popular as the panel featuring a Philadelphia fire marshal and his arson-detecting dog.

A silent auction raised seven thousand dollars for three Philadelphia branch libraries. Friday evening featured a play written by Simon Brett. There was a "Bouchercon Ball" with a jazz band Saturday night. The Mummer's Band, a Philadelphia specialty, performed before the Anthony Awards Brunch Sunday.

Ten years after George H.W. Bush awakened Bouchercon attendees in San Diego, President Bill Clinton arrived at the Wyndham for a political fundraiser. Secret Service guards, with guns, could be seen on rooftops, and the elevators were shut down, stranding people in the lobby or in their rooms during his stay of several hours. I wondered if inconveniencing Bouchercon attendees for political reasons wasn't an impeachable offense.

1999: Milwaukee

If the thirtieth Bouchercon was, as longtime attendee John Apostolou said, "the best organized convention I've ever attended," it was due to Conference Coordinators Gary Warren Niebuhr and Ted Hertel, who devoted three and a half years to make three-and-a-half days run smoothly. "Mischief in the Midwest" was held September 30–October 3 at the Milwaukee Hilton, known when Bouchercon was held there in 1981 as the Marc Plaza. More than twelve hundred people attended, and it was noticed that stuffing the brief cases given to each was becoming time-consuming for the committee and helpful fans. Publishers were now giving out many free copies of books and other promotional material, as were writers.

Bouchercon began Wednesday evening with the "Edelweiss Cruise" on the Milwaukee River, complete with champagne and hors d'oeuvres, for special guests. Max Allan Collins did yeoman duty as American Guest of Honor. He appeared on panels, presented *Mommy,* a movie he wrote and produced, and his band played throughout the Saturday night dance. Reginald Hill was International Guest of Honor. The Fan Guests of Honor were Mary "Maggie" Mason of San Diego and Beverly DeWeese of Milwaukee. Len and June Moffatt were Lifetime Achievement honorees, receiving a special Anthony. As Toastmaster, Parnell Hall did not sing as he had done at so many Bouchercons, but he did read a short story that hilariously incorporated the names of mystery writers and fans.

The program book (196 pages) was especially good, including pictures and articles by the Moffatts about early Bouchercons. There was also the publication of a story by Libby Fischer Hellmann that won Bouchercon's first short story contest.

There were eight tracks of programming, including a panel about Anthony Boucher, others regarding computers, collecting, plot versus character, cooking mysteries, and cultural diversity. Another panel, titled "What Agents Can Do for You," included Dominick Abel, the successful agent who represented many mystery writers and was a frequent Bouchercon attendee. Recognizing that many would like to be published, Bouchercon, in cooperation with the Midwest Chapter of MWA, offered a writer's workshop (eleven sessions) throughout the convention.

Some of the convention spilled over to the nearby Midwest Center, which had room for events that drew large crowds. These included a tribute to Ellery Queen on the seventieth anniversary of the publication of *The Roman Hat Mystery,* the first Queen novel. It took the form of a radio play, "The Adventure of the Murdered Moths," with Ted Hertel achieving a lifelong ambition by playing Ellery. As the play's official "Armchair Detective," challenged to deduce the killer's identity, Max Allan Collins solved the case. On Friday night, Carol and I put on our revised, second edition of "Just in Crime: The Musical."

There were tributes to the late fan Don Sandstrom, in addition to one in writing in the program by his daughter Karen. An auction was held to raise funds for the Sandstrom Memorial Scholarship at Butler University to encourage developing writers; eight thousand dollars was raised. Less serious was the Don Sandstrom Memorial Family Feud, a trivia contest arranged by Ted Hertel's brother Harry. One of the contestants was another of Sandstrom's daughters, Bibi.

When I wasn't speaking as a panelist during a discussion of "The Golden Age," I looked out at the audience and saw that Phyllis White had dropped off to sleep, her head practically resting on my wife's shoulder. It seemed understandable. She was over eighty and traveling across two time zones is not easy, even for younger people. She was ill, and shortly after Bouchercon mystery fans learned that Phyllis had inoperable brain cancer.

Chapter Nineteen

LEFT COAST CRIME (1991–)

One convention a year was not enough for some fans, and people thought of regional conventions that would be more intimate than Bouchercons and involve less travel. The East Coast had Malice Domestic since 1989, and a successful Midwest Mystery & Suspense Convention was held in Omaha in 1990. Bookseller-fan Bryan Barrett decided to plan a San Francisco conference for 1991.

There was uncertainty as to what to call it. Early ads called it "Crime One," but it was later referred to variously as "West Coast Crime Conference," "Western Regional Mystery Conference," and "Left Coast Crime Conference" before the simpler "Left Coast Crime" (LCC), which has proven popular, was chosen.

The program book said it was celebrating two important events in the mystery: the one hundred fiftieth anniversary of what is generally accepted as the first detective story (by Poe) and the fiftieth anniversary of *Ellery Queen's Mystery Magazine*. However, the program also acknowledged the growth of mysteries set on the Pacific Coast. "Perhaps the freshest crimes are being committed in the imaginations of our New West writers, in the solid traditions of Poe and Queen, to be sure, but also on the firm basis of Chandler and Hammett...It is today's Western state inheritors of the tradition—authors, readers, collectors, and critics—that we intend to celebrate here."

The first LCC, February 15–18, 1991, at the Sir Francis Drake Hotel in San Francisco, invited two residents of nearby Sonoma County, Bill Pronzini and Marcia Muller, as Guests of Honor, and Bruce Taylor, owner of San Francisco's leading mystery bookstore, as Toastmaster. Panels dealt with such local issues as the environment and gay and lesbian detectives. The banquet was held at John's Grill, a restaurant Sam Spade visited in *The Maltese Falcon*. A popular event during LCC, as at San Francisco Bouchercons, was Don Herron's Dashiell Hammett Walk.

That fewer than two hundred people attended was due to several factors. The LCC committee did not have access to a mailing list of attendees at other conferences. Also, the Gulf War, with threats of terrorism, had many reluctant to fly. Perhaps the small size of the conference made it so enjoyable for many. As Len Moffatt reported, "Left Coast Crime was fun mostly because we got to visit with friends who stepped right off the pages of *MDM* and *DAPA-EM*." LCC was a reunion for many of those who had attended Omaha in 1990.

Bryan Barrett, who chaired the first Left Coast Crime in 1991 and LCC in 2002

Donna Rankin, treasurer for the first Left Coast Crime, chaired the second in 1992. It remained in San Francisco but moved to the Holiday Inn in Union Square. On Saturday night, the Chinese New Year's parade could be seen from the windows of the room in which authors were autographing books. Two Washington State writers, Earl Emerson and J.A. Jance, were Guests of Honor, and

James Lee Burke came from Montana to be Toastmaster. Peter Davison, then playing Albert Campion on *Mystery!*, attended and was very accessible. Another attendee was Sara Paretsky, wearing a button reading "Don't judge a book by its movie," recognition of the poor reception given *V.I. Warshawski*, the film version of a Paretsky novel. Lia Matera chaired a panel on social issues, always a popular topic in San Francisco. "Fireside Chats," intimate interviews and readings with individual authors, to which attendance limited to fifty people, was successful.

Though some hoped LCC would remain in the Bay area, others were anxious to have it in their backyards, and LCC No. 3 (called "Southern Exposure") moved in 1993 to the Hyatt Regency Alicante, near Disneyland, in Anaheim. Kevin Moore and Kathy Johnson were Co-Chairs. Sue Dunlap and Julie Smith were the Guests of Honor, and Ann and Evan Maxwell were Toastmasters. Attendance reached four hundred. A Sunday night banquet was unpopular with some people because it ended too late for their trip home, and they felt they were forced to spend for an extra night's lodging.

Left Coast Crime returned to the Anaheim location in 1994, with Kevin Moore as Chair. Aaron Elkins was Guest of Honor, with Carolyn G. Hart as Toastmistress. Programming was limited to two tracks, allowing people to see more, with fewer difficult choices. Sex in the mystery was discussed at many panels. In what was becoming an LCC tradition, there was a group autographing session of authors. The Sunday night banquet was held again, and at 3:00 a.m. Monday those staying in the hotel were awakened by an announcement telling them to remain in their rooms because there was a power outage. Some realized the hotel might be legally required to do that, but they wondered why awaken people who were sleeping in the dark. On a prior night during the convention, there was a 4:00 a.m. false alarm.

Left Coast Crime had been meant for locations in the Pacific and Mountain time zones, but some Californians questioned the non-coastal location of the 1995 LCC at the Old Town Holiday Inn in Scottsdale, Arizona. Barbara Peters of Poisoned Pen Press and Bookstore there managed the convention, with Jean and Marty Hanus as Co-Chairs. Writer-fan Jim McCahery, scheduled to attend, died of a heart attack in New Jersey shortly before LCC began. Bob Samoian who had recently had brain surgery, attended his final convention, dying of a heart attack three days after he returned home. He had been as enthusiastic as ever. Others attending were among the walking wounded. Parnell Hall was on crutches due to a torn Achilles tendon, and Don Sandstrom fell down a flight of stairs at the hotel and had to walk with a cane.

Two Albuquerque writers were honored. The convention was called "A Tribute to Tony Hillerman," and he was Guest of Honor; Judith Van Gieson was Toastmistress. Robert B. Parker was a Special Guest. P.D. James was in Scottsdale on a book tour but didn't attend LCC. Neither she nor Parker was at the author signing Saturday night. Again, there were only two tracks of programs. In line with the Southwestern location, panels under the general title "The Modern Gunslinger" were held, but they dealt with mysteries, not Westerns.

Left Coast Crime moved further inland in 1996, to the Clarion Hotel in Boulder, Colorado. Tom and Enid Schantz of Rue Morgue Books there chaired it. Because Boulder is at 5,430 feet, they called this LCC "Murder with an Altitude." Over four hundred fifty people attended. The location provoked some controversy because Boulder had probably the strictest non-smoking code in the United States at that time. Ann Williams of Denver registered, but canceled when she learned the only place she could smoke was in her room. She said, "The pious majority in Boulder has zero tolerance for minority rights." Barry Gardner also railed against the Boulder City Council. Ironically, both Williams and Gardner died in 1996, in their fifties, with cigarette smoking apparently contributing factors. Others who attended said they enjoyed the absence of second-hand smoke, and it was the only mystery convention at which they felt free to go into the bar, normally a smoke-filled place.

Kinky Friedman was Guest of Honor and Nevada Barr Toastmistress. A cabaret was held Saturday night at the Boulder Theater. Some thought Friedman's performance (including a song about mucous) was tasteless and walked out on him. Parnell Hall was a hit with his songs, and Alan Russell and Jeremiah Healy serenaded Left Coast Crime's first Fan Guest of Honor, Mary "Maggie" Mason.

For the first time the "Lefty" Award was given. Saluting the best humorous mystery of the year, it was given to Russell for *The Fat Innkeeper*. The award took the form of a plaster impression of a left hand, "posed" for by Enid Schantz. Panels in Boulder, which had three tracks, included "Collecting the Hypermodern," then at its expensive peak. I explored another aspect in a one-man panel, "Book Collecting for Po' Folks," describing the fun (and bargains) found at library sales, garage sales and second-hand stores.

In 1997, LCC (called "Murder Lurks…") came to the Stouffer Renaissance (formerly Madison) in Seattle, where 1994's Bouchercon was held, with Andi Shechter as Chair; Thom Walls was Vice-Chair. There were joint Guests of Honor, the husband-and-wife team of Jonathan and Faye Kellerman. Because the Kellermans are Orthodox Jews, their participation at LCC was limited to Sunday when their speeches at the brunch were well received. Attendees were disappointed when Jonathan, due to carpal tunnel syndrome, couldn't sign his books, though he did stamp his signature. Lia Matera was Toastmistress.

About 400 people attended. Again, the timing did not please everyone. Advertised as running from Thursday through Sunday, LCC had few Thursday panels. By Sunday afternoon, there were only two panels remaining. Some said that had they but known, they'd not have booked for Sunday evening. At the auction, emcees Bruce Taylor and Parnell Hall raised seventeen hundred dollars for the Northwest Literacy Foundation and a battered-women's shelter.

In 1998 Left Coast Crime ("Crime Crosses the Border") was at San Diego's Bahia Hotel and Resort in the Mission Bay area. The Chairs were "The Left Coast Crime 8 Committee." Elizabeth George, the Southern Californian who writes about England, was Guest of Honor, and local author Alan Russell was Toastmaster. A Lifetime Achievement Award went to another local, novelist-reviewer Robert Wade. A noted San Diego book collector, Willis Herr, was posthumous Fan Guest of Honor.

Left Coast Crime started at Albuquerque's Hyatt Regency Friday, March 5, 1999, but for me it began the night before when, reliving our Mystery Readers' bashes in the Bronx, we had a party for a dozen mystery fans at my home in Santa Fe, seventy miles away.

Harlen Campbell, who had recently published his first mystery, was Chair.

John Dunning was LCC Guest of Honor; Deborah Crombie, a Texan who (like Elizabeth George) sets her mysteries in England, was Toastmistress. Tasha Mackler, formerly a mystery bookstore owner in Albuquerque, was Fan Guest of Honor. She had written a book *Murder by Category,* a subject guide to the mystery.

The theme of this LCC was "the literary mystery," and Dunning tried to stick to the topic in his Saturday night banquet speech. It proved unsatisfying since Dunning couldn't seem to decide whether the mystery should be "escape" or "great literature." The same indecisiveness was present in Campbell's interview with him, in which he opined that the mystery can be "literature" but because it is essentially plot-driven and has rules, it doesn't permit the freedom to explore character that mainstream fiction does. The success of Dunning's own *Booked to Die* (1992), a highly collectible "hypermodern" book, was due to its combination of old-fashioned detective story and book collecting lore, gathered by Dunning in the years he owned a Denver bookstore.

Panels on being published again proved popular as LCC welcomed a new group of hopeful mystery writers. Increasingly, as lobby space at hotels seemed limited, the book room was the place fans gathered to talk, a trend not unpopular with dealers.

In 2000, Left Coast Crime ("Celebrating Mystery, Murder & Mayhem") returned to Arizona, at Tucson's Holiday Inn City Center, and the weather in mid-March was hot. Again there were multiple chairs: "The Left Coast Crime 10 Organizing Committee." Sue Grafton, author of the popular alphabet series, was Guest of Honor. Harlan Coben came from New Jersey to be Toastmaster. George Easter, editor-publisher of *Deadly Pleasures*, was Fan Guest of Honor. Maggie Mason organized "The Easter Egg Caper," gathering egg-shaped pantyhose containers and having George's friends insert notes to him. In what was proving a regular event, Mason's team won the trivia contest, one patterned after the TV show *Jeopardy!* She modestly claimed her success was due to naming her team "The Golden Retrievers," her favorite breed of dog.

George Easter, who founded *Deadly Pleasures*, and Mary "Maggie" Mason, Mystery's trivia ace

More than a dozen fans had an enjoyable dinner at a local Cajun-Creole restaurant owned by Elmore Leonard's son Chris and his wife. A large committee made this LCC a success, with Ellie Warder handling four different functions. The program was varied, though Friday's panels leaned in the direction of police procedure, with two DNA "Fingerprinting Workshops." Literacy continued as the charity of choice, and there were both silent and live auctions to help Literacy Volunteers of Tucson.

Alaska in mid-February seemed a dubious attraction, but there was general agreement that Left Coast Crime at the Anchorage Hilton in 2001 was a good convention. Even the weather cooperated, with temperatures generally in the twenties. (The convention had been jokingly named "Death Below Zero.") Many attendees took the opportunity of their first Alaska trips to spend a few extra days viewing scenery and wildlife; some reported seeing moose on the streets of downtown Anchorage.

To encourage Alaska's native population to read, the local branch of Sisters in Crime organized a project called "Authors to the Bush," in which writers volunteered to go in small planes to remote settlements to promote reading. Dana Stabenow and Linda Billington chaired this convention in which Michael Connelly was U.S. Guest of Honor, Lindsey Davis was International Guest of Honor, and Andi Shechter, active in prior LCCs, was Fan Guest of Honor.

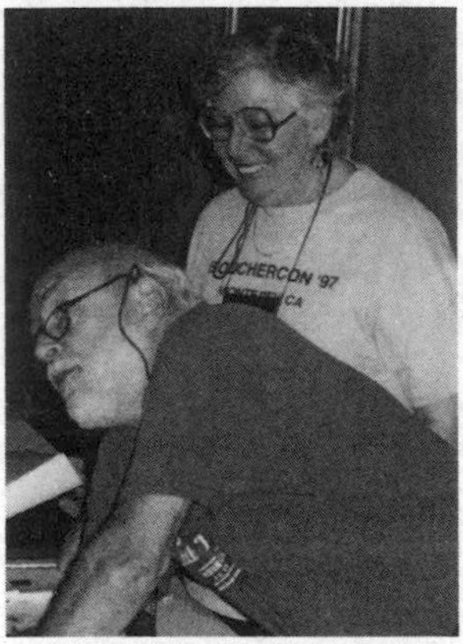

Bill and Toby Gottfried, active in Left Coast Crime and Bouchercon conferences

Recognizing Portland, Oregon's damp climate, Left Coast Crime 2002 at the Columbia River Doubletree Hotel was called "Slugs and Roses." Bryan Barrett and Debbie Cross were Co-Chairs. Laurie R. King and Steven Saylor, known primarily for their historical mysteries, were Guests of Honor. G.M. Ford of Seattle was Toastmaster. Don Herron, possibly the most knowledgeable person about Dashiell Hammett, was Fan Guest of Honor.

Mary Mason saw fewer collectors in the book room, though many who attended took the time to visit the world-famous Powell's bookstore. Few hospitality suites received as high ratings as the one at the Doubletree.

Left Coast Crime came to the Pasadena Hilton in 2003. Mindful of nearby Hollywood, it was called "Lights! Camera! Murder!" One 1991 Bouchercon problem that had not been solved was annoying spillover of sound when the main ballroom was split into two meeting rooms because there were no soundproof dividers. Otherwise, this LCC was a success, enjoyed by its largest crowd to date, about six hundred people.

Robert Crais was Guest of Honor; Jerrilyn Farmer was Toastmistress. Helen Howerton was Chair. The famous radio play *Sorry, Wrong Number* was recreated at the Pasadena Library, with attendees bused there and back. Sue Feder, the great proponent of historical mysteries, was Fan Guest of Honor.

Los Angeles writer-fan Paul Bishop had an interesting conference. After a panel called "Cops vs. Coppers," regarding the U.S. police and their British counterparts, he went to compete in the Los Angeles Marathon, finishing the twenty-six-plus miles in three hours forty-three minutes. He also received "hate mail" from the wife of a judge who was in attendance at his panel. She thought he was being disrespectful to the law, despite his twenty-six years of service in the LAPD.

The Doubletree Hotel in Monterey, scene of 1997 Bouchercon, was the locale for the equally successful 2004 Left Coast Crime, "Sand, Seals, Otters, and Mystery," with about eight hundred fifty attending. Bill and Toby Gottfried were Co-Chairs; Sharan Newman and Walter Moseley were the Guests of Honor. Newman did a slide show on the art, history, and costuming of twelfth-century France, the setting for her historical mysteries. Gillian Roberts was Toastmistress, and Richard Lupoff received a Lifetime Achievement Award. A new award was instituted, the Bruce Alexander History Mystery Award, in honor of the writer who had died three months before LCC. The committee also instituted a one-time award, the Otter, for the best mystery set in the Monterey area. The auction benefitted the Friends of Sea Otters, and the opening reception was at the renowned Monterey Bay Aquarium. Bryan Barrett and Thom Walls, very active in prior LCCs, were Fan Guests of Honor.

El Paso, Texas, was as far east of the Pacific as any Left Coast Crime site and also the farthest south, in this case along the U.S. border with Mexico. (The con title posed the question "Is Something Mysterious Afoot on the Border?") Patricia A. Phillips and Mary A. Sarber were Co-Chairs for LCC 2005, which was held at the Camino Real Hotel.

S. J. Rozan and Paco Taibo II were American Guest of Honor and International Guest of Honor respectively. (Taibo lives in Mexico.) Texas writer Rick Riordan was Toastmaster. Ernie Bulow was the Fan Guest of Honor. He was a bookseller and fan who had written book-length interviews with two of his favorite writers, Tony Hillerman and Lawrence Block.

Brett Halliday, creator of famous private detective Mike Shayne, was the "Ghost of Honor." While Halliday is best known for his Miami, Florida settings, his early work was often set in El Paso or in Mexico. A panel was devoted to Halliday and Shayne, with Ted Fitzgerald, Gary Warren Niebuhr, and yours truly discussing them.

The opening night ceremony was held next door to the hotel at the El Paso Museum of Art, a small venue but one that was worth revisiting. The main tourist highlight for many visitors was El Paso's neighboring Mexican sister city, Juarez. The proximity to Mexico understandably led to interest in *El Dia de los Muertos* (The Day of the Dead), a holiday Mexico celebrates. It was discussed in the convention program book.

The 2006 Left Coast Crime was on a left coast and near a body of water, but it was in Bristol, England! Co-Chairs Myles Allfrey and Adrian Muller had the idea and bid successfully for LCC; they called it "For a Bloody Good Time." Their convention had an attendance of about 500. Anne Perry was the U.K. Guest of Honor. Jeffery Deaver was the U.S. Guest of Honor. A mainland Europe Guest of Honor was Boris Akunin, who said that the first print runs of his mysteries were 500,000 in Russia. Lee Child was Toastmaster and mentioned that Tom Cruise had bought the rights to play his Jack Reacher in films.

Donna Moore was the U.K. Fan Guest of Honor. The U.S. Fan Guests of Honor were Bill and Toby Gottfried of Northern California, two great supporters of LCC from its beginning.

Among the panels there were popular quizzes, one called "Stump the Expert." In another quiz, thriller writers Gail Lynds,

Barry Eisler, and Zoë Sharp were given the task of solving a "cozy" mystery.

The setting in 2006 was the Marriott Royal Hotel. Near it, in Millennium Square, is a statue of Cary Grant, who was said to have stayed at the Marriott when he came to Bristol to visit his mother.

LCC returned to Seattle in 2007, at the Renaissance Seattle Hotel for what was called "Reading in the Rain." Andi Shechter was Chair. Guests of Honor were Gayle Lynds and her late husband Michael Collins (pseudonym of Dennis Lynds, who had died recently). The Toastmaster was Gary Phillips, he of the booming voice. Fan Guests of Honor were Kara Robinson and Diane Kovacs, the two people responsible for DorothyL the popular internet mystery chat site.

In 2008 LCC returned to Colorado, this time to Denver for "Murder on the Rocks" at the Adams Mark Hotel, where the 2000 Bouchercon had been held. Christine Goff and Suzanne Proulx were Co-Chairs. Colorado writer Stephen White was Guest of Honor. Elaine Viets was Toastmistress. Because of her popular culinary mysteries, Joanne Pence was recognized as "Celebrity Chef." Parnell Hall was "Celebrity Singer." The Fan Guest of Honor was Michael Masliah, a devoted attendee at Bouchercons and Left Coast Crime despite an impairment that made walking difficult for him.

Despite winter weather outside, a Hawaiian costume contest was held before the banquet in anticipation of LCC going to Hawaii in 2009.

Like most mystery convention committees, the one for LCC in 2009 devoted two years working on theirs at the Waikoloa Beach Resort on the Big Island of Hawaii. Naming it "Say Aloha to Crime," they also billed it as "The Unconventional Convention." The committee, with Bill and Toby Gottfried, as Co-Chairs, had lots of experience, having put on a Bouchercon in 1997 and a Left Coast Crime in 2004, both in Monterey, California.

The Guests of Honor were Rhys Bowen and Barry Eisler,

two popular writers of very different mysteries. Lee Goldberg, television screenwriter and writer of novels and short stories about Monk, the obsessive-compulsive sleuth, was Toastmaster. Not surprising was the choice of "Ghost of Honor," Earl Derr Biggers, creator of Charlie Chan, the most famous Hawaiian detective. Pam Dehnke and Vallery Feldman were Fan Guests of Honor. Some panels were held outdoors on the beach, beneath palm trees.

Left Coast Crime came back to Los Angeles in 2010, with the theme "Get Booked in L.A." Jean Utley was Chair. Jan Burke and Lee Child were the Guests of Honor. Bill Fitzhugh was Toastmaster. Janet Rudolph was Fan Guest of Honor. For thirty years she had published *Mystery Readers Journal* and headed the Mystery Readers International group. She had also been a member of a mystery-reading group that had met Tuesday nights for over thirty years. At this convention she was auctioneer for an event supporting adult literacy.

A day was devoted to the Crime Lab Project for which Burke has worked to promote forensic science. Tours of labs were limited to seventy-five people and sold out weeks before they were held on the Wednesday prior to the con.

Belying the "wisdom" that no one walks in Los Angeles, there was a walking tour of crime scenes. A special award, called the "Panik," to honor the late Paul Anik, who was to be LCC chair but had died, was given for the Best Los Angeles Noir novel.

LCC, dubbed "The Big Chile," came to Santa Fe, New Mexico, in 2011 at the La Fonda, a leading hotel in that town for almost a century. A thinly disguised version of the hotel had been used in Dorothy B. Hughes's famous Santa Fe mystery: *Ride the Pink Horse*. Hughes and Frances Crane, both of whom had written mysteries set in this area, were "Ghosts of Honor."

Pari Noiskin Taichert was Chair and organizer. Martin Cruz Smith was Lifetime Achievement honoree. Guests of Honor were Margaret Coel and Steven Havill, who write about Colorado and southern New Mexico respectively. Big Steve Brewer, creator of Albuquerque private eye "Bubba" Mabry, was Toastmaster. I was Fan Guest of Honor.

A special award was given out, in addition to the usual "Lefty" and Bruce Alexander Award. The Hillerman Sky Award went to the mystery that best captures the Southwestern landscape.

Each LCC gets to create a catchphrase for itself, sometimes two. LCC 2012 was "Capitol Crimes," logical since it was held in California's capital city, Sacramento. Similarly, "Mining for Murder" was appropriate for the location because of nineteenth-century gold mining nearby. Six hundred people attended.

Former police officer Robin Burcell and Cindy Sample were Co-Chairs.

Guests of Honor were John Lescroart and Jacqueline Winspear. Thriller writer James Rollins was called "Spotlight Guest of Honor." Toastmistress was Harley Jane Kozak. Fan Guest of Honor Noemi Levine earned his being so honored, having been Treasurer at three Left Coast Crimes.

Two pages of the program were devoted to a memorial to Enid Schantz, who had died in August 2011. She was a great supporter of LCC and Bouchercon and had helped put on conventions in Colorado.

Besides the "Lefty" and "Bruce Alexander Awards", a one-time award, The Golden Nugget, was given for the Best Mystery Set in California. Continuing the mining theme, the "Eureka" Award was given for the Best First Mystery.

When panels started at 1:30 p.m. on Thursday, there was the now almost obligatory panel for people attending their first mystery convention. Another tradition is the silent auction, with the prizes prominently displayed so potential buyers can look at them all day long to assess whether they want to bid.

More children were attending Left Coast, and a panel called "Start 'Em Young" was devoted to Children's and Young Adult's mysteries.

Snow, a possibility in Colorado during much of the year, came to LCC, "Where Murder Is the Last Resort," held at the Cheyenne Mountain Resort in Colorado Springs, March 21–23, 2013, though officially it was Spring. Chris Goff and Suzanne Proulx were Co-Chairs for their second Colorado LCC. Guests of Honor were Laura Lippman and Craig Johnson of Longmire fame. David Corbett was Toastmaster. "Ghost of Honor" was Stephen J. Cannell, writer-producer of hit television crime shows, including *The Rockford Files*. Fan Guests of Honor were Tom and, posthumously, Enid Schantz. They had put on conventions and, through their Rue Morgue Press, kept many worthwhile books alive.

Snow on Day One of LCC created problems, as did snow at the end. Special Guest Lou Diamond Phillips, of the *Longmire* series, arrived late after having been stuck most of the day in the Albuquerque airport. Another late arrival was Twist Phelan who got married in Denver just before the convention started. Many writer friends attended the wedding.

Parnell Hall, called the convention's "Troubadour," enlivened this LCC as he had so many other conventions for more than twenty years. He dressed in "drag" to play his series character The Puzzle Lady for a panel "Does This Shoulder Holster Make Me Look Fat?" a feature of a concealed weapon fashion show. He also sang his latest composition "Murder is the Last Resort."

Hardy sightseers among convention attendees traveled to the Garden of the Gods near Pikes Peak, at 14,000 feet, causing altitude sickness among some.

Thanks to the popularity of Monterey, California, as a resort, there were close to a thousand people at Left Coast Crime (called "Calamari Crime") in 2014 at the Portola Hotel and Spa. Two couples (Bill and Toby Gottfried and Lucinda Surber and Stan Ulrich) shared Chair duties. The U.S. Guest of Honor was Cara Black, who writes mysteries set in Paris; Louise Penny of Canada was the International Guest; Sue Grafton was honored as a Special

Guest, and LCC used a variation on her titles, announcing her as "G Is for Guest. Bill Pronzini and Marcia Muller, Guests of Honor at the first LCC, received Lifetime Achievement honors. Collin Wilcox, who had been a popular San Francisco writer, was "Ghost of Honor." Toastmaster was Brad Parks. Fan Guest of Honor was Sue Trowbridge, a website designer and the webmaster for this LCC.

William Kent Krueger, always more cognizant of what writers owe to fan-readers, acknowledged in this convention how intelligent readers help authors, saying "writers only have to give them a snippet, and they take it from there."

In addition to the "Lefty" and Bruce Alexander Awards, "The Squid" was given for the Best Mystery Set Within the U.S. and "The Calamari" for Best Mystery Set Anywhere in the World. Appropriate for a convention featuring seafood, tourists were attracted to the Monterey Aquarium and Fisherman's Wharf.

Portland, Oregon, was called "Crimelandia" for the twenty-fifth Left Coast Crime in 2015. (The name is a take-off on a show *Portlandia,* set there.) L.J. Sellers and Bill Cameron were Co-Chairs. Six hundred fifty people signed up, and there were another thirty on day passes. Guests of Honor were Tim Hallinan and Chelsea Cain. Special Guest was Philip Margolin, like Cain, a local author. The Toastmaster was Gar Anthony Haywood. At 2015 LCC a local Portland group, Friends of Mystery, considered by some America's most active mystery fan group, was collectively Fan Guest of Honor. It was described by Cameron as "dedicated to the study and promotion of all aspects of mystery, including fiction, true crime, and the investigation and solving of crime."

In addition to the "Lefty" and Bruce Alexander Awards, the Rose was presented for the best mystery in the LCC region and the Rosebud for the best debut mystery.

Lucinda Surber and Stan Ulrich helped make this LCC run smoothly. They were Awards Co-Chairs. Stan was Registrar and Treasurer. Lucinda was Publisher Liaison and Volunteer

Coordinator. The weather was uncharacteristic for Portland, with sunshine the first few days. The Auction raised $2,325 for SMART (Start Making a Reader Today), a literacy group.

Among the most popular panels were ones on sex in the mystery, "Is That a Gun in Your Pocket," and "Sweet and Lowdown—A Cozy/Noir Summit."

Many of the blogs written by attendees when they returned home included photos. A few apologized because they had NOT taken any "selfies."

Left Coast Crime returned to Arizona for "The Great Cactus Caper," 2016 in Phoenix. Ingrid Willis, who had chaired the Long Beach Bouchercon, chaired this LCC. American Guest of Honor was Greg Hurwitz. Ann Cleeves was International Guest of Honor and talked of her passion for libraries. She has adapted her fifth D.I. Vera Stanhope novel, *The Glass Room,* into a packet including the script, a CSI report, and even whodunit forms that can be completed by an audience and can be put on by libraries and reading groups. Catriona McPherson, originally from Scotland but now living in northern California, was Toastmistress. Chantelle Aimee Osman, a lawyer, editor, and website creator, was Fan Guest of Honor.

Seven hundred fans registered. Many of them also performed the behind-the-scenes work that goes into putting on a mystery convention: registering people, answering questions, helping at panels, and stuffing book bags given to registrants. The panels included some favorite topics, including bibliomysteries ("Murder on the Books"), discussion and recommendation of favorite books. The biblio-version of speed dating was again present as forty authors rotated among tables of readers, making a "Table-Side Pitch" for their latest books. There were many first-time authors and many fans who longed to be published. A popular panel was "The Transition from Fan to Published Author." Rhys Bowen, with her wonderful sense of humor, moderated the popular "Liars' Panel." The panelists told a story, and the audience had to guess whether it was truthful or a lie.

Left Coast Crime returned to Hawaii in 2017 for what was called "Honolulu Havoc." This time the setting was the Hilton Hawaiian Village, part of the Waikiki Beach Resort in Honolulu. Gay Coburn Gale was Chair. Almost 500 attended despite room rates of $200 and more. Jonathan and Faye Kellerman received Lifetime Achievement Awards. Dana Stabenow of Alaska was U.S. Guest of Honor. Colin Cotterill was International Guest of Honor. Although he has joint British and Australian citizenship, he lives in and writes of Southeast Asia. Laurie R. King was Toastmistress. The "Ghost of Honor" was again Earl Derr Biggers, still, eighty years after he died, the most famous mystery writer who wrote of Hawaii. On Thursday evening they showed two Charlie Chan movies. These films are rarely, if ever, shown on the U.S. mainland now because of political correctness, though Chan is an exemplary father and detective.

Most people who attended took extra time to see the sights, including visiting some of the other Hawaiian Islands. Even during the convention some took time for whale watching, visiting the Pearl Harbor Historic site, touring the Dole Plantation, and the Kualoa Private Nature Reserve. There were three swimming pools at the hotel. Some blamed all these activities for less-than-full attendance at normally popular panels, even though free mimosa drinks were given out at one panel.

Special events included Friday's "Homicide and Hibiscus," solving a mystery for a literacy charity, a new author breakfast, and writers pairing to host a table during the Lefty Awards banquet.

Before the first panel on Thursday, there was what has become traditional: the Speed Dating session. Readers sat at sixteen tables as authors, given two minutes each, rotated around the tables making a pitch for their latest books. Though there was an emphasis on current novels, the past was not forgotten. Martin Edwards, whose *The Golden Age of Murder* (2015) has won Edgar, Agatha, and Macavity Awards, led a Golden Age panel.

In 2018 LCC came to the Nugget Casino resort in Reno, well actually Sparks, a few miles outside Reno, Nevada. It was called "Crime on the Comstock," to commemorate the area's mining history. Guests of Honor were Naomi Hirahara and William Kent Krueger. Todd Borg was the Toastmaster. McAvoy Layne imitated Mark Twain who once lived in this area of the Comstock silver lode. For the first time since1997 Left Coast Crime did not have a Fan Guest of Honor.

The convention was small, fewer than five hundred people, and intimate and friendly. It proved to be a lovefest between the writers who attended and the fans and those who organized it. The chair was Lynn Bremer. Also playing major roles were Lucinda Surber and Stan Ulrich. There were two tracks of programming, but also many five- and fifteen-minute sessions at which fans could talk with writers. The favorite event seemed to be an improvisation "panel" with Naomi Hirahara assigning roles to people to everyone's enjoyment.

The weather didn't entirely cooperate; it was winter after all. It was cold and rainy part of the time, and new snow could be seen in the nearby mountains. Side trips were canceled because not enough people had signed up. The casinos permitted smoking. There was supposed to be a filtered air system, but for many people it didn't work well enough. By arranging a guaranteed number of people, Stan Ulrich was able to arrange a smoke-free bar.

Thirty years ago there seemed to be antagonism between authors and fans. Fortunately, that no longer is true. At LCC authors went out of their way to meet fans, and to treat them to drinks. For example, a group of six authors who call themselves "The Chicks on the Case" and say they write "kick-butt cozies" gave a cocktail party for fans. Kent Krueger, always a writer who appreciates his public, sent a warm "Thank You" to those who had run the convention. He said, "The world awaits with all its uncertainties and challenges but because of my time here in Reno the rivers of goodwill I've been swept up in for days and the great outpouring of affection I've felt, I return to that world with my heart full of energy and my spirits buoyed with hope."

Chapter Twenty

DEADLY PLEASURES (1993–)

With *The Mystery FANcier* in its last stages, Bill Deeck contemplated editing and publishing a replacement. He considered *Mysterious Maunderings* as a title, then later *The Criminous Connoisseur.* However, his announced plans in *MDM* and *TMF* failed to draw much response, let alone the balance of two-thirds articles and checklists and one-third reviews that he hoped to achieve. The material Deeck had received was turned over to George Easter, a lawyer who lives near Salt Lake City, for the fan magazine he called *Deadly Pleasures* and launched with the Spring 1993 issue.

The first issue of Easter's quarterly magazine contained twenty pages. By his second issue, he doubled that. Each issue had interviews, usually with the author who was the subject of its cover article. In the early issues, articles about and reviews of older books took up considerable space. Bill Deeck's review column, "The Backward Reviewer," took four pages in the first issue and five in the second. Easter quickly put together a stable of leading fan writers, including Philip L. Scowcroft and Martin Edwards from England. His early reviewers and writers also included Allen J. Hubin, Don Sandstrom, Sue Feder, Barry Gardner, and Maryell

Cleary, who wrote "Vintage Crime." Ubiquitous as ever, I moved my "It's About Crime" column from the defunct *TMF*.

Early in his publishing career, Easter started two participatory features that made *Deadly Pleasures* distinctive. One was his "Quarterly Question," which continued until issue No. 48, when he "retired" it since response to it had become sporadic. The last question was: "What is the best mystery/crime novel you have read this decade-so far?"

In his third issue he started what is arguably *DP*'s most popular feature, "Reviewed to Death." Easter obtains multiple copies of a new book and sends them to his regular reviewers. It is fascinating to see how differently six or more people review the same book.

Another feature enjoyed by many readers was "Atlantic Asides," a column by Mat Coward, like Edwards, a British fan-reviewer as well as a writer of fiction.

Deadly Pleasures kept growing, to fifty-six pages in No. 4 (Winter 1994), to 64 pages in No. 10 (Fall 1995), reaching 88 pages in No. 38 (Spring 2003), though it has since stabilized at eighty-four pages. It soon became apparent that what its readers most want is reviews of current books. Articles on older writers and books became less frequent. Mary "Maggie" Mason, who wrote a column on collectible books of the 1990s, switched to a review column. *DP* developed a new crew of reviewers, including Mason, Ted Hertel, and Larry Gandle, who reviewed first mysteries and each year's Edgar nominees.

Gradually, the number of new reviews (and previews) increased, taking up more than 70 percent of *Deadly Pleasures*. With the exception of Philip L. Scowcroft, hardly anyone wrote about older books, though I usually included reviews of some in my column, "It's About Crime." The reviews of new books have been invariably positive, something that did not jibe with my own reading of many of them. Finally, I stirred up some debate with a letter Easter published on his website and in *DP*'s letters column. I said there was not enough about past mysteries, too many current reviews, and too little controversy in *DP*. I also criticized Mat Coward's column for being less about crime fiction than about politics and the criminal justice system, usually discussed from a decidedly anti-American viewpoint. Eight readers responded, all saying I was wrong and that they liked *DP* as it was. Mat Coward left after issue No. 45 (Fall 2005), and I felt bad and blamed myself. I had only wanted him to write a mystery-related column because he is a very good and humorous writer.

Those who disagreed with me pointed out that space was too precious to waste on poor books, hence their reviews were generally positive. I let that sink in for a few years, then decided to test it by analyzing the books "assigned" in the "Reviewed to Death" column for twenty issues. There, books they didn't like still had to be reviewed. I found that almost two-third of the books in "Reviewed to Death" received an above average rating from reviewers other than myself. I found only about 30 percent of those books above average. I found 58 percent of the books below average. My fellow reviewers found only 22 percent below average. I printed my findings in a letter in issue No. 63 (Fall 2010) because I feel it is almost as important for a reviewer to tell potential readers what to avoid as it is to recommend. I received no reaction. Differing tastes in reading has not prevented *Deadly Pleasure*'s fans from becoming close friends. One of the highlights of Bouchercons occurs when contributors to *DP* get together.

Since 1997 *Deadly Pleasures* has given out the Barry Awards, honoring one of its most popular reviewers, the late Barry Gardner. These awards, which recognize Best Novel, Best First Novel, Best Thriller, and Best Paperback Original are voted on by *DP* readers, and presented at Bouchercon. Lack of response led to the Short Story Barry, for which I had been the one-man nominating committee, being canceled.

Since 2001 *Deadly Pleasures* has given out the Don Sandstrom Memorial Award for Lifetime Achievement in Mystery Fandom at Bouchercon.

Russ Isabella gave up his post of Associate Editor to pursue other interests. He was replaced by Dr. Larry Gandle, who, besides his medical practice, has at various times reviewed all the nominees for Edgar, Thriller, and CWA Dagger Awards. As a result of this self-imposed "job," he concluded that there were too many overly long books being published and some were of indifferent quality. Gandle has proven he is one of *DP*'s tougher reviewers, one who doesn't hesitate to use "DNF" (Did Not Finish) when he considers it appropriate. He eventually cut back on some of those categories, but in Issue No. 78 (Spring 2016) he still reviewed eighteen books, the Edgar nominees in the Best Novel, Best First Novel, and Best Paperback Original categories. He also has a *DP* review column "Lookin' for a Few Good Books." He cut back to eight books in Winter/Spring 2017 but reviewed thirty-five and twenty-three books respectively in the next two issues.

Gandle has wisely written about fans investing in the so-called "hypermodern" books of the 1990s, for example Sue Grafton's *"A" Is for Alibi* and Patricia Cornwell's *Post-Mortem,* hoping to make money. Many of these books have decreased in value. His advice: "Collect only what you love and don't consider it a true investment."

Many have talked about encouraging the next wave of fan writers. Gandle's daughters, Cassandra and Lauren, when they were teen-agers, reviewed Young Adult mysteries for *DP*. Eleven-year-old Kyle Dreher became an occasional *DP* reviewer, starting with John Connolly's *The Gates* in issue No. 59 (Fall 2009).

For a short while *Mystery News* joined *Deadly Pleasures* in sponsoring the Barry Awards. When it ceased publishing in 2009, *Deadly Pleasures* benefited by acquiring two of their reviewers, Maddy Van Hertbruggen, who reviewed in the column "Her Madjesty's Decrees," and David Magayna, who reviews audio mysteries as well as books.

Many of *DP*'s columnists have been writing for it for many years. Among them are Ted Hertel's "From the Waterfront," formerly "I Cover the Lakefront," "Maggie's Cozy Mystery Café" by Maggie Mason, "A Bevy of Mysteries" by Bev De Weese, who eventually gave up her column. "History Mystery Potpourri" has had many contributors, though Sally Sugarman is currently writing it alone.

One of the more unusual *DP* reviewers is Steele Curry, who spends his summers on the Greek island of Skiathos. Curry reads about thirty to thirty-five books each summer on his terrace, which overlooks the Aegean Sea. Then he reviews many of them in his column called "A Greek Reading Feast."

Besides emphasizing reviews of new books, *DP* is definitely thriller-oriented. Easter said in 2010 that we are in "The Golden Age of Thriller Fiction." Recently, there has been more interest shown in the pages of *DP* in older books and writers. Until his death in 2016 Roger M. Sobin discussed older crime films in his column "Real to Reel," one that had outlived *DAPA-EM* and *Mystery News* in which it had appeared. George H. Madison has written a series of articles about Golden Age detectives such as Hercule Poirot, old films including those based on Cornell Woolrich's works, and the many mystery writers whose work pays homage to Rex Stout's Nero Wolfe.

Beginning in 2016 Brian Ritt's articles about the important writers of paperback originals, including Jim Thompson, Gil Brewer, and David Goodis, have appeared in *DP*. George Easter tracked down and interviewed Canadian writer Ted Wood, once very popular, who hadn't published any books in over twenty years. The interview tells much about the publishing industry today.

Major portions of Mike Ripley's column "Getting Away with Murder" are from the online edition of *Shots Magazine* and are reprinted with its permission. He discusses the current crime scene in England, as well as reviewing books. However, Ripley is clearly a fan as well as a popular author. Because George Easter is an admitted Anglophile, Ripley's column is not the only portion of *Deadly Pleasures* to focus on British mysteries. Issues may contain up to six pages of reviews of English mysteries, and several pages are often devoted to lists of "What's New in the U.K."

Once a year Easter asks his contributors to pick their favorite book of the previous year and also to select a past favorite and a book they read that provided them with "unexpected pleasure."

The "*DP* Calendar" is one of the most complete listing of meetings and conventions to come. The magazine provides much information about current trends in publishing, e.g., it was one of the first sources to write about e-books. *DP* also takes note of deaths in the mystery community with heartfelt pieces about Ed Hoch, P.D. James, Robert Barnard, Barbara Seranella, and others.

Chapter Twenty-One

OTHER FAN MAGAZINES, ORGANIZATIONS, AND CONVENTIONS: 1990S

Australian Fan Magazines (1990–2003)

Distance and expense keep Australian fans from attending many mystery conventions, though I have met Graeme Flanagan, Gayle Lovett, and Graeme Windsor in the United States. Much of the interest in Australian mysteries is in the hardboiled school, and that was the main focus of *Mean Streets*, the Australian quarterly journal that started in October 1990 and had an unfortunately short life. It was edited and published by Stuart Coupe of Bondi Beach, a suburb of Sydney.

Its first issue featured articles on Alan Yates, Australia's most prolific mystery writer under his "Carter Brown" pseudonym. However, much of the magazine was devoted to American writers, though Coupe had an interview with a new hardboiled Australian writer Marele Day. There were also articles on the "mean streets" of Los Angeles and about Sue Grafton, Elmore Leonard, James Crumley's Milo Milodragovitch, and paperback cover art, mostly for U.S. books. The last was balanced by an article by Graeme Flanagan on Phantom Books, Australia's leading paperback publisher of the 1950s and early 1960s. There were two short stories, including one by Peter Corris featuring his private eye Cliff Hardy. Australia's leading anthologist, Stephen Knight, wrote an overview "Old Crime in New Form: Australian Thrillers Today."

Flanagan, from Canberra, started his own magazine, *PI News*, in 1991, and, as the title indicates, it was mainly about private detective fiction. It included news, checklists, and interviews. Its last issue, No. 8, was dated July 1993. Another Australian magazine, also now defunct, was *Crime Factory*, which lasted for nine issue between 2001 and 2003. It covered worldwide English-language crime writing, with an emphasis on the hardboiled. To the usual mix of articles, interviews and reviews was added occasional graphic art fiction.

Mostly Murder (1990–1998)

Its format was that of a tabloid newspaper. Jay W.K. Setliff of Dallas was editor-publisher of *Mostly Murder*, which began in 1990 and contained mostly reviews, except for the occasional interview. Its reviewers included Barry Gardner, considered one of the best fan reviewer, as well as Dallas booksellers Geraldine Galentree and Barry and Terry Phillips. *Mostly Murder* lasted until the May/June 1998 issue.

Midwest Mystery & Suspense Conventions (1990–1992)

Despite having lost its Bouchercon bid for 1990, Omaha had ambitions for 1993, and its committee, led by "Chuck" Levitt of the Little Professor Book Store, decided to prove Omaha's credentials by holding a convention. Don Cole, an important member of his committee, admitted that the first Omaha convention "did start out as a protest con, though we were not ready to admit it, but it quickly became an entirely new concept, a general fan convention of a smaller and more intimate nature."

Fans at Omaha: Orietta Hardy-Sayles, Leila Dobscha, Bob Samoan, Linda Toole, Marv Lachman, and Gary Warren Niebuhr

Though Malice Domestic preceded Omaha by a year, it was limited to one subgenre.

Omaha succeeded in its goal—not in the protest since it occurred three months before Bouchercon, and some people attended both—but in providing a memorable, relaxed convention. Cole described it as "not a regional, as such, but a new national convention for the mystery fan." Indeed, in addition to a large Midwest contingent, fans and writers came from both coasts, as well as the Southwest and Rockies. It was held May 25–27 at the Holiday Inn Central, in whose labyrinthine corridors attendees frequently became lost. Jeremiah Healy reported he called Room Service and, after placing his order, was asked for directions to his room.

Four hundred ten people attended in 1990, but *MDM* correspondents were most noticeable. They took over the lobby, moving the furniture into a circle, talking and laughing late into the night. Ann Williams reported, "I never found myself wanting for a rowdy group in which to make a total fool of myself. But then what are conventions for?" Ori Hardy-Sayles couldn't remember ever laughing as hard. The imaginary fan George Kramer, invented at the 1989 Bouchercon, was discussed and became "real" as Bob Samoian took out a subscription to *MDM* in his name and wrote letters for him. In one letter "Kramer" claimed that his first mystery was going to be published by "Orange Grove Press," an imaginary California publisher. Relying on information in *MDM*, Allen J. Hubin was going to include Kramer in his bibliography, but I spotted the entry in time to assure him it was fake news.

Omaha was a relatively inexpensive convention, with early registration thirty-five dollars. The Saturday night buffet banquet was only eighteen dollars. Clive Cussler was Guest of Honor, and Jim Huang's *Drood Review of Mystery* was honored as a fan publication. At the banquet, authors were seated at various tables, allowing them to mingle with fans. Barbara Paul, who sat at my table, seemed unfamiliar with the hilarity and inside jokes of mystery fans, though she had attended science fiction conventions. The only drawback of the banquet was a long-winded welcome by the representative of Omaha's mayor, one more appropriate if attendees were voters in that November's election.

Panels were good in Omaha, including Ellen Nehr leading a discussion of "Little Old Ladies of Crime." When Joan Hess missed the beginning of that early Sunday panel, she got caught up in Omaha's atmosphere and picketed the room, saying she had been thrown off the panel. Gary Warren Niebuhr moderated a hometown private eye panel, and there was a panel called "Murder in the Classroom," about how mysteries are taught at the college level. Half-hour autographing sessions after panels were a popular feature, allowing fans to get books signed without missing the program.

The funniest moments of the Omaha con occurred in the lobby Saturday night after the banquet. At least four honeymoon couples appeared in full wedding regalia, though all drove up not in limousines, but in red 4x4 trucks! Ronnie Klaskin asked what drew honeymooners to this Holiday Inn and was told they had big Jacuzzis. Using my best Raymond Chandleresque voice, I repeated *"The Big Jacuzzi"* to sound like his *The Big Sleep*. Niebuhr thought it would be a great title for a private eye story and said he would write it.

This convention resulted in more bonding among fans than any other. Cole said, "It was like a family reunion," and Klaskin said, "*MDM* is becoming quite a family at these conventions." When, on Sunday morning, a rumor circulated that Mike Nevins had suffered a heart attack, there was genuine concern until he appeared, albeit pale. He had had a severe gall bladder attack.

If the contributors to *MDM* unofficially dominated the first Midwest convention, they were officially recognized at the second, May 24–26, 1991, at the same Holiday Inn. Bob Napier, *MDM*'s publisher-editor was honored, along with Mary Higgins Clark, Guest of Honor. There was an *MDM* breakfast, and *MDM* 72 1/2, a special issue roasting Napier. Niebuhr reported, "We spent the con signing each other's magazines as if we were graduating from high school."

The previous year's "How to Get Published" panel, moderated by Parnell Hall, was repeated, with a second hour allotted to it because it had been so popular. At the banquet, for the first time, Hall sang "You Gotta Kill 'Em," his song about methods of murder, one he would repeat at other conventions.

At the third (and last) Midwest convention, May 29–31, 1992, *The Big Jacuzzi* was published, but it was not a novel—or even a story—by Niebuhr. Having difficulty in converting the title into fiction, he agreed to publish it and co-edit it with Ori Hardy-Sayles. Following ground rules Niebuhr set, six fans submitted mystery parodies, all of which were titled "The Big Jacuzzi." (Each contributor claimed to have written the title story.) The 1990 event of the brides and grooms pulling up in pickup trucks was part of each story. The entire print run sold out quickly, and it became a short-lived cult classic, with successful authors asking the amateur fan-parodists to autograph copies they bought.

A popular Friday night panel was the first of many to come on forgotten private eyes. Beverly DeWeese spoke of Fredric

Brown's Ed and Am Hunter, Mike Nevins discussed William Ard's Timothy Dane, and I recalled Thomas B. Dewey's "Mac." Especially popular was "Gat Heat," hosted by Robert J. Randisi, who adapted the format of "The Tonight Show" to the mystery with hilarious results.

George Easter truly became part of fandom while attending his first Omaha convention in 1992. Though a longtime collector, he learned the meaning of "booking" and was part of several expeditions to bookstores before the convention began, some that were fifty miles away in Lincoln, Nebraska. Meeting other fanatical collectors, he said, "What a relief to know that I am somewhat normal—even if it is only among a very small group of people."

Though most would return to Omaha for Bouchercon in 1993, those who attended the final Midwest in 1992 left with feelings of sadness, though getting to and from Omaha led to many travel horror stories. Ori Hardy-Sayles had her return flights canceled all three years. In 1992 my luggage spent the first day of the convention in Jackson Hole, Wyoming.

Don Cole had been largely responsible for the convention, telling Levitt, who chaired it for three years, about fandom in the first place. Calling 1992's convention the "last of an era," Cole said, "We pride our con as being the 'down home' convention," and those who enjoyed its relaxed atmosphere agreed.

Perry Mason Fandom (1990–2014)

About 1990, twenty years after Erle Stanley Gardner died and his best-known sleuth was no longer a staple of network television, Jim Davidson, a thirtyish word processor from Berkeley, California, founded The National Association for the Advancement of Perry Mason. (In 1987 two other fans, Brian Kelleher and Diana Merrill, had published *The Perry Mason TV Show Book,* describing every case seen on the small screen until then.) Davidson had at least 125 members, who paid ten dollars yearly and received the *NAAPM Newsletter*. After running the club for ten years, Davidson gave it up due to other "personal commitments." However, he kept his interest in Perry Mason and in 2014 published an e-book, available on Kindle, *The Perry Mason Book: a Comprehensive Guide to America's Favorite Defender of Justice.*

DorothyL (1991–)

As fans sought more ways to communicate more quickly, it seemed clear that the internet would be turned to, leading to its famous chat group, DorothyL where one could write, see one's posting published later that day, and get responses the next day. DorothyL was created in July 1991 by two librarians, Diane Kovacs and Ann Okerson. When Okerson dropped out, Kara Robinson, another librarian, became co-moderator. There eventually came to be over two thousand members and at least fifty new messages each day. Members would review books and movies but also would discuss their personal lives. Betty Webb has described members as "sort of a family," wording previously applied to *DAPA-EM* and *MDM*. There were DorothyL events at several Bouchercons, and in 2005 Kovacs and Robinson received the MWA Raven Award. They were Fan Guests of Honor at Left Coast Crime in 2007.

With the advent of hundreds of blogs, DorothyL's role is far less critical to fan communication. It was once described as "The oldest and largest mystery email discussion group on the internet." The official website has not been updated since January 2015. It currently says, "This site is undergoing re-construction indefinitely. Will update when and if we have time."

Mid-Atlantic Mystery Book Fair and Convention; GoodisCon; NoirCon (1991–)

Deen and Jay Kogan, responsible for the 1989 Philadelphia Bouchercon, put on the Mid-Atlantic Mystery Book Fair and Convention, November 8–10, 1991, at Philadelphia's Holiday Inn on City Line Avenue. More than 200 attended. There were no banquets or award ceremonies, but there were good panels and lots of socializing. William L. DeAndrea said in TAD, "It had that some kind of neighborhoodly block party feeling that the World Convention (Bouchercon) had grown out of."

The second Mid-Atlantic in 1992 moved to a different Holiday Inn, in Philadelphia's Center City, near Independence Hall. Ronnie Klaskin found it "relaxed and intimate." Real crime intruded on crime fiction when author Tony Fennelly's fur coat and cash were stolen from her hotel room.

The third Mid-Atlantic was obviously difficult for Deen Kogan because Jay died November 5, 1993, less than a week before it began. However, she bravely helped to make it a fine convention for 334 who registered, plus eighty daily admissions. Later, in *MDM*, Deen thanked those who had offered condolences and said, "Jay thoroughly enjoyed the genre and it was an important segment of our life." Ann Williams called the convention "a mellow blend of people" but commented on the presence of three hundred fifty noisy teenagers at the hotel; they were among seven thousand in Philadelphia for a Catholic Youth Organization convention. When a priest in the elevator apologized to her for their noise, she wittily replied, "That's all right Father; I forgive you."

In 1994, Deen Kogan capped membership at four hundred to allow "lots of interaction in an informal setting." At the convention she sold *The Mid-Atlantic Mysterious Cookbook* to benefit the Friends of the Free Library in Philadelphia. The popularity of Mid-Atlantic forced her reluctantly to raise the membership limit to four hundred fifty in 1995. 1996 saw the first official reception, a Friday night cocktail party. In 1997 Mid-Atlantic, which had always been held in November, moved to October 3–5 to avoid conflict with Bouchercon. Due to Kogan's work in running the 1998 Philadelphia Bouchercon, Mid-Atlantic was not held in 1998 or 1999.

Resuming October 13–15, 2000, Mid-Atlantic had a different hotel, the Wyndham Franklin Plaza, site of the 1998 Bouchercon.

There was now a Sunday lunch, with special guests Warren Murphy, S.J. Rozan, and George Pelecanos honored. Gordon Magnuson found it the "best organized of all conventions." Because of the proximity of Washington, DC, site of the 2001 Bouchercon, Mid-Atlantic was not held that year.

The 9th Mid-Atlantic, September 27–29, 2002, opened with a Friday night reception dinner. It included presentation of the International Association of Crime Writers' Hammett Prize to Alan Furst. An unusual panel on Feng Shui demonstrated how to structure an office to help one's writing. On Sunday, Jonathan Gash conducted a writing workshop, and there was a "High Tea" to honor the mother-son writing team of Caroline and Charles Todd, who publish under the latter name.

Deen Kogan's involvement with Bouchercons in 2003 and 2005 caused her to put Mid-Atlantic on hold. She resumed in 2006 with Co-Chair Dr. Louis Boxer and the name now changed to GoodisCon, honoring the late Philadelphia writer David Goodis, whose work exemplifies noir fiction. Indeed, in 2008, though the focus was still on Goodis, the convention was now called NoirCon. One of the awards presented was the David L. Goodis Award, given to Pelecanos, whose work is in the noir tradition.

NoirCon was scheduled for November 2018, but Deen Kogan's death early in 2018 caused it to be canceled. Boxer, who worked for many years with Kogan, said he hoped that someday it can resume.

Sherlock Holmes, The Detective Magazine (1991–2006)

This started as *The Sherlock Holmes Gazette* in May 1991, changing to *Sherlock Holmes, The Detective Magazine* with issue number 20. At first it contained only articles, reviews and news. The first twelve issues were only about Holmes, but by issue number 13 there was material in the section called "Other Great Detectives," including Nero Wolfe, Philip Marlowe, Albert Campion, and Hercule Poirot. Beginning with issue 21 a Sherlockian pastiche was featured in each issue. Mike Ripley started his popular column "Getting Away with Murder" in issue 28.

There were other title changes. Beginning with issue number 47 it was called simply *Sherlock*. David Stuart Davies was editor for issues number 15 through number 65. Teddy Hayes was editor for issue number 66, when most articles were not Sherlockian. Davies returned for the last two issues, now titled *Sherlock Magazine*, and the magazine ended its run in 2006, only publishing Sherlockian material in the last two issues.

ClueFest (1992–2003)

First held at the Radisson Suites Hotel in Dallas during Easter weekend, April 17–19, 1992, ClueFest came as close to being a true fan convention as any. Caryl Thompson underwrote it to please her mother, Terry Thompson, a mystery fan who bemoaned that other conventions were too far away and expensive to attend. Wilson Tucker was Toastmaster, and Bill Crider was "Literary Guest of Honor." Mari Hall called it a "relax-a-con" as no one seemed to worry about preparation for panels, which Hall said "were decided when we arrived; most were audience participation… wherever two or three people gathered we had a panel."

Texas fans and writers James Reasoner, Joe R. Lansdale, and Bill Crider

Attendance was sparse, perhaps thirty people. Writer James Reasoner said, "I went as a fan, not as a guest, and there were times I felt like I was the only customer there. Everybody else was either a guest or a member of the convention staff."

My involvement with ClueFest began in 1993 when I was Non-Fiction Guest of Honor, due to my writing about mysteries. Sandy Cupp was its First Fan Guest of Honor, though she admitted her interest was limited to supporting her husband, Scott Cupp, a serious fan, collector, and bookseller.

Though in *MDM* she had criticized Caryl Thompson's lack of mystery convention experience the year before, Mari Hall was chosen to handle 1993 programming. Once more ClueFest's panels were non-structured, with participants recruited at the last minute. Attendance again was meager. I doubt I saw more than thirty-five people, and few were from out-of-state.

ClueFest began growing in 1994, when it was held at the Ramada Park Central, August 5–7. Barry Gardner jokingly predicted "The audience might actually outnumber the panelists on occasion this year." About 150 attended, with Bill Crider as Toastmaster. Book Tree, a Dallas bookstore operated by brothers Barry and Terry Phillips, co-sponsored it with Thompson. A highlight was a Friday night pizza party at Gardner's home. ClueFest was getting more out-of-state attendees, and Gardner's guests included Len and June Moffatt, and Bruce Taylor from California, and Steve Stilwell of Minnesota.

During its first three years there had been complaints about all three ClueFest hotels. The 1994 meeting room even lacked air conditioning! In 1995 ClueFest was held at the Harvey Hotel in suburban Addison, and there was general approval of that site. Barry Gardner was Fan Guest of Honor in 1995 and again invited visitors to a Saturday night barbecue at his house. Attendance at ClueFest was not huge, though there were at least a hundred people. Pat Hawk, the reigning expert on pseudonyms, moderated what was probably the first panel on that subject.

The Fan Guest of Honor in 1996 was Terry Klebba of suburban Dallas. Though she was not active in writing about the mystery, few fans were as avid collectors and as supportive of mystery booksellers as she. Marlys Millhiser of Colorado was a most amusing Toastmistress. This proved to be easily the most successful ClueFest so far, with attendance of about two hundred seventy-five. Panels included repeats on pseudonyms and collecting, plus a new one called "Sex and Violence: Where I Draw the Line."

Barry Gardner drove visitors to a legendary store in Denton, Texas: Recycled Books and Records. For the third year in a row, he and his wife Ellen hosted mystery fans. After ClueFest, he drove Bruce Taylor and Steve Stilwell to various Texas bookstores. Then, only four days after ClueFest, Barry died at his desk of a heart attack. Though he only became part of mystery fandom in 1992, he had, in the words of Art Scott, become "a dear friend, now irreplaceable" to fandom. Barry had informed his wife and his cardiologist that, as a smoker, he was going to live his life the way he wanted to. In the last week of his life, he smoked, enjoyed himself at a mystery convention, went booking with friends, and wrote reviews. He went as he wanted to.

Attendance in 1997 was two hundred forty-two, but some people, including Bruce Taylor, said that Barry's death made it too sad an occasion to attend. Dr. Karen Ross, a pathologist, was Fan Guest of Honor. Parnell Hall was the amusing Toastmaster. At the banquet, Bill Crider paid a touching tribute to Gardner, whose widow, Ellen, attended for the first time. She became active in fandom because it was important to Barry.

ClueFest 1997 remained, in the words of Don Sandstrom, a "laid-back and friendly convention," with only two tracks of programming. Popular panels included "Tough Guys and Dangerous Dolls" and "They Made Me This Way—Books that Shaped Me." The annual auction to help the Dallas Public Library was a success.

Walter Satterthwait and Charlaine Harris were the Fiction Guests of Honor at ClueFest in 1998. Dean James and Jan Grape were Non-Fiction Guests of Honor. Barbara Burnett Smith was Toastmistress, and Richard Centner was Fan Guest of Honor.

After ClueFest had announced its 1999 dates, July 7–9, EyeCon in St. Louis, organized by Robert Randisi of PWA, said it had selected the same weekend. Randisi stressed that this was not deliberate, just a scheduling mix-up. Predictably, attendance at

ClueFest in 1999 was down. There are only so many fans to attend mid-summer mystery conventions in hot, humid locations. Bill Crider was Non-Fiction Guest of Honor for his fan writing. Tony Fennelly was Toastmistress and gave a hilarious talk at the luncheon banquet. Fan Guest of Honor Teresa Loftin moderated six panels!

Diane Day and Steve Brewer were Guests of Honor in 2000. Maxine O'Callaghan was Toastmistress. Lauri Hart was Fan Guest of Honor. Reed Andrus, recently moved from Arizona to the Dallas suburbs, attended his first ClueFest, moderated two panels and participated in a third. Though Brewer and O'Callaghan write of private eyes, Andrus felt most authors attending were a bit too cozy for his taste. Still, he enjoyed it "despite hats and cats and amateur sleuths."

Bill Crider, who had attended every ClueFest, was Special Decade Guest of Honor at its tenth anniversary in 2001, held at the Harvey Hotel in another Dallas suburb, Plano. Frances Butt was Fan Guest of Honor. There was discussion of the increasing separation between new electronic publishing and traditional books with advances and print runs.

The popular Jan Burke was chosen for Fiction Guest of Honor in 2002, but the invitation was withdrawn by ClueFest's organizer, Caryl Thompson, because Burke had agreed to be Guest of Honor at Deadly Ink. Though Deadly Ink is in New Jersey and was scheduled a month prior to ClueFest, her appearing there was regarded as a conflict of interest. Joyce Spizer, who was the Non-Fiction Guest of Honor, doubled as Fiction Guest of Honor. Bill Mark was Fan Guest of Honor, while Texas private eye writer Rick Riordan was Toastmaster.

Tony Fennelly was the popular Fiction Guest of Honor in 2003, while Bill Crider, wearing yet another hat, was again recognized, this time as Fan Guest of Honor, the fourth time ClueFest honored him. Attendance, at about 100, was down from the high point in the 1990s. ClueFest was canceled for 2004 and 2005 because Terry Thompson was in poor health. It never resumed.

Shots on the Page (1992–1997)

The growth in conventions was not restricted to the United States. In Nottingham, England, where hopeful plans were being made for a Bouchercon, the committee, the staff of the Broadway Media Centre, in May 1992 arranged their three-day mystery convention, Shots on the Page, to run concurrently with Shots in the Dark, a ten-day festival of crime films that included the British premiere of *Silence of the Lambs*. They then went to Toronto and bid successfully for the 1995 Bouchercon.

Julian Symons, celebrating his eightieth birthday that weekend, was Guest of Honor at the first Shots on the Page. Ironically, the greatest praise went to a panel with Barry Pike and Stephen Leadbetter on past writers such as John Rhode, whom Symons had famously called "humdrum." The panel was so popular it lasted one half-hour past its allotted time and only ended when the cleaners for the conference room arrived.

Also popular with fans was the panel "Collecting: Is There a Cure?" It included Bob Adey, Tony Medawar, Peter Tyas, and Donald Rudd, all subscribers to CADS, as were many others in attendance at the convention. For delegates attending this first "small" British convention, the pleasure came from meeting and chatting with authors and other fans.

At the 1993 Shots on the Page, Sara Paretsky was Guest of Honor, and Michael Gilbert British Guest of Honor. In addition to the panels, there were "Extra Shots," a popular series of shorter talks by writers, organized by Peter Lovesey. In 1994 James Crumley was Guest of Honor. At the mystery quiz, now an annual event, Geoff Bradley was made scorer, not participant, because as Ethel Lindsay said in her convention report, "It was felt that any team that had him would have an unfair advantage."

Shots on the Page lasted through 1997, though the last convention was a more limited event, despite yeoman efforts by Maxim Jakubowski, who put together the entire program. Financial aid in the form of grants had ceased.

Adrian Wootton, principal organizer of "Shots" and the Nottingham Bouchercon, moved to an important position at the National Film Theatre on London's Southbank. In 2000, with Jakubowski, he organized Crime Scene, a London film festival with a mystery component. Attendance was about 650, with movie fans far outnumbering mystery readers. Crime Scene, which continues, includes celebrations of mystery writers whose work has been adapted for film and television, including Agatha Christie and Georges Simenon.

Mystery Review (1992–2003)

This was a Canadian quarterly, started in 1992 by Barbara Davey of Ontario, that lasted about ten years. In addition to reviews, it published articles and interviews. A feature was its history of Canadian mystery writing. It ceased publication in 2003 due to Davey's illness; she died in 2004.

Murder & Mayhem (1993–1994)

I am reminded of Mickey Rooney and Judy Garland saying, "Let's put on a show, in the barn," when I think of *Murder & Mayhem*, the publication of a Kansas City couple, Fiske and Elly-Ann Miles. It started in the spring of 1993 as a pocket-sized (4 x 9 ¼-inch) publication, subtitled "A Mystery Fiction Newsletter." In October 1993 they gave away sample copies of the first three issues at the Omaha Bouchercon. I met them, and their enthusiasm was engaging, so I subscribed.

They finished their first volume with three more small issues, now referred to as "A Pocket Guide to Mystery Fiction." With their second volume (and seventh issue) they converted *Murder & Mayhem* to a slick, full-sized magazine and began to publish visually appealing articles, including in that issue a well-illustrated one on New York City mystery bookstores and one on the Malice Domestic convention. *M & M* was now designated "The Mystery Readers Guide." The eighth issue had features on ClueFest and

Seattle mystery bookstores. The ninth contained an impressive article on the 1994 Bouchercon.

Possibly the most memorable aspect of Murder & Mayhem is the brief Fiske Miles held for the concept of "objective reviewing" standards. He claimed, "The path to a more objective review is for reviewers to separate the question of whether they like a book from the question of whether that book is well-written." He never was able to explain to my satisfaction—or that of anyone to whom I spoke—the criteria for deciding a book is well written, or why anyone should continue to read a mystery he or she didn't like. Many letters in *M & M* responded to Fiske Miles's unfavorable review of Michael Connelly's *The Concrete Blonde,* which most readers liked but which Fiske criticized for reasons that seemed merely politically correct: Connelly's having an overweight lawyer and a female whose actual first name was "Honey." It appeared that Miles had never heard of a woman so named, not even the Ficklings' detective Honey West.

The dispute was fun, but just when things were getting interesting, publication ceased after that undated ninth issue, and the mystery was whether *M & M* would ever resume and whether subscribers would receive the rest of their issues or a refund. A decade after it disappeared, with some internet detective work, I got in touch with Fiske Miles through a still-active email address on the *Mayhem* website he had established but not updated since 1997. He said, "We stopped publishing because it was running us into bankruptcy…I realize some subscribers may imagine we somehow absconded with the funds, took a trip to Tahiti, whatever. The fact is that the subscription money paid for only a small portion of the publication expense. We ended up having to make financial arrangements with our printer to repay production expenses (which ran into thousands of dollars). We regret that people who subscribed to the magazine did not receive all of the issues for which they had paid. However, the financial resources for the publication have long since been depleted." Obviously,

Fiske and Elly-Ann didn't realize what was involved in putting on a fan magazine in the barn.

Southwest Mystery/Suspense Convention (1993)

Some assumed the Southwest Mystery/Suspense Convention was a continuation of Omaha's Conventions of 1990–1992, but this gathering, called "Deep in the Heart of Texas," was put on by different people at Austin's Hyatt Regency, May 28–30, 1993. Elmer and Jan Grape, then owners of Austin's mystery bookstore (she is also a writer), were Co-Chairs. Jan also served on seven committees, and her hard—though seemingly effortless—work resulted in a smooth convention for about two hundred fifty people.

Loren D. Estleman and D.R. (Doris) Meredith were Guests of Honor. Lifetime Achievement Awards went to Robert J. Randisi, founder of PWA, and Joan Lowry Nixon, winner of many Edgars for young adult mysteries. Sharyn McCrumb, was called "Mystress of Ceremonies," and the banquet featured a Texas barbecue. Parnell Hall was ready to sing "Achy Breaky Heart" at the banquet, but fortunately no one asked him.

As one member of a panel of fanatical collectors, Richard Moore got off the best line of the convention when he said, "I wanted my wife to know, I may be bizarre, but I'm not unique." During a reviewers' panel, Carolyn Banks upset several fans by giving away the ending of a mystery. In the dealers' room, Pat Hawks introduced the first edition of his compendium of pseudonyms, covering over ten thousand authors, including many mystery writers. One panel, part of three-track programming, was a dance demonstration of the Texas Two-Step.

Shortly before this convention, someone committed suicide by jumping from the sixteenth floor of the atrium. This didn't keep people from frequenting the bar in the atrium, but the outdoor terrace overlooking the Colorado River was so delightful it attracted many fans for talk and drinks each night. One night, a saw-whet owl perched on a small potted tree on the terrace and remained for a half hour, long enough for identification by mystery fans who were also birders. The hotel was also near the Congress Avenue Bridge, from under which emerged each evening at dusk over a million bats, reputedly the largest urban concentration in the world.

This was the first mystery convention for Barry Gardner, and he was overjoyed to put faces to the names he had only read in fan magazines. He summed up his experience by writing, "the real highlight was just sitting around and talking and listening to you all, and I wouldn't have missed it for the world."

Shots (1994–)

Shots, a magazine originally named *A Shot in the Dark,* was started in 1994 by Bob Wainwright. Copies were given to all of the delegates at Shots on the Page that year. The magazine was renamed *Shots* in 1999 by its new Editor Mike Stotter, who is still Editor. In 2002, after ten quarterly issues, it became an online e-zine that includes crime fiction. Ali Karim, its Assistant Editor, does frequent interviews. Other features, in addition to book reviews, are mystery film reviews, essays on American mysteries, and occasional true crime essays.

St. Hilda's Mystery and Crime Conference (1994–)

Beginning in 1994, Oxford took advantage of empty dormitories in summer to create St. Hilda's Crime and Mystery Weekend (now referred to as a Mystery and Crime Conference), started by novelist Kate Charles and Oxford's Alumnae Officer Eileen Roberts. The first year only twenty-five people attended, and most were female. More recently attendance has been about 125 people and gender is more evenly divided.

There is no website for St. Hilda's; it thrives on word-of-mouth (or blog postings), and many people return every year. The setting is an attraction. St. Hilda's, until recently the only remaining all-female college in England, is "on the banks of the River Cherwell...in a pleasantly secluded area away from the noise and bustle of the city (Oxford)" There is virtually no commercialism here; authors are not trying to sell books. Business is limited to an occasional agent or editor as speaker. "Small, intimate, interesting, and thought-provoking" were some of the adjectives Ayo Onatade used in her history of St. Hilda's first ten years.

What makes it unique is that there are no panels. Invited authors prepares papers and speak about learned, albeit often humorous, topics. It is considered a serious academic event, and it is an honor to be invited to give a paper. The result is they are prepared, unlike other conventions where panelists seem to be ad-libbing.

The Guest of Honor gives the conference lecture. Each conference has a different theme. In the past, Robert Barnard has spoken about Margery Allingham, and Simon Brett discussed the Detection Club. In 1997, quite appropriate for the setting, "Murder in Academia" was the topic. In 1998, it was "Men and Women in Blue: The Police Detective in Fiction." In 2017 the theme was "Another Crime, Another Place: The Role of Location in Crime." The twenty-fifth conference in August 2018 had Sara Paretsky, Lindsey Davis, and Mick Herron among the speakers.

More than at other conferences perhaps, authors and fans mingle here, and enough free time is allowed for this. All attending stay in the same quarters and take their meals together. There is a Friday night dinner and drinks reception and a farewell lunch on Sunday. There are occasional field trips, such as one to St. Cross, the church where Lord Peter Wimsey married Harriet Vane in a Dorothy L. Sayers novel.

Magna Cum Murder (1994–)

Fandom also mixes gracefully with academia at Magna Cum Murder, the popular name for what was once called the

Mid-America Mystery Conference and now officially is the Magna Cum Murder Crime Writing Festival. It was the idea of Joanna Wallace of the School of Continuing Education of Ball State University in Muncie, Indiana, and has been organized since the beginning by Kathryn Kennison. Magna has proved popular despite being held in October, the traditional month for Bouchercon. Muncie, its original site, is different from other convention locales. A small Midwestern city, it was the basis for "Middletown," the classic sociological study in the 1920s and 1930s by Robert and Helen Lynd.

The first Magna was held October 28–30, 1994, with Ralph McInerny, an author and professor at Notre Dame University, as Guest of Honor. Two hundred sixty-five attended. Many praised the convention site, the Hotel Roberts, especially its lobby, described as being "out of an Edward Hopper painting." Some events were across the street at Muncie's Convention Center. Outstanding was "The Panel from Hell," with Joan Hess and Sharon McCrumb reprising their 1991 Bouchercon panel, aided by Les Roberts, Parnell Hall, and Jeff Abbott.

From the beginning Magna has honored many people. Hess and McCrumb were "Luminaries," and Michael Z. Lewin was labeled "Mystery Master." Instead of being called banquet emcees, Don Sandstrom and Nancy Pickard were Master and Mistress of the Revels, using the fifteenth-century title given the officer of the English royal household responsible for entertainment at Court. Sandstrom was also the Fan Guest of Honor, a title Magna sometimes calls Reader Guest of Honor.

Gary Warren Niebuhr was Fan Guest of Honor at the second Magna, in 1995, when more than three hundred fifty attended, and he started the conference with his slide show on the history of the private detective in fiction. Emphasizing that fans use their time and money to attend conferences and buy books, Niebuhr said, "Every author should realize that the fans who attend these conferences are their support organization and their safety net, as well."

Mary Higgins Clark was Guest of Honor in 1996, and a memorable moment to many was her joining in the singing in the Roberts lobby, accompanied by Les Roberts (no relation to the hotel) at the piano. Donald E. Westlake, as "Mystery Master," was interviewed by Sandstrom, who was given the academic-sounding title "Host Emeritus." Parnell Hall sang "If It Ain't Fried, It Ain't Food," using lyrics from Westlake's *Baby, Would I Lie?* Hall and Dorothy Cannell were Master and Mistress of the Revels. A radio mystery contest was held, with the winning play performed live at the banquet and over the local Public Broadcasting System station. Maggie Mason, fandom's outstanding trivia player, won the Trivia Bowl. Sandstrom and Neil Albert reprised the EyeCon panel called "Big Macs," discussing John D. MacDonald and Ross Macdonald respectively. B.J. Rahn and Jeanne M. Dams were outstanding in a panel on the "Golden Age." In keeping with the academic setting, one track consisted of papers presented by professors or doctoral candidates, for example one by Jan Steffensen on Scandinavian mysteries.

In 1997 though Magna ended only a few days before the Monterey Bouchercon, its loyal fans did not forsake it. James Crumley was Guest of Honor and Lawrence Block was Mystery Master. The Arsenic and Oolong Society of Indianapolis, a mystery reading group supportive of Magna, was collectively Fan Guest of Honor. Sadly, one of their most active members, Don Sandstrom, died shortly before Magna began. Kathryn Kennison said about him, "We could never have done it without him and every single Magna cum Murder is a memorial to our beloved friend and mentor." Each year the Spirit of Magna Award is given in Sandstrom's name.

Magna has continued to draw leading mystery writers as Guests of Honor. They include Michael Connelly, Andrew McCall Smith, Harlan Coben, Louise Penny, Sue Grafton, and William Kent Krueger, among others. Magna no longer has a Fan Guest of Honor.

Magna gives considerable attention to true crime. In 1998 Jerry Bledsoe was True Crime Luminary. In 2001, Clark Davenport and Jim Ebert became Magna's first Forensic Guests of Honor.

For eight years (2000–2008) Jim Huang was Magna's program director and was responsible for many innovations. For example, one year he suggested that all attending read Agatha Christie's classic *And Then There Were None* in advance. There were discussions of the book, and a film version was shown.

Magna invariably sold out the Hotel Roberts, its site from its first year until the hotel closed in 2007. For several years afterward most of the events were held at the Muncie Conference Center. Those attending stayed at various motels, not a satisfactory arrangement because of the traveling. By 2013 Magna had moved to the Columbia Club, a private club, in downtown Indianapolis on the city's Monument Circle, that has guest rooms.

The secret of Magna's success was succinctly stated by Lev Raphael, Master of Revels in 2001, when he compared it to a weekend house party with several hundred close friends. William Kent Krueger described Magna as "both intimate and vibrant." (Attendance is capped at about four hundred people.) Recognizing Kathryn Kennison's warmth and ability to make friends, Terence Faherty said, "Magna is the only conference I know that begins and ends with a hug."

CT (Crime Time) (1995–)

CT, which began in 1995 as *Crime Time,* was a well-illustrated journal that also included fiction and material regarding films and television. It had fifty-four print issues until 2008 when it became another fan journal to go online. Barry Forshaw, who took over as editor with issue No. 14, remains as editor.

BuffCon (1995)

A convention in Buffalo, New York, BuffCon, was held only once, in May 1995. It was organized by Douglas Anderson, who published a detective novel with a Buffalo setting in 1993. The Guest of Honor was Lawrence Block, who was born in Buffalo.

EyeCon (1995–1999)

Cap'n Bob Napier declaring Barry Gardner the winner of the 1995 EyeCon debate

Some fans, and even writer Donald Westlake, were wondering whether the private eye story had grown stale, even moribund, in the '90s. Gary Warren Niebuhr, its most dedicated fan, put on EyeCon, the first convention devoted to that subgenre, in Milwaukee June 15–18, 1995. Sue Grafton was Guest of Honor, and Les Roberts the Toastmaster. There were three auctions during the convention to raise funds so Milwaukee County libraries could purchase copies of Hubin's bibliography. Almost all who attended thought EyeCon was a great convention, justifying eighteen months of work by Niebuhr and his committee. Attendance was three hundred twenty-five, including Naomi Hoida from Japan.

There were panels called "Dead Folks' Dues," about dead writers, and an Art Scott slide show. Much attention centered on the EyeCon debate between George Kelley and Barry Gardner on whether the private eye story was dead; Kelly said it was. Bob Napier officiated and even wore a bow tie, as do boxing referees. Kelley was preaching to the uncommitted since people attending a private eye convention, especially writers in that field, were not especially open to his idea. He hoped to prove his point by giving out paper for the audience to list their favorite private eye stories. He planned to use a timeline to show that most favorites were not recent. Unfortunately, some of the audience grew restive at what they perceived as a pedantic approach and became rowdy, with several turning the sheets into paper airplanes, which they threw. Some who were more open to being convinced, such as John Apostolou, felt that Kelley might have had a better chance of proving his point if he had stated, as Westlake once did, that it has lost its vitality, not that it was totally dead. Referee Napier said afterward that he regretted not explaining the ground rules in advance but that he had assumed both participants were there to debate, not lecture, as he felt Kelley had done. Letters about the debate filled pages in *MDM* afterward, with Michael Seidman criticizing Kelley, who defended himself. This led Gardner to comment, "The debate about the debate is turning out to be a hell of a lot more interesting than the debate was."

Jane Ellen Syrk and Don Newhouse of Murder and Mayhem Bookstore in Indianapolis planned another EyeCon convention for July 25–27, 1997; Marcia Muller and Bill Pronzini were to be Guests of Honor. There was a conflict between the planners and Private Eye Writers of America over who would get space in the dealers' room. PWA wanted more of a voice in deciding which dealers were included and threatened to withdraw from EyeCon. What seemed negotiable got out of hand. Syrk and Newhouse realized they could not have EyeCon without PWA, so they decided to cancel it. Niebuhr wrote in *MDM*, "I just wish someone could have mediated between PWA and EyeCon '97 so that those who love this form of writing could have had a place to go in July."

A second EyeCon was held (sponsored by PWA this time), July 8–11, 1999, at the Adam's Mark in Randisi's home city, St. Louis. Loren D. Estleman was Guest of Honor, and Maxine O'Callaghan, whose Delilah West in 1974 anticipated more famous, later female P.I.s, received the Eye for lifetime achievement. "Friends of P.I." Awards were given to Michael Seidman and Joe Pittman.

Historicon (1995, 1999)

Recognizing the growing popularity of historical mysteries, Tom and Enid Schantz of Rue Morgue Books put on Historicon in Boulder, Colorado, in 1995. Edward Marston was Guest of

Honor. A second Historicon was held there in 1999, with Steven Saylor as Guest of Honor. Attendance at each was limited to one hundred people.

***Mystery Collectors' Bookline* (1995–1999)**

Fans are often collectors, and many were caught up in the "hypermodern" book craze of the early 1990s, in which recent books such as Sue Grafton's *"A" Is for Alibi,* Patricia Cornwell's *Post Mortem,* and John Dunning's *Booked to Die* sold for high prices. In February 1995, David M. Brown of San Rafael, California, started *Mystery Collectors' Bookline,* a magazine designed to identify "hot" books, usually an author's first since these, due to relatively small print runs, become most valuable.

Though there were reviews in *Mystery Collectors' Bookline,* the language used more often related to books' value than to their quality. For example, regarding one recommended book, it said, "the buzz on this title is loud and clear coming from every direction." Many of the books *Mystery Collectors' Bookline* recommended were forgotten only a few years later. The hypermodern era soon ended (and with it *Mystery Collectors' Bookline*) as collectors, some of whom tried to be sellers, found they couldn't get their investment back—let alone make a profit.

***Tangled Web* (1995–1999) and *Tangled Web Internet Crime & Mystery Journal* (1997–)**

Tangled Web, the magazine, was not connected to the similarly titled website. Andrew Osmond was the publisher and also contributed articles. Like CADS, another British fan magazine, *Tangled Web* did not offer subscriptions. Osmond notified those on his mailing list when an issue was available, and, if interested, they sent money. It began in 1995 and lasted through 1999, with nine issues published. There were no replies to inquiries regarding issue No. 10, so it is apparently defunct.

Tangled Web Internet Crime & Mystery Journal was started in

1997 by brother and sister Ralph and Liz Lees and was regarded by Kate Derie in *The Deadly Directory* 2004 as "U.K.'s crime & mystery fiction website." It has thousands of pages in its archives of reviews, author profiles, and bibliographies. The Lees also sell books on the internet.

***Mysterious Women* (1995–?)**

Late in 1995, Kathleen Swanholt of Walnut Creek, California, began *Mysterious Women,* "A Quarterly Newsletter for Fans of Women Mystery Writers." It included articles, reviews, interviews, and bookstore information. Swanholt may have been the only editor whose mother, Alma Connaughton, wrote articles. She said in her second issue that she was expecting an article by her mother on Lilian Jackson Braun, but "Mom decided to do Amanda Cross instead. I may be Managing Editor but, let's face it, in this life Mom will always outrank me." *Mysterious Women* was later published by Sara Berger of Amherst, Massachusetts but has now been discontinued.

***Murder Most Cozy* (1995–2004)**

This bimonthly newsletter on "cozy" mysteries and their creators was published by Jan Dean of Diamondhead, Mississippi, who also offered an annual "Cozy Crimes, Cream Teas & Books, Books, Books" tour of the British Isles. As its title indicates, it offered considerable time for visiting bookstores. When she ceased publication, she offered subscribers the choice of refunds or back issues.

The Ngaio Marsh International Society (1996–2004)

Nicole St. John of Midland Park, New Jersey, founded this group in 1996 to celebrate the work of the famous New Zealand writer. It had a semiannual newsletter, *Harmony,* and an annual journal, *Promptbook,* the latter recognizing that Marsh was once an actress and later a well-regarded theatrical director. The society was discontinued in 2004.

The Friends of Chester Himes (1996–2005)

Established in 1996, in Oakland, California, was a group, formed by Janette Faulkner, to honor this writer. They held an annual conference, presented papers, panels, and films that focused on African-American writers such as Himes. They gave the annual Chester Himes Award, and had a writing contest for high school students. Their tenth and last conference was in 2005.

AZ Murder Goes… (1996–1999)

In the United States, as well as England, booksellers, for obvious reasons sponsor conferences. In 1996 Barbara Peters and Robert Rosenwald of the Poisoned Pen bookstore and publishing company started an annual Scottsdale, Arizona, conference, AZ Murder Goes…beginning with *AZ Murder Goes…Classic.* A book containing the papers submitted by those attending was published in 1997. (After the ellipsis is a word or two telling the theme of each year.) The other two conferences/books were *AZ Murder Goes…Professional* (1998), following five authors on the path to having their books published, and *AZ Murder Goes…Artful* (1999). Barbara Peters edited or co-edited the books. About one hundred writers and fans attended each conference.

The Harry Stephen Keeler Society (1997–)

Francis M. "Mike" Nevins, fan of Harry Stephen Keeler and more

Once, Francis M. Nevins seemed to be Harry Stephen Keeler's only fan, as he kept his memory alive with amusing articles such as "The Wild and Wooly World of Harry Stephen Keeler." Nevins was really recommending Keeler's work, despite its convoluted plots and the inordinate length, over seven hundred pages, of some of his books. If he was ever alone in his enthusiasm, Nevins no longer is. Since 1997 there has been the Keeler Society, founded by Richard Polt of Cincinnati, which issues *Keeler News* five times yearly. Membership in the Society is free, though it is supported by the sale of various items of "Keeleriana," such as T-shirts and mugs. At the same time, Ramble House, a small publisher, began reprinting the works of the prolific Keeler. Ramble House is no longer in business.

Love Is Murder (1998–)

Love Is Murder began as what was called a writers conference in Rosemont, Illinois, a Chicago suburb in 1998 and has continued its mid-winter spot, eventually combining with a Midwest MWA annual conference, so that its title now is Love Is Murder on Dark and Stormy Nights. They have had fan-friendly moments, and in 2005 they named a "Fan of Honor." It was Pat Ruocco, a librarian who leads the "Murder Among Friends" book group at her library and has been Fan Guest of Honor at Malice Domestic. Despite its original title, more than romantic crime is involved. Headliner-Guests have included Lee Child, Jeffery Deaver, and William Kent Krueger. Barry Eisler did a karate demonstration.

Dead on Deansgate (1998–2003)

Dead on Deansgate, which took its name from a local street, began in Manchester, England, in October 1998 as a replacement for Shots on the Page. It was first organized by Britain's Crime Writers Association and Waterstone's bookstore (located on Deansgate). Waterstone sold books by the participating authors; there were no other dealers. The panelists were mainly authors. Fans were relatively few, though Geoff Bradley of CADS was among those who attended. Deansgate adopted the practice of having an American Guest Author, in addition to an International Guest of Honor. Those honored have included Ruth Rendell and Janet Evanovich. Though attendance was about three hundred, it has not been held since 2003, and many lament its passing.

***Dastardly Deeds* (1999–2000)**

A short-lived publication was *Dastardly Deeds,* a colorful newsletter whose contents displayed a sense of humor. It described itself as "A Tainted Newsletter for Readers, Collectors, Booksellers and, yes, even Authors, gasp!" Paul Petrucelli was publisher, and Diane Plumley was called "Editor-in-Grief." Its contents included columns on collecting "hypermodern" books and writers of the past. There were interviews with popular writers such as Dennis Lehane, and also with some who were less well known, including Alan Beechey.

Bloody Words (1999–2014)

Called "Canada's Mystery Conference," it started in Toronto in 1999, moving to Ottawa in 2003. Later, it was held in Victoria, British Columbia, and returned to Toronto with about 225 in attendance. The guests of honor have usually been Canadians and have included L.R. Wright, Medora Sale, Howard Engel, and Peter Robinson. However, Loren D. Estleman has been honored, and in 2003 Val McDermid was International Guest of Honor. It was last held in 2014.

Chapter Twenty-Two

BOUCHERCONS: 2000–2009

2000: Denver

Because it can snow in Denver even in late September, Tom Schantz and Rebecca Bates, Co-Chairs, wisely scheduled 2000 Bouchercon for September 7–10. The setting was the Adam's Mark Hotel, and attendance was about 1,250. Elmore Leonard was Guest of Honor, and Jane Langton received a Lifetime Achievement Award.

The program book recognized that the primary interest of many (possibly most) attendees was recent mysteries. However, it said in the welcome, "Even if you never read anything published before 1990, come prepared to learn something about what has gone before." Panels among the eight tracks, which included "Forgotten Paperback Writers of the 1950s," drew surprisingly good crowds. Most panels were directed at new writers, especially those still unpublished. I counted twenty-one panels about the "business" of writing and being published, including "After Your First Book Is Published," "Studio Publishing: Self and Small Presses," "Foreign Rights and International Markets," "E-Publishing Roundtable," and "Self Publishing."

Steve Stilwell was Fan Guest of Honor, and his reputation for "chatting up" attractive females made him an ideal target for a hilarious, standing-room-only "roast." Of course his allegedly lecherous instincts received much attention, but Bill Deeck got the biggest laugh when recalling the 1987 Bouchercon by uttering two words: "The Magician."

In addition to the Anthonys, awards were given out by a virtual alphabet of organizations, including IACWNA (International Association of Crime Writers North America), PWA (Private Eye Writers of America), MRI Mystery Readers International, and *DP* (*Deadly Pleasures.*) The last named magazine gives out the Barry Awards honoring the late Barry Gardner. There were several receptions and a Bouchercon Ball, with a jazz quartet, though it was sparsely attended because it was scheduled opposite the popular auction and a Colorado Rockies baseball game, at which a block of seats had been reserved for Bouchercon attendees. Probably no one gives more at auctions to be named in future mysteries than Mary "Maggie" Mason. Even pets were an excuse to give to charity. After Denver, Deen Kogan said, "I am well on my way to having my Doberman, Miata, become the most Tuckerized animal in detective fiction."

This seemed the best attended Anthony banquet, perhaps because its price was included in the cost of registration. Unfortunately, the food was far from good. Val McDermid was a popular Toastmistress, singing a Scottish murder ballad while accompanying herself on the guitar. I paid tribute to Phyllis White who was too ill to attend. One of the Anthony categories, for Best Critical/Biographical work, mixed literary apples and oranges when it pitted two fan magazines against two biographies and the third edition of Willetta Heising's bibliography, *Detecting Women,* which won. In addition to the Anthonys, there were "Millennium Awards" voted by fans for the best series, mystery writer, and novel of the twentieth century. The winners, respectively, were Hercule Poirot, Agatha Christie, and *Rebecca.*

2001: Washington, DC

Many things changed after September 11, 2001, including Bouchercon. At the end of July 2001, more than 1,400 had signed up for the convention due to be held November 1–4 at the Hyatt Regency in Arlington, Virginia, only about a mile from the Pentagon, one of the terrorists' targets. Some people canceled, but attendance was still healthy at over 1,300, and that included a large contingent of British writers and fans. One of the most moving moments was a toast to Americans by International Guest of Honor Peter Lovesey. Co-Chairmen Adolph Falcón and Bill Starck said in the program book, "We thank you for your understanding and patience… These have been difficult times for the Washington, DC, area and by attending 'A Capital Mystery' you are helping to make a capital difference in restoring the region's wellbeing."

Kenneth Wishnia said, "New Yorkers like me had just left one city that was attacked for another city that was attacked so none of us were feeling particularly safe. A group of writers and fans led by fellow New Yorker S.J. Rozan…had a spontaneous panel on the subject of our immediate post-9/11 feelings and how this affected our work as crime writers…we had a very intense, honest, and emotional discussion. One of the best 'panels' I've ever been to."

The American Guest of Honor was Sue Grafton. Book dealers Lew and Nancy Buckingham were Fan Guests of Honor, though they had a minimal record of fannish activity. Edward D. Hoch received a Lifetime Achievement Award, and Michael Connelly was Toastmaster.

Halloween night, before the convention's official opening, saw one of the worst events in Bouchercon history, one comparable to the infamous happenings in the Twin Cities, previously described. Billed as "An Edgar Allan Poe Halloween," it disappointed most who had come to see David Keltz's one-man performance as Poe. There were flashing strobe lights and blaring sound, making it difficult to watch a preliminary costume contest. Keltz's appearance was delayed so long, I left with a headache before he arrived.

Thursday night, on the other hand, was memorable for me. Presentations were made of three awards, the Herodotus for Best Historical Mystery, the Macavity from Mystery Readers International, and the Barry from *Deadly Pleasures*. I won the Macavity for my critical work, *The American Regional Mystery*, and received an even greater surprise during the Barry presentations. George Easter gave me the first Don Sandstrom Memorial Award for Lifetime Achievement in Mystery Fandom. Because Don had been a good friend, it was especially appreciated.

There were seven tracks of programming on Friday and eight on Saturday. Taking advantage of many British writers present, there were panels called Cops: Brits vs. U.S., British Crime at the Cutting Edge, Today's Traditional British Mystery, and a panel on British royalty in mysteries. There was a Meet the Brits Reception on Friday night, sponsored by the Crime Writers Association.

There were also panels on publishing trends, two panels on forensics, and an interview with the daughter and granddaughter of Dashiell Hammett. Called "Down Memory Lane," there were three panels regarding writers of the past, and the enthusiastic panelists brought so much material, someone described them as "overprepared." One panelist, John Apostolou, said, "It helped that none of us was trying to sell his or her latest book." He was recognizing that many authors at Bouchercon were there to promote their work, not as fans. Bouchercon had become an important event in "the industry," and almost one-fourth of the program book was taken up by advertisements, mostly from publishers. Publishers also provided fifteen free books, leaving registrants who were travelling by air wondering how to fit them all in their luggage.

2002: Austin, Texas

Texas, scene of other mystery conventions, had its first Bouchercon in Austin October 17–20, at Marriot's Renaissance Hotel. Subtitled

"Longhorns of the Law," it was co-chaired by Karen Meschke and Willie Siros. George Pelecanos and Mary Willis Walker were the Guests of Honor. Following a lead from Malice Domestic, this Bouchercon also honored someone who was dead, designating Barry Gardner of Dallas as Fan Ghost of Honor. Though a prolific professional author, Bill Crider of Alvin, Texas, was Fan Guest of Honor. He had been a true fan long before he was published. Crider and Judy, his wife, won an Anthony for Best Short Story. When Richard Moore could not attend due to a shoulder fracture, Crider stepped in for him on short notice on a panel. Crider's interview, by Joe Lansdale, was one of the highlights of the convention.

Chris Aldrich and Lynn Kaczmarek, publishers of *Mystery News*, at Bouchercon 2002 in Austin, Texas

Still another Texan, Elmer Kelton, was the "Special Guest," though he is mainly a Western writer, with only one criminous title in Hubin's bibliography. George Easter of *Deadly Pleasures* presented the second Don Sandstrom Award to Gary Warren Niebuhr, one of the most enthusiastic of fans.

With attendance at 1,438, there were long lines to register. The free books from publishers were so many that they filled two bags. The many glitches in this convention began even before it opened. The committee was confused as to when the book dealers room would open. Not only were some panelists not told of their assignments, but even some moderators weren't informed. Len Moffatt arrived at 4:00 p.m. Thursday and was told he was on a "History of the Mystery" panel at 4:30 p.m. The program book only gave the names of panels, not telling who the panelists were. Luckily, some attendees got that information from the Bouchercon website. Despite often chaotic conditions, the committee members weren't always present when problems needed to be solved.

There were several "Forgotten Authors" panels. Mine did not have a moderator, so I stepped into the breach. Ted Hertel found that his "Forgotten Authors" panel had been forgotten. There was a meeting from an entirely different convention in his meeting room. He found another room, but it had no chairs at all, let alone a table for the panelists. Posting signs and helping to move furniture in, he and his panelists (John Apostolou and Crider) persisted and gave a good presentation, albeit to only about twenty people.

Forgotten "Forgotten Authors" panel: John Apostolou, Ted Hertel, and Bill Crider

The dichotomy between panels that active fans attended and those popular with people who are mainly readers grew. Hertel jokingly described the latter as having panelists who say, "Hi, My name is Big Name Author. My new book is called Bestseller. It's available in the dealers' room." "Trufans," a term borrowed from science fiction, were to be found, in far smaller numbers, at panels in which S.S. Van Dine, R. Austin Freeman, Philip MacDonald, George Harmon Coxe, Robert Reeves, and Day Keene were discussed. Trufans also went to the panel about such old-time radio detective shows as "The Adventures of Ellery Queen."

The banquet was far briefer than most and rather bland. Sparkle Hayter, as Toastmistress, did not sparkle.

Despite problems, reactions among the attendees were positive. For many, Bouchercon remained about people: old and new friends. Also, the hotel was comfortable, the weather mild, and good shopping and restaurants were a short walk away. Many went on a combined bus and boat tour of Austin called the "Duck Adventure" and were given duck whistles. Later in the spacious hotel atrium, one could hear duck callers serenading each other.

2003: Las Vegas

The thirty-fourth Bouchercon came to Las Vegas October 16–19 with a predictable emphasis on gambling. Attendees were even given rolls of nickels in their registration package, and many spent some time at the "slots." Gambling metaphors abounded in the program, and a separate booklet, *The Gleam in Bugsy Siegel's Eye* by Barry T. Zeman, a bibliography of mystery fiction about Las Vegas and gambling, was distributed. The site was the Riviera, one of Las Vegas's oldest hotels. Many attendees found it run down and signs in bathrooms offering "free needles" didn't inspire confidence that they were intended for diabetics.

Many of the 1,641 people registered found this hotel with its multiple towers confusing. There were long walks, through corridors filled with cigarette smoke, to the meeting rooms. There was no place to sit and chat near the meeting rooms or even on the way except, of course, in the casino. Also, there was no hospitality suite. Everyone paid a 3 percent "energy fee" on their hotel bill to allow Las Vegas to keep its casino lights on twenty-four hours a day.

Deen Kogan, who had put on two Bouchercons in Philadelphia, saved this one by agreeing to chair it, but her nerves seemed somewhat frazzled throughout. A live-cast radio mystery during the opening reception was almost impossible to hear, not surprising at what essentially was a cocktail party with several bars. It should have been presented as a separate production. A highlight of the reception was the third Sandstrom fandom award to Mary "Maggie" Mason.

The dealers' room was more crowded than at any previous Bouchercons, and there was wonder that the fire marshals didn't close it. Some potential book buyers avoided it. One person suggested that whoever planned the dealers' room forgot people needed aisles in which to walk.

James Lee Burke was American Guest of Honor, and Scottish writer Ian Rankin was International Guest of Honor. Ruth Rendell was saluted for her "Exemplary Body of Work," and Janet Hutchings, editor of *EQMM,* was cited for her "Contribution to the Field." Jeff and Ann Smith of Baltimore were Fan Guests of Honor. They represent what is most generous in fandom. Unlike some honored in the past, who have also written for pay, they are not involved in the commerce of the mystery. They are devoted readers, contributors to *DAPA-EM,* and loyal Bouchercon attendees. In Las Vegas, they threw their suite open to mystery fans every night.

On the Wednesday before Bouchercon officially opened, there was a Writer's Workshop conducted by Jeremiah Healy and Gayle Lynds. During Bouchercon, there were again many panels on the "business" of writing and being published. Other panels were about Las Vegas, its history, and gambling scams. There were true crime panels including another with a police dog and its handler. Two panels were about the internet, and another on audio books. Perhaps the most unusual panel was "Walter Sickert Is Innocent, OK!" in which two British academics disputed Patricia Cornwell's book in which she "identified" that British painter as "Jack the Ripper." Highly popular was "Wanted for Murder," a show in which Liza

Frequent volunteer Beth Fedyn takes a well-deserved rest

Cody, Peter Lovesey, and Michael Z. Lewin amusingly demonstrated how a mystery is developed.

The annual auction benefited the libraries of Las Vegas and Clark County. People were bidding up to two thousand dollars to be a character in an Ian Rankin or Lee Child book. Mostly thanks to Beth Fedyn, it was a great success, raising $22,347. Child was Toastmaster, but he was in no way responsible for the Sunday brunch that featured barely edible food. Again, flaws did not prevent those attending from enjoying Bouchercon.

2004: Toronto

Disagreeing with Thomas Wolfe, many who enjoyed the 1992 Toronto Bouchercon found that they could go home again—or at least enjoy another Bouchercon there. Once again Al Navis stepped in when there were no other bidders, assuming financial risk. With no "seed" money from prior Bouchercons, Navis used his own money for expenses until registration money arrived. While 1,350 people attended at the Metropolitan Conference Center on October 7–10, some stayed at 1992's site, the Royal York, and ate at Marché, the delightful restaurant that attracted so many attendees that year.

Ted Fitzgerald, frequent Bouchercon attendee and one of the winners of the Don Sandstrom Award

Navis's choice of Fan Guest of Honor Gary Warren Niebuhr was an inspired one. Not only was he deserving because of more than two decades of activity, but he provided the most entertaining moments during the convention, especially when interviewed by Ted Hertel. In 1992 Gary had entertained some of us with a brief dance from *The Wizard of Oz*. In 2004 he did a hilarious five-minute reprise of the entire movie. Gary was also amusing and gracious in his acceptance speeches when winning the Macavity and Anthony for his critical work *Make Mine a Mystery*.

The professional Guests of Honor were Lindsey Davis (British), Jeremiah Healy (American), Peter Robinson (Canadian), and Bernard Cornwell (Lifetime Achievement Award). Natasha Cooper was Toastmistress and amusing if a trifle effusive. Despite not being a private eye writer, Donald E. Westlake won PWA's "The Eye" for lifetime achievement. Ted Fitzgerald was the fourth winner of the Don Sandstrom Award. The award for best fan magazine is not given every year. It was in 2004 and was won by *Mystery Scene*, edited by Kate Stine.

"Been There, Done That" was the title of one of the panels, and one must admit that in thirty-five years of Bouchercons most topics have been covered—many times. However, Navis and his programming chairman Peter Sellers did come up with some unusual topics, including a live production featuring jazz music and a demonstration/seminar by a professional fighter. At two panels "All-Nighters: Books You Can't Put Down" and "Precious Gems" (about underappreciated writers) one could see the audience busily taking notes for future reading. I first spoke about regional mysteries at the 1974 Bouchercon. This year, I led a panel with five regional novelists. I stirred up some controversy by raising the question of whether we have now gone too far in the direction of regional realism at the expense of detection and plotting.

There was four-track programming, plus another experiment called "20 on the 20" in which every twenty minutes a different author spoke about his or her work or read from it. All that was missing in three and a half days of full programming was a lunch hour.

2005: Chicago

The weather was ideal for Chicago's third Bouchercon, September 1–4, at the Sheraton, but not so throughout the United States as Hurricane Katrina was expected to strike, with significant loss of life and property damage. Understandingly, those attending

Sadly missed, Bill and Judy Crider laugh at a Lachman story, while Steve Stilwell reads the first edition of this book

who lived in Louisiana, Mississippi, and Texas had their attention to this Bouchercon, called "Wicked Times in the Windy City," diverted to weather conditions at home.

Hal Rice of Rockford, Illinois, had successfully bid for this Bouchercon, but he died in 2002 in an auto accident. Hal's widow Sonya co-chaired the convention with Deen Kogan who again stepped in, using her considerable convention experience to rescue Bouchercon 36; it was listed in the program as a production of Kogan's Society Hill Playhouse in Philadelphia. The program paid tribute to Hal as "The Man of Many Faces." He was the loving husband of Sonya, the father of five and grandfather of 26, a successful businessman, the host of many Bouchercon parties, a fan with a passion for the mystery in its many aspects, probably most of all in short stories.

Dennis Lehane was the American Guest of Honor; Jonathan Gash, M.D., of England was International Guest of Honor. Marcia Muller and Bill Pronzini received Lifetime Achievement Awards. Harlan Coben was Toastmaster.

Beth Fedyn was Fan Guest of Honor. She modestly called herself "an accidental fan," maintaining that "if it weren't for dogs and books I wouldn't have any friends." Not true. She has volunteered to perform various tasks at mystery conventions since 1981, reviewed books, edited the newsletter of Milwaukee's Cloak and Clue Society, and organized fan events. The other main fandom award, the Don Sandstrom, went to Bill Crider.

Other mystery fans got attention, especially in the program book. Louis M. Boxer wrote on "Collecting Mystery Books: The Passions, the Friendships, the Disease." Boxer admitted that book collecting is not a hobby but a way of life that some consider pathological. He even compared being a bibliophile to alcoholism by listing the twelve steps of bibliophiles, without suggesting a cure.

Rick Kovalcik wrote "Why (I) Read?" Carol Fitzpatrick wrote "It's ALL About the Reader."

Panels of special interest to fans included "Past Master," moderated by Beth Fedyn, in which she, Beverly De Weese, Ted Hertel, Gary Warren Niebuhr, and Maggie Mason discussed some of their favorite, now-forgotten writers. Four of the five were from Milwaukee.

It was the hundredth anniversary of the birth of the two authors, Frederic Dannay and Manfred B. Lee, who wrote as "Ellery Queen." Janet Hutchings, editor of *Ellery Queen's Mystery Magazine* led a panel on "The Influence of Ellery Queen." In "We Read Before We Write," chaired by George Easter, five editors of mystery fan journals shared some of their favorite "reads." Given a half-hour on Saturday, I gave a brief history of Bouchercon.

The programming included some old standbys of other Bouchercons, including a demonstration by the Chicago P.D. of police dogs, interviews of the Guests of Honor, a basketball game, organized by S. J. Rozan. Harlan Coben excelled as Toastmaster at Saturday night's Anthony Banquet, held on the eightieth floor of the Mid-America Club on Randolph Drive. Unmindful of children in the audience, Dennis Lehane's speech at the banquet included too many four-letter words.

There is a tourist side to Bouchercons. While many fans are

happy to remain at the convention site, especially the book-selling room, many choose to wander. In Chicago, the Art Institute is an especially attractive museum, with its emphasis on Impressionist art. Walking the streets and looking up, one can see the work of some of America's leading architects.

2006: Madison, Wisconsin

About twelve hundred people attended this Bouchercon (called "A Prairie Plot"), held September 28 to October 1 at the Madison Concourse Hotel. This was the third Bouchercon, in its relatively short history, held in Wisconsin. Al Abramson was Chairman. Mary-Helen Becker was important in the early stages of the event, as were Gary Warren Niebuhr and Ted Hertel who had put on the Milwaukee Bouchercon in 1999.

Nevada Barr was the American Guest of Honor, and M.C. Beaton of England the International Guest of Honor. Robert B. Parker received a Lifetime Achievement Award, but he wasn't able to come to Madison. He was replaced by Joseph Wambaugh, author of popular Los Angeles police procedurals, as a Special Guest. Jim Huang was Fan Guest of Honor. William Kent Krueger was Toastmaster and also won his second consecutive Anthony for Best Novel. Janet Rudolph received a "Special Service to the Field" Award for her work with Mystery Readers International. She also received the Don Sandstrom Award. *Crimespree*, published by Jon and Ruth Jordan, received the award as Best Fan Publication.

This convention celebrated the twenty-fifth anniversary of the founding of Private Eye Writers of America (PWA) and the twentieth anniversary of Sisters in Crime.

Among the more interesting panels were "Don't Touch That Dial" about old-time radio and "The Changing Face of Gay and Lesbian Mysteries." There were two panels about crime laboratories plus another on forensic anthropology.

The awards ceremony was especially satisfying. Full disclosure: The first edition of this book (the first and only history of mystery fandom) won an Anthony in the Critical/Non Fiction category. It was a book I could not have written were there not so many enthusiastic mystery fans to write about.

2007: Anchorage, Alaska

Bouchercon went to Alaska in 2007, successfully using the experience its committee gained while holding Left Coast Crime there in 2001. Bouchercon, jokingly also called "Bearly Alive," was held September 27–30 at the Hilton Hotel and the Egan Conference Center. The chairs were Dana Stabenow, who writes a series of Alaska mysteries, Dee Ford, and Kimberley Gray.

Thomas Perry was American Guest of Honor. Diana Gabaldon was a Special Guest of Honor. James Sallis received a Lifetime Achievement Award. Though Barbara Peters is involved in publishing and selling books, she is also a fan and was selected as Fan Guest of Honor. Jim Huang received a Special Services Award and also shared the Anthony for *Mystery Muses*, which he had co-edited with Austin Lugar. Beth Fedyn received the Don Sandstrom Award.

Panels about crime in Alaska were prominent throughout the weekend. One police officer spoke of his experience chasing a suspect on a dog sled and rescuing a hostage from a glacier. Another panel featured two Alaska judges.

At Left Coast Crime, authors had flown "into the bush" to encourage reading and writing among young Alaskans. In 2007 at Bouchercon, with the help of Sisters in Crime, there was "Authors in the Schools." Some writers stayed over to Monday visiting schools in Point Hope and Hooper Bay, Alaska.

Other panels were more similar to those usually expected at Bouchercon. At a panel of reviewers one member of the audience asked whether they read the books they reviewed in their entirety. Anthony Rainone said that not only did he read the entire book, but he read it twice. Rainone had been selected by *Crimespree* Magazine as its "contributor of the year."

2008: Baltimore

In 1975, members of the business community, anxious to improve the public's perception of Baltimore, nicknamed it "Charm City." Bouchercon in 2008 (held October 9–12 at the Wyndham Baltimore Hotel in its Inner Harbor) was called "Charmed to Death." Lawrence Block was given an award for "Distinguished Contribution to the Genre." The American Guest of Honor was Laura Lippman, who is from Baltimore. John Harvey of Nottingham, England, was the International Guest of Honor. Thalia Proctor of England was the Fan Guest of Honor. Though she has worked in mystery bookstores and as an editor, she considers herself primarily a fan.

Bill and Toby Gottfried shared the Don Sandstrom Award. George Easter, originator of that award, was surprised when without his knowledge his fans gave him a Sandstrom Award too.

The Lifetime Achievement Award for non-writing activities went to the Poisoned Pen Press and Bookstore couple Barbara Peters and Robert Rosenwald. Mark Billingham of England was Toastmaster. The convention chairs were Ruth Jordan and Judy Bobalik.

If anyone was worried about the next generation of mystery fans, there was reason to be less concerned. Ali Karim of England brought his fifteen-year-old son, already a fan of Harlan Coben and others. Larry Gandle's daughters were reviewing Young Adult mysteries for *Deadly Pleasures*. Gandle summarized the appeal of the weekend succinctly: "Seeing old friends who share the same passion for the mystery genre and book, and meeting new ones is truly what Bouchercon is about."

Every panel was named after a pop song. There were six tracks of panels. Some topics, for example tackling social issues, were among those already discussed at Bouchercons, inspiring the panelists to search for new approaches. Others were more unusual, for example, Young Adult mysteries, the place of food and wine in mysteries, and one about Edgar Allan Poe, who died in Baltimore. Arguably the most novel panel of all was "If You Attended Bouchercon in 1908." The idea of

Roger M. Sobin, it tried to re-create the mystery world of the early twentieth century.

2009: Indianapolis

"Elementary, My Dear Indy" was the name given to this Bouchercon October 15–18 at the Hyatt Regency. Attendance was estimated at about two thousand people (including a goodly number of youngsters) at a convention chaired by Jim Huang and Mike Bursaw, better known as "Mystery Mike."

Michael Connelly was Guest of Honor. S.J. Rozan was Toastmaster. Kathryn Kennison, who had been putting on the successful Magnum Cum Murder convention for fifteen years, was Fan Guest of Honor. Art Scott, for over thirty years editor of *DAPA-EM*, received the Sandstrom Award. Wendelin Van Draanen, creator of thirteen-year-old girl detective "Sammy" Keyes, was "Honored Youth Author." Al Hubin, who is probably most responsible for mystery fandom as we now know it, received a Lifetime Achievement Award. The Derringer Society for Short Fiction presented a new award, The Edward D. Hoch Memorial Golden Derringer for Lifetime Achievement to Clark Howard.

This was the first Bouchercon since the great recession of 2008, and that was reflected during the convention, especially in the much more meaningful Welcome in the Bouchercon program by Huang and Bursaw. They recognized that "We gather in a time of change and turmoil that applies to the publishing and selling of mysteries, with books as we have known them and new forms such as electronic books." The world situation was even reflected in a panel when an author from Iceland, one of the nations hit hardest by the recession, was asked about his country's future. He humorously replied, "We still have fish."

Some panels presented new approaches to familiar topics. Bouchercon 101 on Thursday and Friday did not focus on people who had not been to Bouchercon before but rather on the day's schedule and an introduction to some writers. Other topics included a private eye panel moderated by Robert Randisi, founder of PWA, a slide show by Raymond Benson on James Bond, and a panel on the role of alcohol in mysteries. Among the humorous panels was "Dirty Rotten Liars: The Game Show" with Liza Cody, Peter Lovesey, and Michael Z. Lewin (an Indianapolis native).

Recognizing that many current mysteries involve crafts, a Craft Room was set aside and authors were invited to demonstrate their crafts, for example, scrapbooking and knitting.

Celebrating Rex Stout, an Indiana native, those who registered in advance were given a copy of a Nero Wolfe novel, *Some Buried Caesar*, to read. It was later discussed at a panel. The Wolfe Pack held their annual banquet at Bouchercon.

It had become traditional for publishers to provide copies of books, which are then stuffed in the book bags given out at registration. Many of these are books in which the registrant is not interested, so books are either left in the hotel rooms or put out for exchange. This year there was a Bouchercon Book Bazaar from 9:00 to 11:00 a.m. in the lobby on Sunday. Books were placed at tables near their authors who would sign them. Each person could get up to five books. It was a splendid idea that almost worked. There was not nearly enough room, so that there was a virtual gridlock. It was an idea that went back for consideration in the future by Bouchercon committees.

Chapter Twenty-Three

BOUCHERCONS: 2010–2018

2010: San Francisco
"Bouchercon by the Bay" was held for the third time in San Francisco. Rae Helmsworth was Chair. About fourteen hundred attended. American Guest of Honor was Laurie R. King, author of the Mary Russell/Sherlock Holmes mysteries. Denise Mina of Scotland was the International Guest of Honor. The award for Distinguished Contribution to the genre went to Lee Child, creator of the Jack Reacher series. Bill Pronzini and Marcia Muller received Lifetime Achievement Honors. Few mystery authors are better at writing about San Francisco than they.

Eddie Muller, especially knowledgeable regarding noir films, was Toastmaster. The Fan Guest of Honor was Maddy Van Hertbruggen, incisive reviewer of mysteries in *Mystery News* and *Deadly Pleasures*. In 1999 she created the Yahoo online mystery fan group called 4 Mystery Addicts, which by 2010 had thirteen hundred members. Cap'n Bob Napier, former publisher of *Mystery & Detection Monthly*, received the Sandstrom Award.

Once fans at conventions gathered in hotel lobbies, even moving furniture to fit the size of the group. By 2010 fans mainly "hung out" in the hotel bar or the book room. Wherever people gathered, there was much discussion of e-books and whether they were good for the writers and readers.

In 2010, fans occasionally left the convention hotel, especially in a city as popular with tourists as San Francisco. There was Don Herron's Dashiell Hammett Tour, reduced to two hours from its usual four. Some took the boat trip to Alcatraz Island. PWA's Shamus Awards dinner was held at the Empress of China restaurant in Chinatown. The Wolfe Pack held its annual banquet at the Payne Mansion. The meal, including five wines, consisted of the menu Stout used in his Nero Wolfe novel *Too Many Cooks*. Gayle Lynds was the keynote speaker. Her subject: "Nero Wolfe, the Spy." She included his "history" in Montenegro in World War I.

Saturday night there was a reception by the local Baker Street Irregular groups, The Scowrers and Molly Maguires. Anthony Boucher had been a member of each.

Lee Child held his annual party for the large group of fans informally known as "Reacher's Creatures." He picked up the tab for about a thousand people. Before Tom Cruise played the role, there had been a Jack Reacher lookalike contest to select the man who looks most like what his readers thought Reacher should look like. Child paid to fly the winner, Duncan Munro, to San Francisco.

There was also a party celebrating the eightieth anniversary of the Nancy Drew mysteries that had created so many fans.

The panels were exemplary, and those who didn't wander off had plenty to whet their interest. William Link, the surviving member of the duo that created *Columbo* and *Murder, She Wrote*, revealed that Jean Stapleton, of *All in the Family* fame, had been considered before Angela Lansbury got the role of Jessica Fletcher. The perennial favorite book panel continued to be popular. This time it was moderated by Ali Karim of England.

As part of the plan to create future readers, a high school class was given the five Barry short story nominees to read and select their favorite. Some of the students then attended Bouchercon.

2011: St. Louis

Bouchercon September 15–18 was also called "Murder Under the Arch," after St. Louis's most famous structure, the Gateway Arch. It was also referred to as the "Spirit of St. Louis Bouchercon" and the program book's title was *The Girl Who Came to Bouchercon.* Nearly1,600 people attended at the Renaissance St. Louis Grand Hotel.

Robert Crais and Charlaine Harris were the American Guests of Honor. The International Guests of Honor were Colin Cotterill and Val McDermid. Lifetime Achievement honors went to Sara Paretsky. Ridley Pearson of St. Louis was Toastmaster. Two St. Louis writers, John Lutz and Robert Randisi, were selected as Special Guests/Local Living Legends.

Jon Jordan was chairman of this Bouchercon. He had originally worked with David Thompson, a fan who was also a bookseller (Murder by the Book in Houston) and publisher (Busted Flush Press). David died, far too young, only a few days before Bouchercon began. His widow, McKenna Jordan, no relation, worked on the convention. The David Thompson Special Services Award was created by the Bouchercon Board in Thompson's name, and went to Ali Karim of England whose passion for the mystery was coupled with his knowledge of it and willingness to volunteer.

The Fan Guests of Honor were the husband-and-wife duo of Kate Stine and Brian Skupin, publishers of *Mystery Scene* magazine. Beverly De Weese received the Sandstrom Award.

Ruth Jordan and Judy Bobalik, who had chaired the successful Baltimore Bouchercon, handled the five-track programming. Subjects included comedy in crime fiction, forensics, sex, diversity, food, noir films, and recommended books. They also considered the continuing popularity of Agatha Christie and Alfred Hitchcock.

In what may have been the sign of a trend, for the first time an Anthony was awarded for the Best Graphic Novel.

J. Kingston Pierce in his blog *Rap Sheet* said of the bars at Bouchercon, "It's there that interpersonal links are most easily made and the best strange convention stories shared."

Authors formed teams for charity bowling to benefit the St. Louis Library. The library also benefited from the Saturday Night auction that raised twenty-nine thousand dollars. Laura Lippman bid a large amount to have a character named after her appear in a Charlaine Harris novel.

2012: Cleveland

"Crime Fiction Rocks" was the slogan for Bouchercon 2012, probably indicative of younger fans than those who had founded it more than forty years before. (The favorite music of many fans in the 1960s and 1970s seemed to be classical or show music.) In 2012, Bouchercon's opening ceremonies were held at the Rock and Roll Hall of Fame, and the program proudly called Cleveland "the birthplace of Rock and Roll." Many attendees said the slogan was "cool." A thousand people attended the opening ceremonies, and it was, predictably, very crowded.

Marjory Mogg, a librarian, chaired this Bouchercon, held at the Cleveland Marriott Renaissance Hotel October 4–7, 2012. Mary Higgins Clark received a Lifetime Achievement Award. The American Guest of Honor was Elizabeth George. Robin Cook was honored for "Distinguished Contribution to the Genre." Les Roberts, who not only lives in Cleveland but writes of it in his Milan Jacovich mysteries, was Special Cleveland Guest. He wrote a paean to Cleveland for the program, one that may have surprised people who only knew negative things about Cleveland, such as the Cuyahoga River catching fire. John Connolly from Ireland was Toastmaster. Doris Ann Norris, a librarian and frequent Bouchercon attendee, was Fan Guest of Honor. In writing about Norris and calling herself a "fan of the Fan Guest of Honor," novelist Elaine Viets told of how helpful Norris had been to mystery writers. She not only volunteered to take Viets around Ohio to promote her book, but she rented a car so that Viets wouldn't have to ride in Norris's car, which betrayed the fact that she was a heavy smoker.

It was long overdue that Allen J. Hubin received the Don Sandstrom Award for his services to the genre over the last forty-five years. Recognizing the role Len and June Moffatt had played in the first three Bouchercons and later ones, they received the David Thompson Memorial Special Service Award.

Again, there was much talk about e-books, especially among the writers. A Thursday panel was called "The Great E-book Revolution" and subtitled "How to find great e-books when there is such a flood out there." It was said that "real" publishers have been signing contracts with authors who have had success with e-books.

Mike Bursaw, a pro-active Co-Chair of the Bouchercon Board, announced that a Best Practices Manual has been created and will be passed on to future Bouchercons along with the By-Laws that govern the conventions.

The recent recognition that future readers must be attracted was evidenced in the panel "The Popularity of Y.A. (Young Adult) Books," subtitled "How do authors appeal to young readers and keep them interested in reading?" Other panels dealt with the legacy of Rex Stout, food ("Cooking Up a Murder"), and romantic suspense.

Tourist opportunities were many, including a visit to The Horseshoe Casino for those from states without casinos. Some opted for after-hours tours of the Rock and Roll Museum. The Shamus Awards were given at a dinner cruise on the *Nautica Queen*.

There was evidence of how much Bouchercon means to people who attend. Charles Todd, male half of the mother and son team, was in obvious pain due to back surgery but attended. Lynn

Chandler Willis showed that authors can be fans too, blogging after the convention, "I could spend hours detailing my fan-girl moments with all the greats."

2013: Albany

Albany proved a less than happy location for Bouchercon 44 ("A New York State of Crime") September 19–22, 2013. One problem was that it did not have a hotel large enough for the fifteen hundred attending. Most events were held in the Convention Center in the Empire State Plaza, which was far enough from hotels that considerable walking (often uphill) or cabs or shuttle buses were needed. Having the convention scattered caused people to miss events due to the logistics of getting there.

Sue Grafton received a Lifetime Achievement Award. The International Guest of Honor was P. C. Doherty. Tess Gerritsen was the American Guest of Honor. Steve Hamilton was Toastmaster. Chris Aldrich and Lynn Kaczmarek, editors and publishers of *Mystery News*, were Fan Guests of Honor, although Lynn was not able to attend. I was awarded the David Thompson Special Service Award, though I also could not attend, for medical reasons. Ali Karim of England won the Don Sandstrom Award for his numerous fan activities.

Writer Lee Goldberg said this was "the worst location and the most poorly organized Bouchercon I've been to." Others complained that locations were hard to find, and the streets they had to walk had many homeless people begging for money. The locale was especially difficult for wheelchairs. The shuttles were old school buses that were difficult for some to board. Also, they left people off far from Plaza entrances. A leading Albany hotel, the Hilton, was described as "woefully unprepared" for this large an event and serving "inedible food." Max Allan Collins was being tactful when he expressed the sentiments of many in describing the venue as "not user friendly." He pointed to the lack of lobby, restaurant, and bar in the convention center. Bars have been called "the beating heart of Bouchercon." The acoustics in the atrium bar at the Hilton made conversation difficult and those at the convention center not much better.

Books are heavy, and having to carry them considerable distances from hotels for signatures was frustrating. Also, hearing that gangs frequented some of the streets near the center cut into attendance for evening events as some people chose to remain in their hotels.

Still, some fans continued to seek the autographs of their favorite authors. The autographing lines were long, and fans were frustrated that they were too long to engage the writers in conversation. George Easter and "Mystery Mike" Bursaw came up with a solution, one that also allowed Mike to sell books. They held "Meet the Authors" sessions in the bookroom, where fans could get signatures and talk to writers.

Judy Bobalik and Jon Jordan were in charge of programming, which generally had five or six tracks. The title of each panel cleverly was a Billy Joel song, for example "Half a Mile Away: Crime Outside the Big City" or "Sleeping with the Television On: Why reading is better than watching."

There were some memorable moments that could be heard. Sue Grafton, nearing the end of the alphabet, said she told her children she would haunt them if they allowed anyone else to continue her Kinsey Millhone series. Chris Aldrich spoke of the people at Bouchercon as "the family of her heart," a phrase that caught on among those who heard it.

2014: Long Beach

Bouchercon came late this year (November 13–16) at the Hyatt Regency, but since its location was Long Beach, California, weather was not a factor in what was called "Murder at the Beach." Ingrid Willis was Chair. J.A. Jance was the U.S. Guest of Honor. A writer of historical mysteries, Edward Marston of England, was International Guest of Honor. Jeffery Deaver received Lifetime Achievement honors. Al Abramson who had played an important role in many previous Bouchercons was recognized as Fan Guest of Honor. Judy Bobalik won the David Thompson Special Services Award. Simon Wood was Toastmaster. Ted Hertel received the Sandstrom Award.

The size of Bouchercon overwhelmed the hotel, and some events had to be scheduled elsewhere. For example, the opening ceremonies were at the Pacific Ballroom, and the Anthony presentations at the Terrace Theater.

The effort to attract the young as mystery readers and, eventually, as writers continued apace in Long Beach. Eoin Colfer of Ireland was the first Young Adult Fiction Guest of Honor. Before Bouchercon opened, more than a hundred authors visited school classrooms in the Long Beach area. Each student received at least one book. There was a "YA Fan Fest" aboard the *Queen Mary,* which is permanently docked in Long Beach harbor, with over twenty YA authors. It was a paid event with a luncheon. Proceeds went to the Long Beach Public Library Foundation.

Some panels were especially helpful to those attending. (There were about sixteen hundred attendees, including two hundred day passes.) Thursday morning had Bouchercon 101, "All you need to know about Bouchercon to get the most out of the convention," mostly for people attending their first Bouchercon.

Some have complained that few panels are geared toward fans. An exception was Friday's panel "All About the Fans: Super Fans and How They Got Involved."

"Speed Dating" came to Bouchercon on Thursday. It has been described as a "frenzied event" in which authors circulate to tables of fans and are given two and a half minutes each to pitch their latest book. Many events at Bouchercons are sponsored by publishers, but this was sponsored by Smith & Wesson.

The success of Bouchercon is increasingly due to the board of directors of Bouchercon, Inc., who contribute their time and effort without being paid. The Board's welcome in the

Bouchercon program, prepared by David Magayna, Board Chair, and Jeffrey Siger, Board Vice-Chair, succinctly summarized what mysteries can accomplish. "Mystery readers can enjoy and learn about cultures, politics, and social viewpoints different from their own and maybe gain a better understanding of the world through their enjoyment of mysteries." In the past the general members' meetings had seemed an afterthought, sometimes scheduled at 8:00 a.m. on Sunday. This year the Board scheduled it on Friday in the middle of the day. Board members were also present at 10:00 a.m. on Saturday for a panel titled "So You Want to Host a Bouchercon," ready to help those so inclined to understand what is involved in this formidable task and how the Board will support them.

The variety of panels at Bouchercon was astounding. Many featured leading experts. Some examples in 2014: "Sherlock Through the Ages," with noted Sherlockian Leslie S. Klinger as moderator; collecting with Otto Penzler as moderator; "Jewish Noir" with Kenneth Wishnia, editor of a collection under that title, a Robert McGinnis slideshow presented by the leading expert on McGinnis's cover art, Art Scott. Other panels were about forensics, e-books, and historical mysteries.

Audiences for some of the "old" panels were small. An example was Thursday's panel on locked rooms, despite Jeffery Deaver, Laurie R. King, and Gigi Pandian being on the panel. Pandian, author of the popular Jaya Jones Treasure Hunt mysteries, writes locked room short stories and always emphasizes that she is a fan as well as an author.

There should have been more people at a panel about Anthony Boucher. One panelist, June Moffatt, knew Boucher personally.

2015: Raleigh

The first Bouchercon to be held in the South (except for one in Texas) was "Murder Under the Oaks," October 8–11 at the Marriott and Sheraton hotels in Raleigh, North Carolina. If one wasn't sure why that title, one had only to look at the seemingly never-ending rows of oak trees between the airport and the hotels.

The American Guests of Honor were Dr. Kathy Reichs and Tom Franklin. The International Guests of Honor were Allan Guthrie and Zoë Sharp. Margaret Maron of North Carolina received the Lifetime Achievement Award. Sarah R. Shaber of Raleigh was the Local Guest of Honor. The Toastmasters were Lori Armstrong and Sean Doolittle. The Fan Guests of Honor were Lucinda Surber and Stan Ulrich, who had chaired or participated in many Left Coast Crime and Bouchercons and write and edit *Stop, You're Killing Me*, arguably the most valuable website for mystery fans. They have also created a website designed to help children to read. The David Thompson Special Service Award went to another married team—Bill and Toby Gottfried, who've attended conventions for over thirty years and have played many roles in putting them on. Jane Lee received the Sandstrom Award. She's a frequent volunteer at conventions who can be found behind the scenes, stuffing books in bags, etc. Al Abramson was Chairman again.

Ali Karim and Kerry Hammond arranged the panels, usually seven tracks worth. J. Kingston Pierce in his blog *Rap Sheet* said about Karim, "Ali seemed to be everywhere simultaneously—not only in the audience at panel discussions, but outside the conference rooms, checking in with authors and comrades, and introducing people to one another in the best networking fashion." Ali also took many pictures, allowing the *Rap Sheet* to present a good pictorial history of this convention.

Dogs are always popular at Bouchercon, and this year there was a panel called "What the Dog Knows: The Science and Wonder of the Working Cadaver Dog." The two panelists Kate Floria and Cat Warren (an unusual name for someone on a dog panel) spoke about dogs trained to locate and follow the scent of decomposing human flesh. They are used in missing person cases in which a dead body might be found by a search.

A panel on political espionage thrillers included two former intelligence officers and a federal marshal. There was little discussion of spy novels but much about Edward Snowden of Wiki-leak fame or infamy. Most of the panelists denounced Snowden.

Most crime novels are about murder. As the worst crime that can be committed it has the gravitas to hold readers' interest. However, some readers have said they would like to read (and hear about) other crimes. They got their wish in Raleigh with a Saturday panel "The White Collar Criminal in Mystery & Thriller Fiction."

Blogs allowed attendees at Bouchercon to share their experiences during or right after the convention. Many said that one of the pleasures of Bouchercon was meeting in person people they had only been in touch with via email or Facebook. Almost all bloggers, especially those new to the convention, commented on the friendliness of their fellow attendees. First-timers described their experiences in superlatives such as "overwhelming" and "epic."

Many important features of recent Bouchercons were carried over to Raleigh, including Bouchercon 101, "Speed Dating," and "So You Want to Put On a Bouchercon?" An anthology of short fiction whose theme is connected to Bouchercon was published. Called *Murder Under the Oaks*, it was edited by Art Taylor, one of the leading current short-story writers. A panel was devoted to it, as was a signing by the authors collected in it.

2016: New Orleans

A Bouchercon in one of America's most popular cities for tourists resulted in attendance of close to two thousand people, nearly a record. "Blood on the Bayou" was held September 15–18 at the Marriott Hotel. Bestselling writer Heather Graham and Connie Perry, a Louisiana native, were Co-Chairs.

Harlan Coben was the American Guest of Honor. Instead of an International Guest of Honor, per se, Craig Robertson of Scotland was designated International Rising Star Guest of Honor. David Morrell received a Lifetime Achievement Award. Julie Smith was the Local Legend. Bouchercon Kids Guest of Honor was R.L. Stine. Harley Jane Kozak and Alexandra Sokoloff were Toastmasters.

The Fan Guests of Honor were Jon and Ruth Jordan who have been involved in putting on many mystery conventions and also publish the fan magazine *Crimespree*. They first met at the 1999 Bouchercon. The Jordans, along with Judy Bobalik, were also responsible for panel programming this year. David Magayna, a fan-reviewer who is active on the Bouchercon Board of Directors, received the Sandstrom Award.

The distribution of books has never been handled better at a Bouchercon. Instead of loading them into a book bag, they were placed on tables, and attendees were given six tickets and allowed to choose the books they wanted. Free copies of *Mystery Scene*, *Strand Magazine*, *EQMM*, and *AHMM* were also available.

Many who attended added days either before or after Bouchercon to sample what makes New Orleans special. There was even a "New Orleans 101," led by Graham before the convention on Wednesday to guide people who had not been to the city before to get the most out of their time. (The usual Bouchercon 101 was held Thursday for those new to the convention.)

Food, of course, was important and was a frequent topic of discussion. Many reported having their first taste of alligator. When people weren't in restaurants or at Bouchercon, they might be seen touring the city's famous cemeteries, the National World War II Museum, or even the remnants of Hurricane Katrina. Oppressive heat and humidity were often noticed. Despite it, the annual Bouchercon basketball game, organized by S. J. Rozan, took place.

Saturday was designated Kids Day, and important writers, including Harlan Coben, R.L. Stine, and Ridley Peterson, went to branches of the New Orleans Library. Special attention was paid to those children who had done best in summer reading programs. There was a Young Adult book panel at the convention on Friday.

Panels were given the names (or variations on them) of songs. It is always hard to pick favorite panels. As usual, many favored the annual dog panel with ATF agents and a detection demonstration by a yellow lab named "Ting," trained by Katherine Barton.

Laura Lippman won easily in "Just a Minute," a BBC game show in which the contestants had sixty seconds to discuss a topic chosen on the spot by the moderator "without hesitating, repeating, or deviating from the subject." Lippman also moderated a panel on "Real Housewives and Other Dangerous Women."

Panels about the past did not draw many people. Admittedly, the one on fandom was early (9:00 a.m.) on Thursday. A panel on Ellery Queen should have done better also. It included the granddaughter of John Dickson Carr, now a mystery writer herself. A panel on the "Golden Age," led by Martin Edwards, did better.

For the third year in a row, an anthology of short stories, *Blood on the Bayou*, was published; it received a signing event. This one was edited by Greg Herren.

The organizers of Bouchercon tried to capture as much of the flavor of New Orleans and Mardi Gras as possible. The Opening Ceremonies were conducted with flashing strobe lights and booming jazz music. The Guests of Honor were given bead necklaces to throw. One spectator was hit in the face, but with no damage. On Friday, the Guests of Honor were escorted to the Orpheum Theatre for the Anthony Awards on elaborate Mardi Gras parade-type floats, throwing beaded necklaces all the way.

Even after Bouchercon was over, many who attended celebrated it in blogs. Several wrote, "I Survived My First Bouchercon," while looking forward to next year.

2017: Toronto

Toronto's Bouchercon in 2017 was called "Passport to Murder," appropriate since terrorism has tightened security so much that a passport is now necessary for U.S. attendees to go to Canada. The Co-Chairs, Janet Costello and Helen Nelson, emphasized in their welcome, "Toronto is known for its multiculturalism, openness and, ironically for our event, its low crime rate. It's the safest major city in North America." Successful Bouchercons were held in Toronto in 1992 and 2004. In 2017 it was at the Sheraton Centre October 12–15.

Prior to the opening of Bouchercon there was a tour to Niagara Falls, one that some fans who went on it called "the tour from Hell" as the bus broke down, and they were stranded for hours in the rain. Probably happier were those who took one of the tours to the Toronto Public Library, with its outstanding Arthur Conan Doyle collection.

Louise Penny was the Canadian Guest of Honor. Megan Abbott was American Guest of Honor. Christopher Brookmyre of Scotland was International Guest of Honor. In a continuing effort to create younger readers for the mystery, Chris Grabenstein was Bcon4Kids Guest of Honor. The "Ghost" of Honor was John Buchan, aka Lord Tweedsmuir, famous for crime novels such as *The Thirty-Nine Steps,* and for being the popular Governor General of Canada from 1935 to 1940. Twist Phelan and Gary Phillips were Toastmasters. Canadian author Howard Engel, creator of the private detective Benny Cooperman series, was named a "Local Legend." *Ellery Queen's Mystery Magazine,* in its seventy-sixth year, was honored for its "Distinguished Contribution," and a panel was held at which its editor, Janet Hutchings, was interviewed, and fifteen *EQMM* authors and fans spoke about their connection to the magazine.

George Easter, publisher and editor of *Deadly Pleasures,* received the David Thompson Special Service Award for "extraordinary efforts to develop and promote the crime fiction field." George, in turn, had created the Don Sandstrom Memorial Award for Lifetime Achievement in Mystery Fandom in 2001. In 2017 the award went to Steele Curry, a devoted mystery reader and reviewer.

The Fan Guest of Honor was Margaret Cannon, who calls herself "a born mystery reader," despite the fact that her mother refused to allow the Nancy Drew books into their house in Arkansas. Cannon taught a survey course on crime fiction at York University and has been a reviewer for the *Globe and Mail,* a leading Toronto newspaper, for over thirty years. She receives mail from readers asking for her recommendations of books to read.

The Bouchercon Board of Directors prior to the 2017 elections had David Magayna as Chair; Dru Ann Love as Secretary, and Stan Ulrich as Treasurer. There are also five elected members, and ten past and future Bouchercon Chairs on the board. The Bouchercon Bylaws and Standing Rules were prominently printed in the convention program book.

Some of the popular events that were repeated included "Speed Dating," that allowed forty-four authors to rotate quickly to tables to promote their books. Similarly, "20 on the 20 Spotlight" allowed fans to meet authors during twenty-minute sessions.

Unusual was a Library Tea on Thursday afternoon in which the many librarians attending enjoyed refreshments and discussion with writers and reviewers. Alarm bells went off in the midst of this, and we were told that the Toronto Fire Department came to check it out. Fortunately, there was no problem that required evacuation or further interruption of events.

2018: St. Petersburg, Florida

Weather is not a factor at most Bouchercons, which are usually put on in autumn, with a few summer occasions, as was this one. Temperatures were in the high 80s, and the humidity was equally noticeable to those who left the hotel to eat or visit a museum. On the last day, the threat of Hurricane Florence caused some people to turn to the Weather Channel and eventually cancel plans for sightseeing further north along the Atlantic shore.

Scheduling Bouchercon at about the same time as a major Jewish holiday did cause some long-time attendees to stay home.

Yet, at least 1,429 people did show up at the Vinoy Renaissance and other nearby hotels. The Vinoy was a fine site, albeit one with as confusing a series of corridors as any since the infamous Omaha Holiday Inn of the early 1990s. Signs weren't always helpful, or accurate. On the first night Carol and I got lost trying to find the hotel's seafood restaurant, but a bellhop personally took us there.

Erin Mitchell was Co-Chair along with Ruth and Jon Jordan, the latter two having much experience in putting on Bouchercons. The three summed up their viewpoint simply, "We love to read and talk to other people who love to read."

There was a long list of people honored. Sean Chercover and Karin Slaughter were the American Guests of Honor. Mark Billingham of England and Sara Blaedel of Denmark were International Guests of Honor. Lifetime Achievement honors went to Ian Rankin of Scotland. Florida Guest of Honor was Tim Dorsey. Lisa Unger was Toastmistress.

The David Thompson Special Service Award went to Lesa Holstine, a librarian and blogger (*Lesa's Book Critiques*).She also reviews for three publications: *Mystery Readers Journal*, *ReadertoReader.com*, and *Library Journal*. Louise Penny said, "Lesa has championed crime writing with intelligence, passion, warmth and insight."

There were two Fan Guests of Honor. Judy Bobalik was Co-Chair of the 2008 Baltimore Bouchercon and has been in charge of programming for four other Bouchercons. Ayo Onatade of London is a reviewer, blogger, judge for CWA awards, and a great supporter of new writers.

Proving that the internet is changing the way fans buy books, there were only four booksellers in the book room.

The program book, in addition to publishing the Bouchercon Bylaws and Standing Rules, contained for the first time Bouchercon Board's Harassment Policy/Code of Conduct. It was designed to help insure that "Bouchercon 2018 should be free of any discrimination, abuse, or harassment." Apparently, there has been anecdotal evidence of misconduct in the past at Bouchercon. The instances of which I'm aware did not occur at Bouchercons and are discussed elsewhere in this book.

John D. MacDonald was "Ghost of Honor." No one wrote as often or as well about Florida. His grandson talked about him at the opening ceremonies and mentioned that his grandfather was one of the first mystery writers to include environmental issues in his books.

Social issues surfaced in Kellye Garrett's acceptance speech after receiving the Anthony as Best First Novel for *Hollywood Homicide*. Garrett had done research and spoke of her finding few minority writers had won awards in the past.

Larry Gandle was surprised when he won the Don Sandstrom Award. He claimed not to deserve it, but he does for his work as Associate Editor of *Deadly Pleasures* and his other fan activities.

A new award, the Bill Crider Award for Best Novel in a Series, honored one of the most popular writer-fans, who had died early in 2018. It was won by Sue Grafton, who had also died since the 2017 Bouchercon, for the twenty-fifth book in her Kinsey Millhone series. Crider's daughter, Angela, both a mystery writer and an attorney, presented the award.

There were five tracks of either panels or interviews. None was especially fan-centered, with the possible exception of a Friday 9:00 a.m. panel on *Ellery Queen's Mystery Magazine*. The panelists, Dale Andrews, David Dean, Brendan DuBois, Josh Pachter, and Sarah Weinman all have had stories in the magazine and were clearly fans of the magazine, now in its seventy-seventh year, and cared about its future.

Other panels of special interest included Digging in the Dirt-Archeological Protagonists; the annual Liars Panel with Laura Lippman especially convincing; Michael Connelly's interview of the very funny (he was once a stand-up comic) Mark Billingham.

The Business Meeting, scheduled in prime time, drew its largest attendance to date, an estimated four times greater than any previous one. Fans were able to vote for new members of the Bouchercon Board as well as future sites. Nashville projected for 2021 had to withdraw, but it was replaced by an equally attractive location: New Orleans. Minneapolis was selected for 2022.

As you read this book, you may be at Bouchercon's fiftieth anniversary in Dallas in 2019. The research and writing necessary for this book had to be completed in 2018, but rest assured, some fan of the future will eventually cover 2019 while updating this history of mystery fandom.

Chapter Twenty-Four

OTHER FAN MAGAZINES, ORGANIZATIONS, AND CONVENTIONS: 21ST CENTURY

The International Sister Fidelma Society (2000–)
Paul Tremayne is the pseudonym of Peter Berresford Ellis. His seventh-century nun-detective is the subject of a fan group started in 2000 by David Robert Wooten of Little Rock, Arkansas. Ellis has said in praise, "The Fidelma Society seem to know more about the books than I do." Three times a year Wooten puts out a journal, *The Brehon,* its name taken from the system of law in which Sister Fidelma was trained. He sells Fidelma-related material to keep the organization going.

A bed-and-breakfast in Cashel Town, Ireland, has been renamed The Sister Fidelma Bed and Breakfast. The idea of a meeting of her fans who belong to the Sister Fidelma Society, began at the 2006 funeral of Ellis's wife, Dorothy Cheesmur Ellis, a great booster of the series and the inspiration for Fidelma. Since then, it has been held biannually. The last meeting was in 2017.

Nancy Drew Sleuths (2000–)

Nancy Drew Sleuths was established in 2000, with Jennifer Fisher as president, for the purpose of "fostering the legacy of Nancy Drew." Nancy Drew has been an inspiration to many writers, lawyers, and teachers, including Hillary Clinton and Laura Bush. The group started as an online discussion group, but now holds an annual convention, one that has been held in various cities, including Boston, New York and Las Vegas. One annual meeting was conducted as part of a cruise to the Bahamas. They publish a bimonthly magazine, *The Sleuth*. Lifetime membership in the group is thirty dollars. Fans of the Hardy Boys have been invited to join.

At each convention, a theme book is selected (one of fifty-six hardcover Nancy Drew books published between 1930 and 1956), usually one that has a specific locale. In April 2018 the convention was at Key West, Florida, following *The Clue of the Black Key*. The website says, "and we do things that Nancy Drew and her chums did in the books." In one of the convention activities, collectors of the Drew books meet "to trade books and stories." Since there have been so many editions of Nancy Drew books, many members search for specific editions.

Some of the costs are defrayed by selling "Officially licensed Nancy Drew merchandise." The organization donates Nancy Drew books to libraries "for today's generation to discover Nancy Drew mysteries."

Crime Scene (2000–)

Adrian Wootton, principal organizer of "Shots" and the Nottingham Bouchercon, moved to an important position at the National Film Theatre on London's Southbank. In 2000, with Maxim Jakubowski, he organized Crime Scene, a London film festival with a mystery component. Attendance was about six hundred fifty, with movie fans outnumbering mystery readers. Crime Scene, which continues, features celebrations of mystery writers whose work has been adapted for film and television, including Agatha Christie and Georges Simenon.

Mayhem in the Midlands (2000–2010)

Omaha, Nebraska, was a center of fandom in the early 1990s with three regional conferences and a Bouchercon, previously discussed. Few of the people who worked on the earlier Omaha conferences were involved when Mayhem in the Midlands started in 2000. It was sponsored by the public libraries of Omaha and Lincoln. An anthology, *Mayhem in the Midlands,* with stories by authors who attended in 2000, edited by Robert J. Randisi and Christine Matthews, was published in 2002. Guests of Honor, such as Dennis Lehane and Jan Burke, have come from outside the Midwest. A highlight of the 2003 banquet was Burke singing "Makin' Mayhem" to the tune of "Makin' Whoopee." In 2009 a panel of spouses, some of whom were only fans because they are married to writers, took place. The organizers of this conference avoided the maze-like Omaha Holiday Inn, holding their conferences at the Omaha Sheraton. Reports from the convention have emphasized surprise in finding how many good restaurants Omaha has. It was last held in 2010.

Deadly Ink (2000–)

Originally a one-day conference, Deadly Ink, in New Jersey, starting in 2000, has been described as New Jersey's "biggest little convention." Its first Guest of Honor was Parnell Hall, who lives in New York, but later Jan Burke of California and Steve Hamilton of Michigan have been honored. This conference was first held in Mount Arlington and then in Parsippany and New Brunswick, New Jersey. It has expanded to a three-day event. In 2018 it was held in Rockaway, New Jersey, with Debby Buchanan as Chair.

Cape Fear Crime Festival (2001–2007)

Cape Fear is not only the title of two movies based on a John D.

MacDonald novel but also was the site of the Cape Fear Crime Festival, first held in 2001 in Wilmington, North Carolina. It was a joint effort of local publishers, booksellers, and the New Hanover County Library. Margaret Maron, North Carolina's most famous mystery writer, was keynote speaker at the first conference; later events have had Carolyn G. Hart of Oklahoma and Parnell Hall in that capacity. It was held until 2007 but stopped when a sponsoring bookstore closed and the library had budget problems.

Give Me That Old-Time Detection **(2002–)**

A welcome visit to the past is provided in this fan journal that Arthur Vidro started in the autumn of 2002. It has a punny title. (Think of the gospel song "Give Me That Old-Time Religion.") Vidro's interests rest in the writers of detective fiction's "Golden Age," including Rex Stout, Stuart Palmer, John Dickson Carr, Ngaio Marsh, and Ellery Queen, but he is also a fan of the suspense writer Cornell Woolrich. He has also printed articles on Hillary Waugh, who wrote an outstanding series of police procedurals, and Julian Symons, known for his psychological suspense novels.

Asked why he started *Old-Time Detection,* Vidro replied, "Because after years of immersion in the subject matter, it was time to be more than just a fan. I wanted to contribute to the cause."

Vidro is especially a fan of Ellery Queen who has been the subject of at least five cover articles in *Old-Time Detection,* as well as having one issue devoted almost entirely to him. When Vidro and his wife moved from Long Island, it was partly coincidence that they settled on Ellery Street in Claremont, New Hampshire, the small town that Ellery Queen used as the basis for Wrightsville, the New England village that Queen wrote of, beginning with *Calamity Town* (1942).

The magazine that Vidro publishes three times a year is reminiscent of the early days of fan magazines. Its fans are enthusiastic.

Although Vidro has only about one hundred subscribers, he publishes more letters from readers than other American fan magazines (seventeen in the Summer 2006 issue). Vidro retypes every article himself, as Al Hubin did when *The Armchair Detective* began. Unlike other publisher-editors, he doesn't have a website.

Vidro's love for the great mysteries of the past shows throughout his magazine. The classic detective puzzle is its main focus, with in-depth articles on Philip MacDonald, T.S. Stribling, C. Daly King, among others, and reviews. Forgotten writers are brought back in *Old-Time Detection*. For example, Stribling is virtually unknown now, though he once won a Pulitzer Prize for a novel, and his detective Professor Poggioli is considered one of the great sleuths of the past. Vidro has printed material about Stribling in his magazine, including his correspondence with Frederic Dannay, and he has edited a collection of Stribling short stories.

In the days before talking films and television, the crime play was very popular on Broadway and in London's West End. That is no longer true, though Agatha Christie's *The Mousetrap* is the exception. Vidro published a long series, eighteen articles, that I wrote about theatrical mysteries. They eventually became a book, *The Villainous Stage* (2014).

Occasionally *Old-Time Detection* publishes fiction, for example the stories of William Brittain, whose detective stories about a teacher, Mr. Strang, are examples of old-time detection. Vidro also sponsored a contest, publishing three detective stories that had never been printed before.

In the Spring 2018 issue Vidro published the results of a poll of *Old-Time Detection* readers as to their "Favorite" mysteries. These results were compared to a 1973 poll of *The Armchair Detective* readers. About a third of *OTD*'s readership, thirty-one people, voted. With few exceptions, the books and stories selected date from mystery's so called "Golden Age" between the World Wars.

Murder in the Magic City (2003–)

The Southern branch of Sisters in Crime, Crosshaven Books, and the Homewood Library jointly sponsor Murder in the Magic City, which started in 2003 in Birmingham, Alabama, and is held at the Homewood Library. "Magic City" refers to the "magical growth" in population of Birmingham since the end of the Civil War, from one hundred people to two hundred fifty-thousand. The conference was held in 2018 on February 3. Lunch and a "goody bag" were included in the forty-dollar registration fee.

Harrogate Crime Writing Festival (2003-)

Though relatively recent, the Harrogate Crime Writing Festival in northern Yorkshire already has gained great popularity. The brainchild of popular author Val McDermid and agent Jane Gregory, it added a crime-fiction conference to the various other arts festivals that take place in Harrogate. Though it has its share of panels and interviews, Harrogate also emphasizes entertainment, and there are quiz programs and a "Cabaret of Crime," in which writers sing and tell jokes. In 2018 McDermid was a member of the "Fun Lovin' Crime Writers Band," performing at the Saturday night Cabaret. Others who have entertained include Simon Brett, and Mark Billingham, a former stand-up comic. On Sunday there is often a popular quiz "I'm Sorry I Haven't a Cluedo," presided over by the humorous Mike Ripley.

In 1926 Agatha Christie disappeared, and for eleven days much of England wondered about her fate. She turned up at the Swan Hydropathic Hotel, now called the Old Swan Hotel, a spa in Harrogate, using someone else's name and apparently suffering from loss of memory. With this history, it is fitting that the Old Swan is headquarters for one of England's most prestigious crime meeting: Theakston's Old Peculier Crime Writing Festival, usually called the Harrogate Crime Festival, although the Theakston brewery has been important in sponsoring this meeting since 2004. Their ads for it typically say, "Your only crime would be to miss it." In 2017 the Old Swan held an exhibition featuring original artwork and items from the Christie archives, including original correspondence between Christie and her publisher, Collins. The Swan now has a plaque proclaiming "Agatha's Retreat" on its ground floor.

Harrogate started in 2003 at the Majestic Hotel. It later moved to the Crown Hotel before settling in at the Swan in 2011. Unlike most American conventions, at which paying one registration fee permits entrance to all events (except occasionally a banquet), Harrogate, the city of many festivals, sells individual tickets, some for the weekend, others for individual days, some for a particular lecture, interview or panel. In 2017 and 2018, 16,500 tickets were sold each year. The crime writing festival was reported to generate 3.5 million pounds for the city. Most events at this sold-out convention have at least five hundred people present.

Major names frequently are featured, such as J.K. Rowling (of Harry Potter renown) and David Suchet who plays Hercule Poirot. It was at Harrogate that Rowling revealed that she was writing mysteries as "Robert Galbraith." Unlike the U.S. where programming is the job of the fans who make up the convention committee, in England important writers take on that task. For example, Ann Cleeves was in charge of programming in 2014; Lee Child was in charge in 2018 and brought his friend, fellow bestselling author John Grisham, who doesn't often appear at conventions, but agreed to be a "Headline Star" in 2018. Child interviewed him at the Royal Hall on Friday. Grisham received an award for "outstanding contribution to crime fiction." Child displayed remarkable patience and staying power in 2018, posing for countless "selfies" with those attending.

There are other awards given at Harrogate, starting with the first night when the Theakston Award for the best British novel of the past year is given. That is voted on by fans, though the Harrogate committee has input. Among the winners have been McDermid, Denise Mina, and Billingham.

Fans also vote for the Dead Good Reader Awards, presented each year since 2015. They are often in unusual categories, for example, following a current trend, there was an award for the book with the "Most Unreliable Narrator."

Fans obviously are attracted to this event. Writers in their blogs often emphasize that they are readers too. "Reader" seems to be the word favored over "fan," perhaps because the latter is, after all, short for fanatic. There seem to be fewer fan-based activities at British conventions, including the absence of a Fan (or Reader) Guest of Honor at Harrogate.

When Val McDermid received an award for "Outstanding Contribution to Crime Fiction," she said, "And in everything we do we include the readers because writers without readers are redundant." She called Harrogate "the most vibrant and popular event of its kind anywhere in the world...because we're inclusive." In publicity there was mention that "fledgling writers and established superstar authors mingle in the hotel bar." In 2018 Lee Child also said, "Readers are the most important people."

One of the Harrogate highlights every year is McDermid's New Blood Panel consisting of the four writers she has picked for her favorite debuts. Other panels recur every year, but some are one-offs, like the panel in 2011 that feature three ex-convicts. One had been a football hooligan; another had been convicted of murder.

There is basketball at most Bouchercons. At Harrogate there have been football matches (the British, not the American variety), with Northern English writers pitted against the South.

There is much emphasis on the first day of Harrogate on writing, especially for those still unpublished. It is referred to as "Creative Thursday." There are workshops for which many sign up, and there is a "pitch" session at which writers promote their latest books in hopes of interesting an agent or editor. Obviously, it is important for writers to attend though it may mean a stressful weekend. Rebecca Whitney blogged, "...there were many more events I'd have loved to attend, but there was the ever-important job of catching up with other authors, publicists, agents, and editors in the bar..." Some of the conversation at Harrogate is about getting published and book deals. Invariably, before one becomes a mystery writer, one is first a mystery reader. Typical is novelist Stephanie Marland who in her blog *Crime Thriller Girl* describes her mystery reading.

Fans don't have quite the same pressure, but they want to attend events and write them up for other fans. Among the Super Fans who have written about Harrogate and other conventions is Ayo Onatade, a clerk for a judge, who spends much time as a freelance critic, interviewer, and blogger. Similarly, for Ali Karim, a scientist when earning a living, Ali doesn't seem to be interested in censoring his reports, and they joyously detail his drinking and his late night bar conversations, usually about mysteries. His knowledge of the mystery is profound. He was a previous winner of the Theakston Quiz, a part of every Harrogate. In 2017 he came second, and his teammates jokingly blamed him for losing because of his "swigging all that gin."

The Great Manhattan Mystery Conclave (2004–2009)

The Great Manhattan Mystery Conclave was not expected to be a continuing conference; it was first held in 2004 to celebrate the centennial of the Manhattan, Kansas, Public Library. Among the guests were Nancy Pickard of Kansas. It was a success, so further conclaves were held, chaired by Marolyn Caldwell, who advertised it as celebrating "the small town mystery" and its writers and fans. Attendance was seldom more than a hundred. In contrast to New York City's Manhattan, it was called "the little apple." An anthology of authors who attended, *Manhattan Mysteries,* was published in 2005. The conference was last held in 2009, with Earlene Fowler as Guest of Honor.

***Crimespree Magazine* (2004–)**

Crimespree Magazine has been edited by Jon and Ruth Jordan of

Milwaukee since 2004. It is a bimonthly publication that aims to attract a diverse group of readers. Answering the rhetorical question as to who *Crimespree* is, the Jordans said, "Collectively, we are mystery/crime fiction readers from all over the map. A shared passion for the genre has drawn us together."

Each issue includes articles about writers and interviews with them, short stories, for which *Crimespree* cannot pay, true crime (one issue had an interview with a private detective), and information about small press publishers and book stores. That Jon Jordan would include many interviews is not surprising; in 2003 he published an Anthony-nominated book, *Interrogations*, that contained twenty-five interviews with current writers. Though its emphasis seems mainly on the hardboiled, *Crimespree* occasionally delves into the past, as with an article by Ted Hertel on Ellery Queen, and Ruth Jordan's piece on Father Brown. Issue 67, in 2018, celebrates the one hundredth birthday of Mickey Spillane and remembers the late Bill Crider.

One of the things *Crimespree* does is report on conventions. "I Was a Mystery Convention Virgin" by Sue Kelso told about her first convention: Omaha's Mayhem in the Midlands. Ann R. Chernow's report on the Harrogate Crime Writing Festival showed the same enthusiasm demonstrated when people wrote about early Bouchercons and included that oft-used line "You had to be there!" when words seem inadequate to capture a delightful experience.

Crimespree's circulation is between two thousand and twenty-five hundred. The Jordans remain very busy, putting out the magazine as well as being involved in conventions as they were in co-chairing the 2018 St. Petersburg Bouchercon.

ConMisterio (2005–2006)

People in Austin, Texas, who put on the 2002 Bouchercon launched a new convention, ConMisterio, in July 2005 with Karen Meschke and Lillian Butler as Co-Chairs. Kate Derie, who operated the famous mystery website *Cluelass.com,* was Fan Guest of Honor. Jon A. Jackson and Earlene Fowler were the Guests of Honor. Joe Lansdale was Toastmaster. Linda Landrigan, editor of *Alfred Hitchcock Mystery Magazine,* was "Professional Guest of Honor."

ConMisterio returned to Austin in 2006. Jan Grape was Fan Guest of Honor. She had been slated to share that honor with her husband Elmer, but he died on December 29, 2005 and was fondly remembered as "Ghost of Honor." Margaret Maron and James Crumley were Guests of Honor. Publisher Dennis McMillan (Black Lizard Press) was a "Special Guest." Bill Crider was Toastmaster.

ConMisterio had good publicity, including a long newspaper article about it a week before it started. Two contests took advantage of Austin's reputation for popular music. In both the winners would be among those who could name five songs about crime. After two years, ConMisterio could not show a profit, and Meschke announced that it would not be held in 2007, nor was it held thereafter.

New England Crimebake (2005–)

It has become increasingly clear that many mystery readers would like to be mystery writers. Though fans are welcome, many small conventions aim for writers. For example, the New England Crimebake, usually held Veterans' Day weekend in Boston, advertises that it "offer numerous opportunities to meet with agents, editors, and authors." Opportunity for networking and manuscript critique are also mentioned. It has been sponsored by Sisters in Crime and the Mystery Writers Association and has been held since 2005. Registration is limited to two hundred fifty, and activities are not planned for fans.

Murder in the Grove (2005–2008)

Murder in the Grove in Boise, Idaho, was sponsored by Partners in Crime Boise, a Chapter of Sisters in Crime, and Coeur du Bois, a Chapter of Romance Writers of America. It has not been held since 2008.

Murder & Mayhem in Muskego; Murder & Mayhem in Milwaukee (2005–)

This was launched by Jon and Ruth Jordan, Erica Ruth Neubauer, and Penny Halle in 2005 in Mukego, a Milwaukee suburb. It was held at the town's Public Library, with the help of the Friends of the Library (FOL). It was a one-day, intimate conference with a single track and was described at "fancentric." In 2013 it was decided that since those attending paid, holding the conference was inconsistent with rules that mandated that FOL events be free to the public.

Murder and Mayhem moved to Milwaukee in 2014 to a former church, now the Irish Community Center. Those attending sit in pews while listening to panel discussions. People attending say it has lost none of its casual and relaxed attitude.

***Ellery Queen's Mystery Magazine* Fandom (2005, 2016)**

Anthony Boucher famously said, "Ellery Queen *is* the American detective story." He was recognizing Queen as author, editor, detective, collector, and scholar. Queen is the pseudonym of two cousins, Fredric Dannay and Manfred B. Lee. In 2005 the magazine celebrated the one-hundredth anniversary of the birth of Dannay and Lee with a conference at Columbia University in New York City, where an exhibition of Queen memorabilia was held. Queen's son and Lee's granddaughter both spoke, as did many fans of Queen, including Francis M. Nevins, Edward D. Hoch, Steve Steinbock, Jeffery Marks, and Douglas G. Greene. Queen's fair play puzzles were, for many readers, the entry path into mystery fandom, and they remain loyal to him.

The 2005 meeting was termed the *EQMM* Centenary Symposium, though the magazine was not one hundred years old. In 2016 it was seventy-five years old, a remarkable achievement for any magazine now. The magazine celebrated in its pages during the year and invited its fans to a celebratory symposium held at the Butler Rare Book and Manuscript Library of Columbia University on September 30, 2016. There were remarks by Queen fans and an exhibition, running from September 26 until December 23, including magazines, artwork, and correspondence by Dannay.

ThrillerFest (2006–)

Despite the cost of staying at a midtown New York hotel, some fans do attend the Thrillerfest conference each summer to meet favorite authors. That organization started in 2006 meeting at the Arizona Biltmore in Phoenix, where the July temperature was close to 110 degrees. Later meetings have continued to be in July, but in New York at the Grand Hyatt Hotel. Its members include some of the most successful writers in the genre, people such as James Patterson, Joseph Finder, and David Morrell. A short story anthology titled *Thriller* was published, though to unenthusiastic reviews in the *New York Times Book Review.*

Early in the history of this conference more fans, including George Easter, Larry Gandle, Ali Karim, Maggie Mason, and Mike Stotter, attended. Karim wrote of the sad feeling at the end of one of these conferences, words that could apply to more fan-oriented meetings: "You feel at home talking to people who share the same passion, the thrill of turning pages, the smell of books, the excitement that the printed word can generate in your mind, and the pictures they print in your imagination."

CrimeFest (2008–)

After a successful Left Coast Crime in 2006, Bristol became a fixture on the convention circuit in July 2008. Adrian Muller and Myles Allfrey have continued to chair Bristol, now joined by crime writer Donna Moore as a co-host. It is called CrimeFest, though its full title is: The International Crime Fiction Convention. It also uses the catchy phrase: "Where the Pen Is Bloodier Than the

Sword." People who attend are called "delegates," a term that in the U.S. connotes an election convention. A female toastmaster, like Natasha Cooper, is referred to as a "toasttrix." Attendance is often at least five hundred. J. K. Rowling, who has become a mystery writer, was a Guest in 2014. Maj Sjöwall, the legendary Swedish writer, was a special guest in 2015.

Nine different awards are given each year, including two for children's books. A Last Laugh Award goes to the best comic mystery. Like other English conventions, there is no Fan Guest of Honor, though, of course, many fans attend.

One can get a good idea of what CrimeFest is like by reading the report that Super Fan Ali Karim wrote on the first convention in 2008 for the *Rap Sheet* blog. He mentions the heavy luggage that many fans bring to conventions if they want to have books signed. Karim collects first printings of Advance Readers Copies. Almost all conventions provide free books to those attending, but also sometimes prize books go to those in the audience who ask "the most intriguing questions" at the end of panels.

Karim's description of how he spends his time at conventions includes lots of drinking, almost non-stop talking about mysteries, and very little sleep. He, like other true fans, seems to thrive on that regimen.

A feature of CrimeFest is at least one panel on "Forgotten Authors." An example is John Creasey who had seven hundred forty-three rejections before making a sale, yet ended up with over six hundred books published. Leading historian Martin Edwards often leads these and is called a "participating moderator." At American conventions, occasionally the moderator participates in the discussion. Often, they seem to be there only to direct traffic.

A feature at the 2015 CrimeFest (and later meetings) was "Pitch an Agent," in which authors get to describe books possibly to attract that necessary person in the publishing process: the agent. Another panel that year was called "Emerging Indie Voices," and it emphasized self-publishing.

That year not only did John Curran resurrect two forgotten authors, J.J. Connington and Henry Wade, but he celebrated "125 Years of Agatha Christie," interviewing Christie's grandson Mathew Prichard and Sophie Hannah who was selected by the Christie estate to carry on with Hercule Poirot books.

"No Spoilers" is an unwritten rule at conventions, one that is occasionally violated by authors. In 2017, with one hundred fifty authors present, Caro Ramsay made up a paddle saying "No Spoilers" that she threatened to use.

In 2018, to mark a tenth year for CrimeFest, a celebratory anthology, *Ten Year Stretch,* edited by Martin Edwards and Adrian Muller, was published. The book was the idea of Canadian mystery fan Jane Burfield who has often attended CrimeFest and offered to sponsor the book, a copy of which went to every delegate attending. All of the twenty stories are new and include authors Simon Brett, Lee Child, Ann Cleeves, Jeffery Deaver, and Ian Rankin. Maj Sjöwall contributed a story written many years ago, but with a translation into English for the first time. Profits go to the Royal National Institute of Blind People, a charity for which CrimeFest has raised funds in the past.

Scandinavian crime fiction is important in Bristol. One of the awards given, the Petrona, is for the best Scandinavian mystery novel. In 2018 the Icelandic Chapter of CWA held an impromptu meeting there. CrimeFest is often international, and in 2017 a panel was called "Wunderbar! The Hidden Wonders of the German Krimi," the last word German for a crime story.

Bloody Scotland International Writing Festival (2012–)

Lin Anderson and Alex Gray wondered why with all its crime writers Scotland did not have a conference. That led to the Bloody Scotland International Writing Festival in Stirling, founded in 2012, still alive and doing well as of 2018. Opening receptions have been held in Stirling Castle, followed by a torchlight procession. As at Harrogate, tickets are sold for various events. A record number (8,474) were sold in 2017. The convention website says, "Free standby tickets were made available to the unemployed or those on a low income."

Among some of the unusual features at Bloody Scotland are a field trip to a distillery, a football match between the Scottish writers and the English writers, and the ever-popular "Crime at the Coo," an event at the Curly Coo Pub and cabaret.

Crime Readers Association (CRA) (2012–)

The Crime Writers Association (CWA) founded this group in 2012 to encourage reading of mysteries. Membership is free, and a monthly newsletter is sent via email to members, publicizing books and meetings and publishing interviews with writers. May 2018 was declared National Crime Reading Month in England, and there were events to help achieve CRA's goals. Four thousand mysteries were given away during the month. The CrimeFest convention was held in that month.

NoirWich (2014–)

Still another British mystery convention, NoirWich, has been held since 2014 in Norwich, which is advertised as the "City of Literature." It is presented by the National Centre for Writing (with events at its Dragon Hall) and the University of East Anglia. One of England's leading experts in crime fiction, Barry Forshaw, says that the title of this convention is more than a pun because noir "is a major strand of British crime writing" now.

Important guests at the 2018 meeting included Val McDermid, Benjamin Black, Nicci French, and Paula Hawkins. Reporting on the convention is "Blogger in Residence" Jamie Bernthal. He completed his Ph.D. on Agatha Christie and is researcher for Sophie Hannah who was selected to write new Hercule Poirot novels. There is an organized group, "The Norwich Bloggers," whose job is blogging for various events held in Norwich.

Clouded in Mystery (2014–)

By the twenty-first century, it was rare for a fan journal to be published in the traditional magazine format. (The plethora of blogs about the mystery, which replaced magazines, will be discussed elsewhere.) An exception, beginning in October 2014, was *Prose 'n Cons: A Magazine for Fans of Mystery, Crime, & Suspense*. This is the one-woman operation of Stephanie Hoover, part of what she calls her "History-Tainment Network." The emphasis is on true crime, even offering "the best tours and vacations for lovers of true crime." There are occasional interviews with mystery writers, such as Sara Paretsky and M.C. Beaton. In 2017 Hoover changed the name of *Prose 'n Cons* to *Clouded in Mystery: Myths and True Crime from the U.S. and the U.K.*

Bodies from the Library (2015–)

Following a 2013 exhibition "Murder in the Library," the British Library began to hold a one-day conference about crime fiction. These fit in nicely with another British Library project: reprinting older mystery classics as part of the British Library Crime Classics series. The first conference was held June 20, 2015, and was a success according to those who attended. The choices of topics for author presentations or panels were highly praised. Topics included: "When was the Golden Age?" Oxbridge mysteries, the Detection Club's collaborative mysteries, Agatha Christie's tastes in reading, and books that are "Ripe for Reprint."

Some of the leading lights of the "Golden Age," no matter when you decide that was, were discussed at the second Bodies from the Library, July 11, 2016. They included Anthony Berkeley, Josephine Tey, Ngaio Marsh, H.C. Bailey, and G.K. Chesterton.

The third conference in 2017 began with further consideration of that ever-fascinating topic the "Golden Age." Other talks featured "neglected" writers Ethel Lina White, Elizabeth Daly, Father Ronald Knox, John Rhode, and Edmund Crispin. For the last named, the discussion wasn't about his detective novels but rather about the movie music he wrote under his real name: Bruce Montgomery.

The fourth conference in 2018 had discussion of Richard Hull, Christianna Brand, and Michael Innes, but also included someone who is not well known, especially in the United States. Ellen Wilkinson was a Member of Parliament and later only the second woman to be a Cabinet Minister. Long a fan, she wrote one detective story *The Division Bell Mystery* (1932).

Good news for those attending was that there will be a fifth conference in 2019.

Ladies of Intrigue Conference (2015–2017)

"Featuring Remarkable Women Mystery Writers" is how this conference advertised itself, but it also said, "aspiring crime novelists and mystery lovers are welcome." Organized by the Southern California Sisters in Crime and the Mystery Ink Bookstore in Huntington Beach, California, it has held Sunday events in Santa Ana, California, near the Orange County airport. One of the guests in 2017 was Marcia Clark, prosecutor in the O. J. Simpson case and now a mystery novelist. It was held yearly beginning in 2015 but was not scheduled in 2018.

Mayhem & Murder in Chicago (2017–)

Aware of the success of Muskego/Milwaukee, different organizers initiated a one-day event, held on a March Saturday at Roosevelt University on Chicago's South Side. Promotion for this advertised that "This event is perfect for crime readers and librarians hoping to find new books to read…" The organizers are Dana Kaye, a publicist who specializes in publishing and entertainment, and novelist Lori Rader-Day. About two hundred fifty people attended the first conference at which Sara Paretsky and William Kent Krueger were featured guests. Jeffery Deaver and Gillian Flynn appeared in 2018. Tickets were relatively inexpensive, with a range of thirty-five to sixty-five dollars, depending on whether you were a student and when you signed up.

Miss Fisher's Murder Mysteries Conference (2017–)

Phryne Fisher, the stylish Melbourne, Australia, private detective, created by Kerry Greenwood, is so popular that she has given birth to an annual conference that started in 2017 and was repeated in 2018. The initial conference was held in Las Vegas. The second was in Portland, Oregon, from June 28 through July 1, 2018, and was so popular that it was sold out early in the year. It is organized by a non-profit group: The Adventuress Club of the Americas.

Discussion of the television scripts and the role of Miss Fisher, played by Essie Davis, is important at the event. The convention emphasizes that it also includes costume contests, scavenger hunts, and shopping. Pictures show many of those attending (they are mostly female) in costumes similar to those worn by Miss Fisher in the show that is set in the 1920s.

Alibis in the Archives (2017–)

One of the newest mystery conventions is Alibis in the Archives, first held in June 2017 to celebrate the opening of the British Crime Writing Archives at Gladstone's Library in Hawarden, North Wales. Attendance was limited to seventy-five people, about fifteen of whom were crime writers, as was speaker Martin Edwards, Chair of the Crime Writers Association, President of the Detection Club, and Archivist of both organizations. Enthusiastic about the Archives, Edwards said, "The idea of the weekend is to engage crime fans with the heritage of crime writing, including non-fiction, and to give them a chance to have a look at material in the archives..."

Alibis in the Archives returned in 2018, in partnership with the British Library's Bodies from the Library publishing program. Among speakers were Ruth Dudley Edwards, Martin Edwards,

Simon Brett, Michael Jecks, and Peter Lovesey. Like the St. Hilda's conference, speakers discuss topics; there are not panel discussions. In 2018 Martin Edwards spoke on collecting crime fiction, including that fan favorite the "green Penguin mysteries."

Chapter Twenty-Five

FAMOUS MYSTERY FANS

It is highly unlikely you will see any famous fans at a convention. There are security problems, and they are usually too busy to attend. However, because every aspect of their lives is covered in the media, their reading of mysteries receives publicity.

The first famous fan emerged less than two decades after Edgar Allan Poe wrote what is usually considered the first mystery in 1841. In an 1860 campaign biography, William Dean Howells wrote of Abraham Lincoln, "He is therefore pleased with the absolute and logical method of Poe's tales and sketches, in which the problem of mystery is given, and wrought out into everyday facts by processes of cunning analysis. It is said that he suffers no year to pass without a perusal of this author."

Few remember Arthur B. Reeve now, but his scientific sleuth Craig Kennedy was so popular, especially in the second decade of the twentieth century, that he was known as "the American Sherlock Holmes." When Reeve learned that Theodore Roosevelt liked his work, he sent the former president a specially bound set. Roosevelt is also known to have read Poe and Mary Roberts Rinehart.

An alert White House reporter spotted Woodrow Wilson reading J.S. Fletcher's *The Middle Temple Murder* (1919) and reported it. His report turned it into a book that sold far better than it might have otherwise. After Wilson suffered a stroke, his wife, Edith Galt Wilson, who took on many of the tasks of the president, found time to read mysteries to Woodrow.

Franklin Delanor Roosevelt was probably the best-known Presidential mystery fan. He is the only president who appears in Hubin's bibliography as an "author." During a White House supper, FDR told his guests of an idea for a story that he had not been able to write: "How could a man disappear with five million dollars and not leave a trace?" One of his guests was Fulton Oursler, editor of *Liberty* and, as "Anthony Abbot," a popular American detective story writer. Enlisting six other writers, each of whom contributed a chapter, Oursler serialized *The President's Mystery Story* in his magazine in 1935. It was also published as a book that year and was reissued in 1967 as *The President's Murder Plot.*

After Roosevelt's death in 1945, it was reported that the book he had been reading in bed the night before he died was *The Punch and Judy Murders,* which John Dickson Carr wrote as "Carter Dickson." The Dickson series character, Sir Henry Merrivale, is reported to have been based, at least in part, on Winston Churchill. Roosevelt was also a fan of Sherlock Holmes, as was his successor Harry S Truman.

John F. Kennedy is often credited with promoting the popularity of the James Bond novels in the U.S. The publicity director for Ian Fleming's paperback publisher was surprised at how much better sales were after another of those alert reporters spotted JFK with a Bond novel and was told that Kennedy loved Fleming's books.

Before attention shifted to his sex life, Bill Clinton's reading habits made the news. He was revealed to be a fan of Walter Mosley, Michael Connelly, Dennis Lehane, and Sara

Paretsky. Reporters accompanying Clinton followed him into a Washington bookstore where he bought a copy of Connelly's *The Concrete Blonde.*

In 2018 Bill Clinton made more headlines when he collaborated with best-selling writer James Patterson on a mystery *The President Is Missing*. In it President Jonathan Duncan leaves the White House to foil a cyberterror plot. It quickly reached the top of the New York Times Bestseller list.

Ronald Reagan was reported to read Sherlock Holmes and Tom Clancy.

George W. Bush read his fellow Texan Kinky Friedman as well as John D. MacDonald. Laura Bush is a fan of Elizabeth Ironside, the pseudonym of Lady Catherine Manning, whose husband Sir David Manning was British Ambassador to the U.S. from 2003 to 2007. Bill Crider reported that at a reception in Austin, Laura Bush mentioned Crider's *The Texas Capitol Murders* (1992).

It is not only in the United States that political leaders find relaxation from their duties in mysteries. Former Prime Minister Harold Macmillan read them and wrote Peter Lovesey a fan letter. Margaret Thatcher was known to have watched British crime series on television. She read Agatha Christie and P.D. James.

Love of mysteries is not limited to political figures. Perhaps, as Philip Guedalla, a well-known British historian in the first half of the twentieth century, said, "The detective story is the normal recreation of noble minds." Some of the great names in culture and literature have been readers—and occasionally writers of/or about mysteries. Jacques Barzun is probably the best known. Russell Kirk, a leading conservative philosopher, wrote two mystery novels, the first of which was highly praised by Anthony Boucher. The Nobel Prize-winning French writer André Gide wrote of his love of the work of Dashiell Hammett. In *Six Men,* Alistair Cooke wrote about interviewing the noted philosopher Bertrand Russell on a train between New York and

Washington, DC. After the interview, he observed Russell reading a paperback mystery.

The anti-fan was Edmund Wilson, a noted novelist and essayist, whose series of 1944–1945 diatribes in *The New Yorker,* "Who Cares Who Murdered Roger Ackroyd?" mobilized early mystery fandom to strong response.

Popular entertainers also read mysteries. In the 1950s, *Ellery Queen's Mystery Magazine* advertised that stars as diverse as Steve Allen, Joan Crawford, Eddie Cantor, Ethel Merman, and Beatrice Lillie were among their readers.

Chapter Twenty-Six

SCHOLARSHIP BY MYSTERY FANS

There was a time when scholarly writing about the mystery was done by professionals. Yes, Howard Haycraft and Ellery Queen were fans, but they earned their livelihoods writing and editing. Many of the most active Sherlockian fans, including Christopher Morley, Anthony Boucher, John Dickson Carr, Rex Stout and Queen were professionals, too.

Since the "fan revolution" of 1967, an enormous number of scholarly articles and books about every aspect of the mystery have been written by fans whose livelihood was earned elsewhere. *The John D. MacDonald Bibliophile, The Mystery Reader's Newsletter,* and *The Armchair Detective* were published by people wanting to share information about the mystery and the writers they loved. Publishers of fan magazines were lucky if they didn't lose money. Even when fans were paid for their work, the amount was minimal. I speak from the experience of writing books and hundreds of reviews and articles, as well as co-editing and co-writing books, when I say that financial gain has never been the motive for fan scholarship. After remuneration is divided by hours spent, the scholar has worked at far less than minimum wage.

Early articles and bibliographies in fan magazines were about such major names as Agatha Christie, Raymond Chandler, G.K. Chesterton, Harry Kemelman, and Edgar Wallace. So little had been written about the mystery, that was a logical starting point. Soon material appeared on Freeman Wills Crofts, Margaret Millar, Arthur W. Upfield, and Sax Rohmer who had their champions but were not known to all fans, let alone the general mystery-reading public. Eventually, more obscure author—Cleve Adams, Norbert Davis, C. E. Vulliamy, Ernest Savage, and James Corbett—became the subjects of articles.

In 1976, Mystery Writers of American established an Edgar category for Best Critical/Biographical Work, but fans were already publishing books. In 1971, Francis M. Nevins published *The Mystery Writer's Art,* the first anthology of articles about the mystery in twenty-five years. That year, Norman Donaldson, a chemist, published *In Search of Dr. Thorndyke,* about R. Austin Freeman and his detective. Also in 1971, Jacques Barzun and Wendell Hertig Taylor won a Special Edgar for *A Catalogue of Crime.* Barzun was a famous savant who wrote widely in many areas of culture, while his friend Taylor was a scientist. They wrote as fans, reprinting forty years of notes they sent each other on the mysteries they read.

Their book, revised in 1989, is an annotated bibliography of over five thousand books, essays, and stories of crime fiction and true crime. It is a book about which few are neutral. The authors admit to a bias in favor of detective novels with fair-play solutions. This has made it a valuable book for it introduced readers to little known writers, some of whom were never published in America, especially those who wrote in the "Golden Age" years. Other fans questioned their omission of many American hardboiled writers. Their writing is witty and sophisticated, though there are errors in the first edition, making one suspect that the book was largely printed from the authors' notes, without overly careful review.

Detectionary, destined to become a legend, was also published in 1971. Its origin was a proposal from the Hammermill Paper Company for a book, to be delivered in a few months, to demonstrate their reference book paper. It consisted of brief biographies of the great detectives, helpers, and rogues in crime fiction, as well as brief summaries of important crime novels, short stories and detective movies. The five fans who were the author-editors were Nevins, a law professor; Otto Penzler, a writer for ABC's Wide World of Sports; Chris Steinbrunner, program director of a New York television station; Charles Shibuk, a school teacher; and myself, an administrator at a New York State Agency.

We delivered the book on time and even received our copies. However, before it could be distributed, Hammermill discovered a small defect (a wrinkle) on some pages. It was not fatal to reading *Detectionary* but was if you were using the book to promote your company's paper, so Hammermill destroyed the remainder of the first printing. A second printing in 1972 proved equally unlucky. Though some copies were distributed, most were destroyed in a warehouse in Pennsylvania when a hurricane caused the Susquehanna River to overflow. Copies of either printing became collectors' items, though there was a commercial hardcover edition in 1977 and a paperback edition in 1980.

The first "new fan" to win an Edgar was Nevins who received a Special Edgar for his 1974 book *Royal Bloodline: Ellery Queen, Author and Detective.* Like his earlier anthology and the Donaldson book, it was published by Bowling Green State University's Popular Press. One of the first universities to make popular culture "respectable," it published books by fans about crime fiction, although they never distributed them widely.

In 1973, a major publisher, McGraw Hill, commissioned the first mystery reference book, *Encyclopedia of Mystery and Detection,* to be written and edited by four perpetrators of *Detectionary:* Steinbrunner, Penzler, Shibuk, and Lachman. It won MWA's first Critical/Biographical Edgar.

There had been no bibliography of crime fiction before the "fan revolution," though while Hubin was deciding whether to publish *The Armchair Detective*, another Minnesota fan, Ordean Hagen, was writing *Who Done It: A Guide to Detective, Mystery and Suspense Fiction* (1969). Its main feature was Hagen's attempt to list, by author, every mystery book published in English. There were errors and omissions, and Hagen's death April 5, 1969, before his book was published, denied him the opportunity to add to or correct it. Other sections, also incomplete, included a subject guide of mysteries, lists of plays and screen adaptations, a list of geographical settings, a list of series characters, a list of anthologies and collections, and a bibliography of secondary sources. Despite its faults, Hagen's book is a major work and every feature of it became the basis of later scholarly works by fans.

Al Hubin with his indispensable bibliography at Bouchercon 2003

Shortly after Hagen's death, Hubin began to devote part of each issue of *TAD* to correcting and adding to Hagen's book. Hubin also added many features that made his bibliography easier to use, including separate listings of pseudonymous work, important because so many mystery writers wrote under pen names. Hubin's *The Bibliography of Crime Fiction, 1749–1975*, published in 1979, is generally regarded as the one indispensable reference work. Jon L. Breen said it "has come about as close as humanly possible to achieving the goal of listing every volume of mystery or detective fiction published in English." Later editions updated it, and an edition published in 2003, both as a CD-ROM and in a five-book set, carried it through 2000. Since then, Hubin has worked continuously, with help from Steve Lewis and John Herrington, among others, to correct and add information through 2000. He and Locus Press have issued three CD-ROMs to make this information readily available.

There are other bibliographies that are enormously useful and enjoyable reading because they are annotated. Breen has been a mystery reader and fan from a young age. In his twenties, he began publishing fiction and other material in *Ellery Queen's Mystery Magazine*. He later became *EQMM*'s reviewer. In 1981 he published *What About Murder? A Guide to Books About Mystery and Detective Fiction,* covering 239 books, most of which were published after 1967. This is a short book of 157 pages, but had Breen only included works published before the "fan revolution," it would have been far shorter. So extensive is the later writing about the mystery, much of it by fans, that a second edition covering only 1981 through 1991, listed 565 books and took up 377 pages.

Detective and Mystery Fiction: An International Bibliography of Secondary Sources (1985) by Walter Albert, a fan and former Professor of French, goes beyond Breen because he also lists thousands of magazine articles. There are evaluations of many of the 5,200 entries, but not in the depth Breen's more limited scope allowed. MWA awarded Albert a Special Edgar. The first revision, published in 1997, included only the period 1985–1990 but this had almost 7,700 listings. A final revision, through the year 2000, on CD-ROM, has 10,715 annotated entries.

Other bibliographies were more specific. In 1992 Ellen Nehr published her Anthony-winning *Doubleday Crime Club Compendium 1928–1991,* a lavishly illustrated history of the longest-lasting line of mysteries from any U.S. hardcover publisher. She listed every book they published and described plots and even dust jackets.

There are also bibliographies of individual authors. In addition to working on one for John D. MacDonald, June Moffatt, with the help of Nevins, produced a bibliography of the prolific Edward D. Hoch. She updated it each year. By 2008 when he died, Hoch had published well over nine hundred short stories, as well as novels and nonfiction.

Nevins, with Ray Stanich, compiled *The Sound of Detection*

about the Ellery Queen radio mysteries. The first edition, in 1983, was useful but contained gaps. With old-time radio expert Martin Grams, Jr., Nevins brought it up to date in 2002. Another successful Nevins bibliographic project was reprinting Anthony Boucher's 1940s reviews from the *San Francisco Chronicle*.

Annotated bibliographies have increasingly taken the form of "Companions," books that treat an author's work in considerable depth and provide biographical material. One of the earliest was *The Agatha Christie Companion* (1984), which authors Dennis Sanders and Len Lovallo called a "four-year labor of love." Sometimes the emphasis is on the detective character, as in *The Cadfael Companion* (1991) by Robin Whiteman, about Ellis Peters's Brother Cadfael. A major part of *The Tony Hillerman Companion* (1994), edited by Martin Greenberg, is a two hundred-page "concordance" of all the characters in Hillerman's fiction by Elizabeth A. Gaines and Diane Hammer.

Another example is Sharon A. Feaster's *The Cat Who... Companion* (1998) devoted to the cat mysteries of Lilian Jackson Braun. It includes an interview with Braun, plot summaries of her books, an alphabetical list of characters in the series, and even a map of its setting, fictional Moose County. The format of *The Dick Francis Compendium* (2003) by Jean Swanson and Dean James is similar to Feaster's, but they added some features appropriate to a guide to Dick Francis: a gazetteer to the racing locations mentioned and a list of the horses in the books, and, fittingly for an author who so often "grabbed" readers with his first sentence, a list of memorable opening lines in the Francis canon.

While the Cold War was still hot, Andy East published *The Cold War File* (1981), a listing of the work of eighty authors of spy novels. His range was great, from the literary espionage novels of John Le Carré to such sexy novels of Ted Mark as *The Man from O.R.G.Y.*

One of the most ambitious of all fan-bibliographers was Michael L. Cook of Evansville, Indiana. His first "project" was

Murder by Mail: Inside the Mystery Book Clubs (1979), with histories and complete lists of offerings of the Detective Book Club, the Mystery Guild, and the Unicorn Mystery Book Club. A revision in 1983 updated the offerings of the first two clubs, then still active, and added several lesser-known clubs.

The title of Cook's *Monthly Murders: A Checklist and Chronological Listing of Fiction in the Digest-Size Mystery Magazines in the United States and England* (1982) aptly describes his bibliography of about one hundred periodicals. For the computer age, William G. Contento updated Cook's work in a CD-ROM *Mystery Short Fiction Miscellany: An Index* (2003), including information on short story collections and anthologies.

Two somewhat-related 1983 bibliographies of Cook's were *Mystery Detective* and *Espionage Magazines* and *Mystery Fanfare: A Composite Annotated Index to Mystery and Related Fanzines 1963–1981.* The first book included descriptions of fan magazines, along with hundreds of pulp and digest-sized fiction magazines. The second book covers almost fifty fan magazines.

Cook's most daunting indexing project, one undertaken with Stephen T. Miller, was *Mystery, Detective, and Espionage Fiction: A Checklist of Fiction in U.S. Pulp Magazines, 1915–1974,* published in two volumes in 1988. Cook died June 14, 1988, at age fifty-eight, shortly before it was published. The first volume is a chronological listing of about three hundred-fifty magazines, beginning with *Ace Detective Magazine* and extending to *Zeppelin Stories.* (Yes, in 1929 there was a magazine with the latter title, and it included some mysteries.) The second volume is an alphabetical listing, by author, of about ten thousand pulp stories.

Steven A. Stilwell indexed the first ten years of *The Armchair Detective,* and William F. Deeck updated it through *TAD*'s demise in Vol. 30. Alone, Deeck indexed *The Mystery FANcier, The Poisoned Pen,* CADS, *Mystery Readers Journal,* and *Deadly Pleasures.* With Deeck's death in 2004, the last two fan magazines, still active, cry for some fan to bring them up to date. (Christine R.

Simpson has been indexing CADS.) Deeck's indexes are invaluable to scholars.

John Nieminski was another tireless bibliographer, and his work is more impressive because its 4,212 entries were done with index cards, not a computer. In 1974 he published an index to *Ellery Queen's Mystery Magazine,* covering its first 350 issues. Nieminski was proud of his complete *EQMM* collection, including the fact that all the issues were in mint condition. Not willing to trust his copies to the Postal Service, he bought them at newsstands. (As another fan of *EQMM,* I am continuing his index for the magazine, beginning where he left off in January 1973.) Nieminski also did a complete index for *Saint Mystery Magazine;* his death in 1986 prevented a similar index for *Alfred Hitchcock Mystery Magazine.*

As the mystery became increasingly popular, it was apparent that a high percentage of readers are women. It was also clear that many female readers enjoy reading about female characters. Once, scholarly works were gender-neutral, but then fans began writing books about female authors. Perhaps the first of these was *Silk Stalkings: When Women Write of Murder* (Black Lizard, 1988) by Victoria Nichols and Susan Thompson. Their subjects were female mystery writers, but they did not restrict themselves to those with female characters. Thus, P.D. James and her Adam Dalgliesh are included. A new edition in 1998, *Silk Stalkings: More Women Write of Murder* (Scarecrow Press), added many new writers. Incidentally, the title "Silk Stalkings" was so clever that a cable television network purchased it for a series with female sleuths.

Jean Swanson and Dean James's *By a Woman's Hand* (1994; second edition 1996) is a guide to over 200 female authors and their characters. In *Mystery Women: An Encyclopedia of Leading Women Characters in Mystery Fiction* (in four volumes, published between 1997 and 2003), Colleen Barnett wrote of over 1,100 female series characters. Her numbers testify to their increase since 1980. Between 1860 and 1979, there were 392 female series characters. Between 1980 and 1989, there were about two hundred fifty new ones, and then more than five hundred emerged from 1990 through 1999!

Willetta L. Heising first published *Detecting Women* in 1995, listing living female authors that write mystery series, with biographical information about them and a listing of the books in which their series characters appear. Proving she was an equal-opportunity bibliographer, Heising published *Detecting Men* in 1998. By 2000, *Detecting Women* was in its third edition, having added two hundred twenty-five authors since the second edition in 1996.

The growth of female series detectives was a reflection of a huge increase in mysteries published. Readers wanted recommendations, not only in magazine reviews but also in books. This led to a growth in guides that were not restricted to authors or series characters of one sex. G.K. Hall employed six fans for their Reader's Guide series. First, Susan Oleksiw, who became series editor, wrote the book that was the prototype: *A Reader's Guide to the Classic British Mystery* (1988). It included brief plot descriptions of about one thousand British mysteries. There were also appendices that listed settings, occupations, and the period in which the mystery takes place. Finally, Oleksiw picked 100 outstanding books in her field. Her book was followed by my *A Reader's Guide to the American Novel of Detection* (1993), Gary Warren Niebuhr's *A Reader's Guide to the Private Eye Novel* (1993), Jo Ann Vicarel's *A Reader's Guide to the Police Procedural* (1995), Nancy-Stephanie Stone's *A Reader's Guide to the Spy and Thriller Novel* (1997) and Mary Johnson Jarvis's *A Reader's Guide to the Suspense Novel* (1997).

No subject seems too far-fetched for fans wishing to share their enthusiasm. John Kennedy Melling's *Murder Done to Death* (1996) is the definitive book about parody and pastiche in detective fiction. John E. Kramer wrote *Academe in Mystery and Detective Fiction* (2000) concerning mysteries set on college campuses. Jon

L. Breen's *Novel Verdicts* (1984) is an annotated listing of courtroom mysteries. Though not a lawyer, Breen shows a remarkable knowledge of the law as well as wide reading. He analyzes eighty-six Erle Stanley Gardner novels that have courtroom action. With the growth of legal mysteries following the success of Scott Turow's *Presumed Innocent* (1987), Breen published a second edition of his book in 1999. The number of courtroom mysteries had risen from 421 in 1984 to 790 fifteen years later.

Combining a love of sports and mystery stories, I wrote a series for *TAD,* beginning in 1972, about mysteries with sports backgrounds. It was an idea inspired by an earlier article I published in *World Tennis,* "Tennis and the Mystery Story." Tom Taylor's *The Golf Murders* (1996) is the ultimate book about golf mysteries.

Scholarship is not all humorless. Bill Pronzini, as those who know him are aware, is as much a fan as a writer of fiction. He's a collector of pulp magazines and other mysteries and searches for examples of funny, bad writing, what he calls "alternate classics." He uses these in his "Gun in Cheek" series, one book of which is subtitled "An Affectionate Guide to More of the 'Worst' in Mystery Fiction." Illustrations include: "The next day dawned bright and clear on my empty stomach," from Michael Avallone's *Meanwhile Back at the Morgue,* and "He poured himself a drink and counted the money. It came to ten thousand even, mostly in fifties and twenty-fives," from Brett Halliday's *The Violent World of Michael Shayne.* Bill Deeck, to whom I previously referred, captured the best of the worst of James Corbett in his *The Complete Deeck on Corbett* (2003).

Cover art can be an important bonus to mysteries. A feature of Nehr's book on the Doubleday Crime Club was the color reproduction of ninety-four of their best dust jackets. John Cooper and Barry Pike compiled two books with some of the best British dust jacket art. Art Scott is one of the leading experts on American paperback cover art, and he conducts popular slide shows, with examples, at Bouchercons. Scott is the leading expert on the work of Robert McGinnis, arguably the best artist to illustrate the covers of paperback mysteries. With Dr. Wallace Maynard, Scott published the well-illustrated *The Paperback Covers of Robert McGinnis* (2001). An even more complete representation of the artist's work is found in Scott's *The Art of Robert E. McGinnis* (2014). Equally admired by those with a taste for nostalgia is the artwork that was on the covers of mystery pulp magazines. Among the best collections of these are Lee Server's *Danger Is My Business* (1993) and Robert Lesser's *Pulp Art* (1997).

Definitive biographies of writers have been written by fans. In addition to writing two book about Ellery Queen, Francis M. Nevins won an Edgar for his biography of Cornell Woolrich, *First You Dream, Then You Die* (1988). Nevins had been writing about Woolrich for fan magazines for twenty years and edited collections of Woolrich's stories. In addition to describing Woolrich's ability to write suspenseful prose, Nevins conveys the unusual life led by Woolrich, a recluse full of self-hate who spent most of his life living in hotels with his mother.

Another unhappy life is documented by Jeffrey Marks in *Who Was That Lady?* (2001), the biography of Craig Rice. Marks discusses the question of whether it was Rice who "ghosted" Gypsy Rose Lee's *The G-String Murders.* Rice died at forty-nine, her death hastened by alcoholism.

Doug Greene, expert on John Dickson Carr and founder of Crippen & Landru Publishers

John McAleer spent years researching his definitive, Edgar-winning 1977 biography *Rex Stout,* being fortunate to have interviewed his subject before Stout died. Equally worthy of an Edgar was Douglas G. Greene's *John Dickson Carr: The Man Who Explained Miracles* (1995), but he did not win it or any of the three other awards for which he was nominated.

J. Randolph Cox wrote an exhaustive article on his

almost-namesake, George Harmon Coxe, for *TAD.* He later published *Man of Magic and Mystery,* a guide to the work of Walter Gibson, creator of *The Shadow.* In *Old-Time Detection* for Summer 2017 he wrote a long article about critic, scholar, and mystery writer Robert Barnard.

Richard Martin was a fan of Margery Allingham since he first read her at age seventeen. His 1988 biography of her, *In Her Blood,* is appropriately titled because she came from a family who thought writing the only suitable way to earn a living. There is biographical material about Allingham in *Campion's Career* (1987) by B.A. Pike, but the focus of this British fan is her detective, Albert Campion. Ray B. Browne published *The Spirit of Australia* (1988), about the crime fiction of Arthur W. Upfield. B.J. Rahn edited *Ngaio Marsh: The Woman and Her Work* for the 1995 centenary of Marsh's birth. Marsh wrote her autobiography in 1965, but since she lived another seventeen years, there obviously was much that was not included, but was in *Ngaio Marsh: A Life* by Margaret Lewis, a 1991 biography that involved two round trips from England to New Zealand for research. Biographies of Golden Age writers are seldom published, but a fortunate exception is Malcolm J. Turnbull's *Elusion Aforethought: The Life and Writing of Anthony Berkeley Cox* (1996) a book about the author better known as Anthony Berkeley or Francis Iles.

Since the 1980s, almost every American mystery has had a strong regional element, with detailed descriptions of the geography, speech, dress, and lifestyle of their locations. At times, it seems that this lengthy description overwhelms the mystery plot. My complaint is ironic since in 1970, in *The Mystery Reader's Newsletter,* I started a series of articles on how the regions of the United States are depicted in mystery fiction. I said then that there weren't enough mysteries with good regional descriptions. My series was completed in 1977, having moved to *TAD* when *TMRN* ceased publication. Eventually, despite the vast number of new regional mysteries, I finished revising and updating my articles and published them in a five-hundred-forty-two-page book, *The American Regional Mystery* (2000). Steve Glassman and Maurice J. O'Sullivan have been more pragmatic in writing about smaller areas, with books on mysteries set in Florida and the Southwest.

Many mystery readers and writers have remarked on the influence of the Nancy Drew and Hardy Boys series on their future tastes. An unscientific poll indicates the Drew influence was greater, perhaps because more women read mysteries than men. Fans of these two young detectives series have written, respectively, *The Nancy Drew Scrapbook* (1993) by Karen Plunkett-Powell and *The Mysterious Case of Nancy Drew and the Hardy Boys* (1998) by Carole Kismaric and Marvin Heiferman. Melanie Rehak, also a critic and a poet, wrote *Girl Sleuth: Nancy Drew and the Women Who Created Her* (2005).

Scholarly fans like to play detective when they can, and one of the most fertile areas concerns pseudonyms. Reading the books of two different authors and finding similarities of style, they are wont to guess that one is a pseudonym, and they are often right. Nevins in 1968 demonstrated that two well-known British authors, John Rhode and Miles Burton, were really Major Cecil John Charles Street, writing under both names. More than thirty years later, in CADS, Tony Medawar revealed another pseudonym, Cecil Waye, for Street. When Jon L. Breen speculated in 1974 that Emma Lathen and R.B. Dominic were both the creation of the same authors (Mary Jane Latsis and Martha Henissart), Patricia McGerr was able to confirm that in the next issue of *TAD*. An active scholar of pseudonyms is Texas fan Pat Hawk whose *Authors' Pseudonyms* (1992) has gone through three editions, with sixteen hundred pages and more than sixty-one thousand pseudonym attributions, a significant percentage of whom are of mystery writers.

A unique and useful reference book was *The Deadly Directory*, which was started by Sharon Villines in 1995. Kate Derie, creator of *Cluelass.com*, took over in 1999 and edited it until its last annual edition in 2004. Accurately subtitled by Derie *as "A Resource Guide for Mystery, Crime and Suspense Readers and Writers,"* it provided information regarding mystery booksellers, periodicals, internet websites, and events.

Mystery scholarship remains alive and well, though writing about the mystery now includes stage dramas and musicals that have strong elements of crime. Amnon Kabatchnik wrote a seven-volume series, beginning in 2008, *Blood on the Stage: Milestone Plays of Crime, Mystery and Detection.* Beginning with Aeschylus's *Prometheus Bound* (480 B.C.), these books, which Kabatchnik calls "An Annotated Repertoire," provide plot synopses and details about the production and critical reaction of almost seven hundred plays. Kabatchnik also wrote *Sherlock Holmes on the Stage: A Chronological Encyclopedia of Plays Featuring THE GREAT DETECTIVE* (2008).

Kabatchnik's approach is chronological. As a contemporary of his, and an equal fan of crime on stage, I wrote *The Villainous Stage* (2014) analyzing crime plays according to their subject matter. Among my seventeen chapters are ones titled: "Agatha Christie, Playwright," "Trial and Error: Courtrooms on Stage," "The Spy Who Came Onto the Stage," and "Just in Crime: The Musical."

Curtis Evans has his doctorate in American history, but, as a fan, he loves British mysteries of the "Golden Age." Reacting to critic Julian Symons calling many writers, of whose work Evans is a fan, "Humdrum," Evans wrote *Masters of the "Humdrum" Mystery* (2012) about Freeman Wills Crofts and the two writers best known respectively by their pseudonyms: John Rhode and J.J. Connington.

Evans said, "I wanted to begin a personal project of recovering the lost world of Golden Age British mystery fiction." In addition to writing books and introductions to older books being reprinted, he has a website, *The Passing Tramp,* whose title cleverly uses the frequent habit of the police, especially in the 1920s, of first attributing a murder to "a passing tramp" before seriously investigating those who had motives for murder. Evans has written paeans to novels that are detective puzzles and derided the movement, partially led by Symons, to praise psychological "crime novels" rather than "detective novels." He also questions praising books merely because they are said to have "transcended the mystery genre."

Another great fan, though he is also a lawyer and a professional writer of fiction, is Martin Edwards. His *The Golden Age of Murder: The Mystery of the Writers Who Invented the Modern Detective Story* (2015) is the definitive history of the Detection Club, the organization to which classic British detective story writers, including Agatha Christie, Dorothy L. Sayers, and Ngaio Marsh belonged. The puzzle element was paramount in their books, and they usually provided fair play clues so that fans of this type of mystery could try to guess the solution, before the book's detective.

Edwards's *The Story of Classic Crime in 100 Books* (2017) is a masterful history of crime fiction during the first half of the twentieth century with evidence of vast reading in the field. The current revival of interest in republishing these older puzzle novels is partly due to Evans and Edwards, whose writings have made them sound like the fun they are.

Chapter Twenty-Seven

MYSTERY FANDOM IN CYBERSPACE

Woody Allen famously joked that the trouble with instant gratification is that it takes too long. In the early days of fandom, the letters columns were an important feature of fan journals, and subscribers seemed to have no problem waiting one issue (usually three months) to see their letters or responses to their letters.

By the early 1980s fan magazines often took far longer than three months between issues to publish letters, so fewer readers were writing letters. *Mystery & Detection Monthly* solved the problem temporarily with its almost monthly appearance and lively letters. However, in 2003, after almost twenty years, its regular contributors were down to about a dozen, and it ceased publishing.

By the mid-1990s virtually everyone contributing to *DAPA-EM* and *Mystery & Detection Monthly,* to name two fan groups involving written participation, was using a computer and had email. Whereas once I wrote many letters, I now have only one correspondent to whom I send what is called, pejoratively by some, "snail mail."

Some fans were Luddites and uncomfortable with new technology. A first step for a fan who writes letters, articles, and books was the realization that writing is much simpler with a personal computer. Revisions are more easily made, and mistakes can be corrected without the use of messy correction fluid. I acquired my first computer in 1984 and quickly joined the fan chorus asking, "How did I ever write anything before I got a computer?" Still there are many fans unhappy with reading lengthy material on the computer screen, so the hard copy remains important, and we have not reached the "paperless society" once predicted.

Most of the fan magazines still in print maintain websites; others have ceased publishing paper edition and gone entirely online. Similarly, fans purchase many of their mysteries from online sellers or read books on e-readers.

In the early days of the internet two librarians founded DorothyL, technically called a "listserv," to allow fans to write about the mystery. Eventually, there were 2,500 members. It began in 1991 and is still active, creating an impressive record for longevity. Fans continue to review mystery books and films, comment on trends, and occasionally write about their personal lives. There are few restrictions, except for blatant self-promotion or personal attacks on others (called "flaming") in this very polite group.

Kate Derie, better known as Cluelass

The Mysterious Home Page (MHP), created and formerly owned by Jan B. Steffensen of Denmark, established in May 1995, was the first general mystery website. Kate Derie's *Clulass.com Home Page* website, begun in June 1995, was the second and is often considered as the first major site for the mystery world online. Steffensen sold the *MHP* to Derie in November 2001, and she maintained both websites until October 2008. It included a calendar of events, a list of forthcoming books and conventions, and answers to frequently asked questions (FAQs). While Steffensen only listed website links,

Derie annotated each link with a description of the site. She kept track of over fifteen hundred sites, hundreds of which belonged to individual mystery authors. Neither Steffensen nor Derie currently keep track of this information, which is now readily available via Google and social media.

The range of websites and blogs is wide, and limited space permits me to give only a few examples. Blog is a word that wasn't in any dictionary before the internet, and now there are countless blogs all over the world, many operated by mystery fans. These personal journals have become another way to communicate in cyberspace.

The Gumshoe Site by Japan's Jiro Kimura, established in January 1996, is one of the oldest and best for news. Kimura is especially good regarding information on awards, obituaries of writers, and publishing, especially of short story anthologies. He has printed pictures he took at Bouchercons and MWA banquets.

Interest in the short story seemed to be waning, there being only three magazines that publish them in print editions as well as the occasional book anthology or collection. The internet tried to fill the gap, especially in the hardboiled genre. *Plots with Guns*, started in 1999, was a well thought of online magazine that, despite paying little, attracted "name" writers such as Laura Lippman and Steve Hamilton to contribute to a special issue. When it ceased publication in 2004, its editor Anthony Neil Smith explained why: "Because we're tired and we're busy." "Busy" may have meant seeking paid work.

In 1996 the members of a website devoted to short stories, *Shortmystery-Idigest* voted to become the Short Mystery Fiction Society, which has about eight hundred fans and writers as members and since 1998 has given out the Derringer Awards for excellence in short mystery fiction. At present these awards are distributed during the opening night ceremonies at Bouchercon.

With the revolving door that is blogdom, some of the better short story blogs are no longer around. They follow in the footsteps of print magazines such as *Hardboiled*, no longer published after twenty years. Bob Tinsley of Colorado Springs started the *ShortofIt.blogspot.com* in late 2004. Tinsley, who reviewed short stories on his site, predicted that the future of the mystery short story would rest in "e-zines," and there are some still publishing crime fiction, mostly hardboiled, that fans of the online magazine consider excellent.

Jeff Cohen's *Mystery Morgue* was another e-zine that was once praised but is no longer published. In addition to reviews, articles, and interviews, Cohen featured "Murder by Committee," a serial mystery written by Julia Spencer Fleming, Rhys Bowen, and Robin Burcell, among others. They wrote it in the style of the mystery writers who had inspired them.

Another defunct site, *Thug.lit,* had the distinction of having one of its stories included in the annual *Best American Mystery Stories* series, edited by Otto Penzler. Todd Robinson (a.k.a. "Big Daddy Thug") edited Thug.lit. He claimed it was a "professional amateur online magazine" that published "hardcore hardboiled," a claim supported by a random reading of the level of violence and scatology in its fiction.

Other online e-zines now defunct include *Hardluck Stories* and the amusingly named *Mouth Full of Bullets.* Still active is *Spinetingler Magazine,* originally founded in 2005. It has submission guidelines and has attracted some authors who usually publish in print magazines. It seeks ads and support from its readers and writers. It is one of the magazines that appeal to mystery fans who hope to write mysteries professionally, starting online if necessary.

Kevin Burton Smith's *Thrilling Detective Blog* has been active since 1998. It once included short stories, with authors paid $7.50 per story, but that has been discontinued. Smith still publishes news, reviews, and essays, especially about private detectives. Some are scholarly, for example Marcia Kiser's "Nero Wolfe: A Social Commentary on the U.S."

Bunny Brown of Edmonds, Washington, started *Stop, You're Killing Me (SYKM),* which she described as "A Site to Die For…

If You Love Mystery Books." There was information on new books and pages on hundreds of authors, including lists (often not complete) of their books.

In 1998 Lucinda Surber and Stan Ulrich, of Santa Fe, New Mexico, took it over and turned it into an Anthony-winning website and a valuable reference source. They list a complete bibliography of almost five thousand authors, showing, at last look, almost sixty thousand books and six thousand series characters. They include a complete list of all nominees and winners for fifteen different mystery awards. They also publish a newsletter, list new releases, and publish reviews.

Surber and Ulrich sell books, T-shirts, and coffee mugs to help *SYKM* to operate. They are unfailingly generous, announcing, "And it's perfectly fine with us if you printed our pages for your private use, especially for a trip to your local library or bookstore."

Tangled Web, a leading U.K. website, uses similar language, calling itself "A Website to Die For." Novelist Andrew Taylor termed it "Crime Fiction's Mecca on the internet." It provides news, reviews, author profiles, lengthy interviews, often by Bob Cornwell, and essays, for example one by Natasha Cooper on Josephine Tey. It, like many websites, has links to or ads for online booksellers like Amazon, providing a source of income for sites that are free.

Shots was once a print magazine, but the ezine is now one of the U.K.'s best online publications. It is still edited by Mike Stotter of London, who has a full-time job but still finds time for *Shots*. One of its highlights is Mike Ripley's column "Getting Away with Murder," which brings humor to the internet.

Though most of the interest on websites is in current mysteries, there are sites for fans of older detective stories. *Golden Age Detection,* run by Jon Jermey of Australia, has been "published" electronically more than a thousand times. Its members are often polled, allowing, for example, them to vote on the best and worst final novels of major writers. Another poll concerned the best short stories of all time. Members frequently discuss almost forgotten writers, such as Anthony Wynne.

The Yahoo group *The Golden Age of Detection* has a similar name but an even longer history, since 2001. It is posted almost monthly and has more than five hundred members. Reviews of both new and old books are printed under the heading "Past Offences."

Michael E. Grost of Michigan calls his *Classic Mystery and Detection* "an educational site containing reading lists and essays on great mysteries, mainly of the pre-1965 era." He also publishes his own short stories, which can be read for free, on his "mystery fiction page." His essays show considerable reading. To list but two authors, essays about Helen Reilly and Theodora DuBois cover every book by these once prominent writers, describing their plots and evaluating their strong and weak points. Grost also operates *Classic Film and Television* and *Classic Comic Books* sites.

Other bloggers who specialize in mysteries of the past include Les Blatt with *Classic Mysteries*, Martin Edwards with *Do You Write Under Your Own Name?*, and Curtis Evans with *The Passing Tramp*. They and many other bloggers are responsible for the increase in older books being published, especially the popular series of reprints by the British Library.

Xavier Lechard's *At the Villa Rose* takes its name from the 1910 A.E.W. Mason novel. Lechard's blog is in French but often translated. In addition to being a fan of the Golden Age of detection, he is a fan of psychological suspense and neglected writers such as Mildred Davis.

One of the most popular blogs is Sarah Weinman's *Confessions of an Idiosyncratic Mind*, with its combination of news, quotes from articles about writers, reviews, true crime stories, and lively opinions about controversial topics such as mystery awards and the publishing industry. She calls herself a "writer, editor and Crime Lady." She has written fiction for online magazines but now edits and writes for more mainstream publications.

Sometimes social issues are combined with mystery discussion.

The blog of Richard Valet is called *Black Guys Do Read*, and it is designed to overcome a stereotype that says black men are not readers.

Another important blog, by a writer who was also a fan, was *Bill's Blog*, by the late Bill Crider. He reviewed books, wrote about old paperbacks and old-time radio mysteries, as well as telling about his personal life. In his blog, Bill told how he became what many call "a Super Fan." He was reading Anthony Boucher's *New York Times Book Review* column and came across mention of the *John D. MacDonald Bibliophile* in it. He sent for a copy and ended up subscribing to virtually every other mystery fan magazine. As he said, "I was amazed to discover that there were people who were just as crazy as I was."

Bill checked out about a dozen blogs a day and between 2007 and early in 2018 he wrote a column "Blog Bytes" for EQMM in which he evaluated and recommended blogs. When Crider died, his column was taken over by Kristopher Zgorski, who, in 2018, received a Raven from MWA in recognition of his reviews published in the online website *Bolo Books*. Zgorski said that he sees the Raven "as a vote of confidence for the contribution of book bloggers everywhere." MWA in citing Zgorski's achievements said that he attends "industry conventions such as Bouchercon," thereby again ignoring that Bouchercon was started and continued by fans.

The love that mystery fans have for the printed word is keeping fan magazines alive, but almost all of them also make use of the ease of communicating via the internet. Having good fan magazines to read at their leisure while communicating quickly, when necessary, on the internet may be as close to instant gratification as it is possible for mystery fans.

Chapter Twenty-Eight

THE FUTURE OF MYSTERY FANDOM

There was a time when many mystery writers and editors were pessimistic about their future. In 2019 the mystery is far healthier than ever in the United States and the United Kingdom, and this improvement is rewarding for fans also. There is more for them to read and more avenues in which to communicate with other fans and writers, and I see no change on the horizon.

Mystery conventions will remain popular with fans. While Bouchercon has not grown much larger than, say, Monterey in 1997 or New Orleans in 2016, with about 2,000 attending, it probably won't. For it to expand might detract from the pleasure of those attending by making it more crowded than it, of necessity, already is, with fewer opportunities for fans to interact with other fans. The smaller conventions, that began with Malice Domestic in 1989, have grown but still are small enough to seem relatively intimate. Regional conventions, especially Left Coast Crime, do well, and there are smaller conventions in such varied locations as Alabama, Illinois,

Wisconsin, and New Jersey. I anticipate that all will continue in the foreseeable future.

In my 2005 edition of this book I did not realize how successful conventions in Britain would become and how they would grow. While an already crowded calendar might preclude many more conventions, those that took place in 2018 should do well in the future because they are so varied. Some, like Harrogate and Bristol, emphasize their "fun" aspect, but St. Hilda's and the British Library meetings are scholarly but never dull.

At a 1995 ClueFest panel, I questioned where we would find young fans willing to continue to perform the scholarship and organizing that had been done since 1967. In *MDM*, editor Bob Napier echoed the pessimism of my panel, wondering if active fans weren't an endangered species. However, he and others wisely predicted that with so many mystery readers, there was bound to be "New Blood" and that the internet would be a source of future fans.

It is not a given that all conventions will continue to take place. At least three times in this century there was doubt that Bouchercon would be presented until at almost the last moment, a fan stepped forward to provide the necessary hotel guarantee. Most of the smaller regional U.S. conventions eventually folded, as did Dead on Deansgate in the U.K. Based on the more organized way conventions are now run and the number of bidders at the Bouchercon business meeting in 2018, I predict that most conventions will be with us for a long time to come.

If fewer scholarly articles are being written for some fan magazines, knowledge is being disseminated on the internet in the form of blogs that contain bibliographies, essays, reviews, and convention reports. Though material on the internet may seem ephemeral to some people who prefer paper, one must remember that different generations have different means of communicating. While Hubin's Bibliography remains indispensable, websites such as *Stop, You're Killing Me!* supply bibliographic information, much of it quite current. Reference material in blogs may be readily printed, providing a degree of permanence, at least to those willing to keep material that hasn't appeared in a book. Mystery scholarship will remain alive.

Meanwhile, though there have not been additions, the five major fan journals (CADS, *Mystery Scene, Mystery Readers Journal, Deadly Pleasures,* and *Old-Time Detection*) have remained active for a very long time, each having secured its own niche in fandom, and they are likely to continue to be published. The first three were founded in the 1980s. *Deadly Pleasures* dates from 1993, and the most recent, *Old-Time Detection,* from 2002. However, the internet is so popular among younger fans that I doubt we'll have *new* print journals, and the existing ones may not continue when their editor can no longer publish them.

More mysteries than ever are published—and by more publishers, and that is without tapping the full potential of print-on-demand services. In the late 1940s about 250 mysteries were published each year. According to *Publishers Weekly* about a thousand new mysteries are now published in the U.S. annually. Some worry that quality is not keeping up with quantity, but reviewers on the web and in magazines have no trouble finding books to recommend highly.

Popular at conventions are events for those newly published writers and readers/fans who want tips on how to get published for the first time. As fans anxious to be published increasingly attend conventions and write blogs, we see a younger fan base, and if they are not as interested in the history of the mystery, they are keeping it alive.

Fans with more specific wants are not being ignored thanks to smaller publishers. Crippen & Landru Publishers, in its Lost Classics Series, brings out short story collections by writers such as Helen McCloy and T.S. Stribling, in danger of being forgotten. Douglas G. Greene who founded Crippen & Landru is certainly a fan and a scholar. Since another fan, Jeffrey Marks, has taken over that company, we can expect that reprinting short stories from the past will continue.

The British Library has been reprinting older mysteries, books that I never expected to see reprinted, and they are selling remarkably well. It isn't only nostalgia; readers have found good reading in many older books. Otto Penzler has started to do the same in the U.S. with his American Mystery Classics imprint, reprinting works by Ellery Queen, Clayton Rawson, and Mary Roberts Rinehart in 2018. Given Penzler's long experience in publishing, I anticipate success. However, that may be a reflection of my own taste in reading, since one can't be certain there is a market yet for these classics in the U.S.

Hard Case Press, founded by Charles Ardai, has reprinted books for fans of hardboiled mysteries, including older works, such as the paperback originals of Lawrence Block. It has also printed a new paperback original, an Erle Stanley Gardner mystery (as A. A. Fair) about Bertha Cool and Donald Lam never before published. They have commissioned outstanding artists, such as Robert McGinnis, to provide covers reminiscent of the best art work of the 1950s and 1960s. I don't see quite the market for another publisher reprinting the hardboiled mysteries of, say, the1950s and 1960s. Many of today's mysteries are as hardboiled as anything Spillane and company wrote, and they are better written.

One sign of a healthy future for fandom is the number of mystery discussion groups and blogs. Fans do not have to leave their computers to read about and discuss mysteries, though many of these groups meet in person.

The future of mystery fandom will continue to follow technology, as it has done on the internet. In this era of pay-per-view television, some expected a time when people will "attend" mystery conventions from their homes. Closed Circuit TV has been used at science fiction's WorldCon, which is much larger than Bouchercon. So far, the only time this happened in the mystery was at the 1994 Bouchercon in Seattle when, because the banquet was sold out, the speeches and award presentations were made available, at considerable expense to the convention, on close circuit television to the rooms of the hotel guests. This may be beneficial to people for whom travel is either difficult or overly expensive, but I suspect that most fans would rather show up in person.

Observers at conventions, especially those in the United States, have noticed that many (if not most) of the fans are older, often in their sixties or seventies. On the other hand, those who have been published or want to be published are younger. They may be readers and fans, but they are less interested in promoting fandom than in pursuing their own writing careers.

At this point it may be useful to distinguish among READERS, FANS, and SUPER FANS. Obviously, there are millions of mystery readers. A recent study in England showed the mystery to be the most popular genre among readers, more popular even than mainstream fiction or science fiction. That well may be true in the United States too.

A small number of readers are FANS buying and reading more mysteries than casual readers and willing to spend money and vacation time in attending mystery conventions. They may participate in mystery discussion groups.

Super Fans are a breed apart. If a fan attends one convention, the Super Fan might attend three a year. It is the Super Fan who is willing to devote several years of his or her life to organize and put on a convention. Many of the Super Fans have worked on more than one mystery convention over the years.

Though they may also work on conventions, there are other Super Fans who edit fan journals and or write for them. The people who edit fan journals devote considerable time and money to them, seldom making a profit. Almost as necessary are the Super Fans who often write for these journals or write reference books on the mystery.

The question for all three groups is how to get young people "hooked" on mysteries so that at some point in their future many will read (and buy) them, discuss them, attend conventions and even become the Super Fans of the future.

An informal poll of fans as to how they started to read mysteries reveals that many found mysteries in their homes and decided to try one. Most enjoyed them so much that they are still reading them. However, many homes do not have books, let alone good mysteries. Recent Bouchercons have taken a major step forward, holding events aimed at the Young Adult readers. Having adults telling young readers to read a mystery is unlikely to produce results but making Young Adult mysteries available may work. Thousands of books are given free by publishers to adults attending Bouchercon and other conventions. A good long-term investment would involve publishers giving books to schools to give to students. The books will of necessity be Young Adult mysteries to begin with, but I anticipate that many teens who become "hooked" on mysteries will soon go to the adult mystery shelves.

Of the predictions I've made in this chapter, the one I'm most certain of is that though reading material is increasingly available on the internet, the desire to hold a mystery in one's hands will never vanish.

ACKNOWLEDGMENTS

In my fifty-plus years of mystery fandom, I've been lucky enough to meet dozens of people who have had a profound effect on fandom—and become friends. They are too many to name without risking the sin of forgetting someone. I thank them all sincerely. However, there are some people who must be mentioned:

KATE DERIE, a.k.a. "cluelass," who was involved in this project from its beginning and helped throughout and always with good humor.

ART SCOTT, for his help with most of the photographs in the book, allowing me to show readers of this book many of the fans about whom I wrote.

GEOFF BRADLEY, for his help regarding British fan publications and meetings.

CHARLES SHIBUK, the most important mystery fan to live in the Bronx since Edgar Allan Poe. He has always been ready with encouragement, suggestions, and corrections

With love to **CAROL**, my wife, who read the manuscript and the index many times, improving them more than I can say. She didn't even complain when I monopolized our one computer.

APPENDIX A

Bouchercon: Fan Guests of Honor

1970–1980	None
1981	Al Hubin
1982–1983	None
1984	Marv Lachman
1985	Len and June Moffatt
1986	Chris Steinbrunner
1987	John Nieminski
1988	Bruce Taylor
1989	Linda Toole and Bill Deeck
1990	Bob Adey
1991	Bruce Pelz
1992	None
1993	Don Sandstrom
1994	Art Scott
1995	Geoff Bradley
1996	Ellen Nehr
1997	Bob Napier
1998	Hal and Sonya Rice
1999	Maggie Mason and Beverly DeWeese

2000	Steve Stilwell
2001	Lew and Nancy Buckingham
2002	Bill Crider
2003	Jeff and Ann Smith
2004	Gary Warren Niebuhr
2005	Beth Fedyn
2006	Jim Huang
2007	Barbara Peters
2008	Thalia Proctor
2009	Kathryn Kennison
2010	Maddy Van Hertbruggen
2011	Kate Stine and Brian Skupin
2012	Doris Ann Norris
2013	Chris Aldrich and Lynn Kaczmarek
2014	Al Abramson
2015	Lucinda Surber and Stan Ulrich
2016	Jon and Ruth Jordan
2017	Margaret Cannon
2018	Judy Bobalik and Ayo Onatade
2019	McKenna Jordan

APPENDIX B

Malice Domestic: Fan Guests of Honor

1991–1995	None
1996	Maggie Mason
1997	Judy & Jack Cater
1998	Willis Herr
1999	Tasha Mackler
2000	George Easter
2001	Andi Schechter
2002	Don Herron
2003	Sue Feder
2004	Bryan Baarrett & Thom Walls
2005	Ernie Bulow
2006	Bill & Toby Gotfried, Donna Moore
2007	Diane Kovacs & Kara Robinson
2008	Elizabeth Foxwell, Ron & Jean McMillen
2009	Laura Hyzy
2010	Tom & Marie O'Day
2011	Marvin Lachman
2012	Noemi Levine
2013	Tom & Enid Schantz

2014	Sue Trowbridge
2015	Friends of Mystery
2016	Chantelle Aimée Osman
2017	None
2018	Janet Blizard
2019	P.J. Coldren

APPENDIX C

Left Coast Crime: Fan Guests of Honor

1989	Ellen Nehr
1990	Phyllis Brown
1991	Janet Rudolph
1992	Bill Deeck
1993	Mary Morman
1994	Jim Huang
1995	Dean James
1996	Shirley Beaird
1997	Judy & Jack Cater
1998	Maureen Collins
1999	Carol Harper
2000	Sheila Martin
2001	Andi Shechter
2002	Gerry Letteney
2003	Donna Beatley
2004	Linda Pletzke
2005	Ann Reece
2006	Bill & Toby Gottfried
2007	Lee Mewshaw

2008	Elizabeth Foxwell and Ron & Jean McMillen
2009	Laura Hzyz
2010	Tom & Marie O'Day
2011	Marv Lachman
2012	Ruth Sickafus
2013	Cindy Silberblatt
2014	Audrey Reith
2015	Friends of Mystery, Portland, Oregon
2016	Linda Smith Rutledge
2017	Luci Zahray
2018	Janet Blizard

APPENDIX D

Recipients of the Don Sandstrom Award for Lifetime Achievement in Mystery Fandom

2001	Marv Lachman
2002	Gary Warren Niebuhr
2003	Maggie Mason
2004	Ted Fitzgerald
2005	Bill Crider
2006	Janet Rudolph
2007	Beth Fedyn
2008	Bill & Toby Gottfried, George Easter
2009	Art Scott
2010	Cap'n Bob Napier
2011	Bev DeWeese
2012	Al Hubin
2013	Ali Karim
2014	Ted Hertel
2015	Jane Lee
2016	David Magayna
2017	Steele Curry
2018	Larry Gandle

APPENDIX E

Recipients of the David Thompson Memorial Special Service Award

2011	Ali Karim
2012	Len and June Moffatt
2013	Marv Lachman
2014	Judy Bobalik
2015	Bill & Toby Gottfried
2016	Otto Penzler
2017	George Easter
2018	Lesa Holstine

INDEX

B

C

D

E

F

G

H

I

J

K

L

M

N

O

P

Q

R

S

T

U

V

W

X

Y

Z

ABOUT THE AUTHOR

Photo by Karen Sandstrom Muir

Marv Lachman has been reading mysteries since 1943, when he was eleven. He won Mystery Writers of America's Edgar Award for Best Critical/Biographical Work of 1976, for *Encyclopedia of Mystery and Detection* (with co-authors Chris Steinbrunner, Otto Penzler, and Charles Shibuk). He was nominated for the same award in 1994 for *A Reader's Guide to the American Novel of Detection*, which was also nominated for an Agatha, an Anthony, and a Macavity Award. Lachman won the Macavity Award in 2001 for *The American Regional Mystery* (2000), which was also nominated for an Anthony and an Agatha.

Lachman was given a Raven Award from the Mystery Writers of American in 1997, for his fan-related activities. MWA's Raven is a "special award given for outstanding achievement in the mystery field outside the realm of creative writing." In 2001 he received the first Don Sandstrom Memorial Award for Lifetime Achievement in Mystery Fandom. In 2013 the Bouchercon Board of Directors gave him the David Thompson Special Service Award for his "exemplary life-long service to the mystery and crime fiction community." In 2019 Marv is attending his fortieth Bouchercon.

The first edition of *The Heirs of Anthony Boucher* (2005) won the Anthony Award at Bouchercon in 2006. Marv's most recent book was *The Villainous Stage* (2014), a history of crime plays in New York and London. He lives in Santa Fe, New Mexico, with his wife, Carol.